THE REAL T. E. LAWRENCE

To my dearly beloved friend Bernard C. Burgess, formerly National Trust volunteer guide at Clouds Hill, T. E. Lawrence's former home.

THE REAL T. E. LAWRENCE

HIS LIFE AND LEGACY

ANDREW NORMAN

WHITE OWL
AN IMPRINT OF PEN & SWORD BOOKS LTD.
YORKSHIRE – PHILADELPHIA

First published in Great Britain in 2025 by
PEN AND SWORD WHITE OWL
An imprint of
Pen & Sword Books Ltd
Yorkshire – Philadelphia

ISBN 978 1 03611 125 0

A CIP catalogue record for this book is available from the British Library.

Typeset in Times New Roman 10/12 by
SJmagic DESIGN SERVICES, India.
Printed and bound in the UK by CPI Group (UK) Ltd, Croydon, CR0 4YY.

The Publisher's authorised representative in the EU for product safety is
Authorised Rep Compliance Ltd., Ground Floor, 71 Lower Baggot Street,
Dublin D02 P593, Ireland.
www.arccompliance.com

For a complete list of Pen & Sword titles please contact

PEN & SWORD BOOKS LIMITED
George House, Units 12 & 13, Beevor Street, Off Pontefract Road,
Barnsley, South Yorkshire, S71 1HN, England
E-mail: enquiries@pen-and-sword.co.uk
Website: www.pen-and-sword.co.uk

or

PEN AND SWORD BOOKS
1950 Lawrence Rd, Havertown, PA 19083, USA
E-mail: uspen-and-sword@casematepublishers.com
Website: www.penandswordbooks.com

FSC www.fsc.org
MIX
Paper | Supporting responsible forestry
FSC® C013604

Contents

About the Author

Andrew Norman was born in Newbury, Berkshire, UK in 1943. Having been educated at Thornhill High School, Gwelo, Southern Rhodesia (now Zimbabwe) and St Edmund Hall, Oxford, he qualified in medicine at the Radcliffe Infirmary. He has two children, Bridget and Thomas, by his first wife.

From 1972-83, Andrew worked as a general practitioner in Poole, Dorset, before a spinal injury cut short his medical career. He is now an established writer whose published works include biographies of Thomas Hardy, Beatrix Potter, Paul Robeson, Françoise Hardy, Adolf Hitler, Agatha Christie, Sir Arthur Conan Doyle and Robert Mugabe. Andrew was remarried to Rachel in 2005.

Acknowledgements

I am grateful to the following: Bodleian Library, Oxford; *Daily Echo*, Bournemouth; Dorset History Centre; Forestry Commission; Met Office National Meteorological Archive, Sowton, Exeter; National Cycle Museum; Pen & Sword Books; The Seven Pillars of Wisdom Trust; The Tank Museum, Bovington, Dorset; the Wellcome Trust Library, 183 Euston Road, London.

Steven J. Barker; Valerie Bedford; Ed Bishop; Tom Booth; Peter Bowart; Ed Bristow; Jeremy Brown; Mick H. Burgess; Christopher Donaghy; Michael Dragffy; Nicholas Dragffy; George Forty; Mary B. F. Frampton; Benedicta Froelich; Thomas Gillibrand; J. Richard Harvey; Bob Hopkins; Michaela Horsfield; Bill Jesty; Barry King; Scotford Lawrence; Janetta Mizen; Barbara Peirce; Judith Priestman; Tosun Saral; Joan Self; Louise Seymour-Smith; Stuart Wheeler; Jeremy Wilson.

I am deeply grateful to Jonathan M. Weekly, for his expertise and kindness. I am especially grateful, as always, to my beloved wife Rachel for all her help and encouragement.

Say not the struggle naught availeth,
The labour and the wounds are vain,
The enemy faints not, nor faileth,
And as things have been they remain.

If hopes were dupes, fears may be liars;
It may be, in yon smoke conceal'd,
Your comrades chase e'en now the fliers,
And, but for you, possess the field.

For while the tired waves, vainly breaking,
Seem here no painful inch to gain,
Far back, through creeks and inlets making,
Comes silent, flooding in, the main.

And not by eastern windows only,
When daylight comes, comes in the light;
In front the sun climbs slow, how slowly!
But westward, look, the land in bright!

Arthur Hugh Clough (1819-1861)

(One of 112 favourite poems, from an anthology assembled by Lawrence, each of which he copied out by hand)

Author's Note

I must confess to feeling a special affinity for T. E. Lawrence. My home in Dorset is a mere 18 miles from his former home, Clouds Hill, and 21 miles from his grave at Moreton.

As an undergraduate at Oxford, I was privileged at Jesus College to be shown the cast of a bronze bust of Lawrence by sculptor Eric Kennington in 1926. Also, Lawrence's golden dagger at All Souls College.

As an undergraduate and later medical student at Oxford's Radcliffe Infirmary, I often walked past the house No. 2, Polstead Road in North Oxford, where Lawrence lived with his family during his school and university days.

As a result of the road traffic accident, that resulted in Lawrence's untimely death, it was thanks to neurologist, Sir Hugh Cairns, that the UK government was finally persuaded to make the wearing of crash helmets compulsory for all motorcyclists.

At Oxford, I witnessed in person neurosurgical operations on the brain, performed by the Director of the Radcliffe Infirmary's Department of Neurosurgery Joseph ('Joe') Pennybacker: also, by Pennybacker's colleague, consultant neurosurgeon Mr John Potter, both of whom had been previously mentored by Cairns. On one occasion, the bulb of Mr Potter's surgical headlamp exploded during an operation, showering the unfortunate patient's exposed brain with glass! The operation was witnessed by myself, and some fellow UK and US medical students. Having cleared up the mess, obtained a replacement bulb, and completed the operation, Mr Potter solemnly turned to the American students and declared, 'Please remember, we British can always put up some sort of a show!'

Finally, Nuffield Professor of Orthopaedics Robert Duthie described to me and my fellow medical students how in 1937, motor car magnate Lord Nuffield had personally handed over cheques, to endow Oxford's five Nuffield professorships - of medicine, surgery, obstetrics and gynaecology, and anaesthetics. (An orthopaedic chair, also endowed by Lord Nuffield of which Duthie was the current incumbent, came later.)

In my courting days, my wife-to-be lived in James Street, Oxford, where Lord Nuffield, then plain William Morris, who started from humble beginnings, commenced his bicycle repair business in his parent's garden!

As an undergraduate at St Edmund Hall, Oxford, reading for a degree in Animal Physiology prior to beginning as a medical student at the Radcliffe Infirmary I lived for a year in digs in Juxon Street. My landlady was the delightful Mrs Mulford whose husband Thomas Louis had, as a young man, manned the petrol pumps at William Morris's first garage in James Street.

Lord Nuffield died on 22 August 1963. I had reason to be grateful to British Leyland, which is what William Morris's company Morris Garages became, when an ancient and decrepit Austin Mini motor car, which I purchased from an Oxford psychiatrist, and which I was relying upon to take me to Headington, where one of the exams was being conducted, broke down the night before my medical finals in 1970. In a panic, I telephoned British Leyland. The vehicle, whose brake shoes were completely worn out and whose windscreen wiper, long minus its rubber blade, had cut a deep groove in the windscreen, was collected, repaired, and delivered back to me early the following morning - at no charge to myself!

Of all the highlights in my attempt to discover 'The Real T. E. Lawrence' perhaps the most unforgettable was meeting the current owner of the Brough Superior on which he made his final, fatal journey and, in what was a bittersweet experience, in all the circumstances, setting eyes on this, the most famous motorcycle in the world!

Preface

The county of Dorset in southern England is the one, which more than any other, resonates with the folklore of T. E. Lawrence. In the licenced restaurant of Wareham's Anglebury House there are two plaques (situated above the window seat), one of which reads 'Lawrence of Arabia sat here 1923', and the other 'Lawrence of Arabia spent many a pleasant hour drinking coffee in this seat'.

Mr Cecil Hopkins of Corfe Mullen and Lawrence used to wave, cheerfully, to each other as they passed one another on the Wareham to Swanage road on their respective motorcycles: the former's was an 'OK Supreme', and the latter's a 'Brough' (of which Lawrence was to own a number during his lifetime). Miss Helen Taylor, a former seamstress at Tyneham House, told me that Lawrence, who loved to ride his motorcycle around the area of South Dorset known as Purbeck, grew impatient at the number of gates which he encountered across the roads. Instead of pausing to open them, he chose to ride straight through them!

Visitors to the tiny cottage at Clouds Hill (not to be confused with Clouds Hill Cottage, which is located on the opposite side of the road) find it extraordinary that a man of world renown, such as Lawrence, could have inhabited such a humble abode. And, of course, it is common knowledge that it was between this cottage and nearby Bovington that he met with his fatal accident; the motorcycle on which he was killed being a 'Brough' (or 'Brough Superior'), Type SS100.

To the east of Dorchester (Dorsetshire's county town) lies 'Max Gate', the home of Thomas Hardy and his wife Florence, whom Lawrence loved to visit. In the Dorset County Museum is a lock of Lawrence's hair, together with a letter from Thomas Hardy's wife confirming its provenance. In the Bovington Tank Museum collection is a 'housewife' (pocket sewing outfit) said to have belonged to Lawrence; his camera; his binoculars in leather case; his prismatic compass in leather case; two star and crescent emblems from a Turkish train destroyed by Lawrence's forces in Arabia, and other items associated with Arabia's Hejaz railway. There is also a collection of photographic slides, together with other artefacts.

Finally, Lawrence's grave is to be found in the cemetery of the Church of St Nicholas in the tiny village of Moreton, five miles east of Dorchester. His was a glorious, but tormented life – as will be seen.

Prologue

T. E. Lawrence, soldier and writer, the co-leader with King Faisal of Saudi Arabia of the Arab Campaign during the First World War, became a legend in his own lifetime. And yet to this day there is much about him which remains a mystery: two aspects of his character being of particular interest.

This first is why, having become a famous figure with the world at his feet, did he choose, subsequently, to live a life of obscurity in the lower ranks of the armed services?

The second concerns Lawrence's sexuality. Some of his biographers have been accused of bringing 'sex' into their volumes, for reasons of sensationalism and publicity. To be fair, however, it was Lawrence himself who first raised the subject, by including in his book *Seven Pillars of Wisdom* (an account of the Desert Campaign), details of how he was captured and raped by the Turks. Lawrence, who never married, is known to have engaged in masochistic rituals. So, what was the true nature of, and explanation for his sexuality?

This is the challenge of *The Real T. E. Lawrence.*

Chapter 1

His Mother, Sarah

One may imagine Sarah Lawrence, peering through the tall sash window of her Victorian house in Polstead Road, Oxford. It was a mellow, red-brick building shielded by the leaves and branches of trees which lined both sides of the road. The afternoons were drawing in with the approach of early autumn, and Sarah awaited the return of her four elder sons from school, now that another academic year had begun. Her fifth and youngest son Arnold, remained at home with her, being not yet of school age. Her boys were all bright, intelligent, and promising, and life in Oxford offered everything she could hope for in the way of education for them; far more so than at any of their other previous homes – of which there had been several. In fact, this was the reason that had brought them to the city. Education was immensely prized, both by herself and by her husband Thomas. But it was of particular importance to her, for she had been brought up in a strict Presbyterian household, where learning, religion, and discipline ruled the lives of all within the family.

Sarah sighed, contentedly, as she awaited the return of her boys for tea. Her sons were all doing well at school, but the second eldest, Thomas Edward, otherwise known as 'Ned', was her greatest challenge. He was the one most likely to question her authority, and there were arguments which often resulted in her having to chastise him physically. What was it about him, she wondered? Why could he not be like the others?

Sarah's life had been a hard one. The illegitimate daughter of Elizabeth Junner, she had been born in Sunderland in north-east England in 1861, and when she was only 8 or 9 years old her mother died of drink. Thereafter, she was brought up in Scotland: first by her grandparents, and later by an aunt whose husband was a minister of the church.

Sometime between 1878 and 1880, Sarah crossed the Irish Sea to join the household of the aristocratic Chapman family at South Hill near Castletown Devlin in County Westmeath, Ireland, where Thomas Chapman lived with his wife Edith and their four daughters. Sarah, subsequently, became Thomas's mistress, even though she was fifteen years his junior. Thomas, thereafter, abandoned his wife and family and set up home with Sarah in Dublin, 30 miles away.

According to the Matrimonial Causes Act of 1857, legal separation was permitted only if there had been one act of misconduct by the wife, or two by the husband. Therefore, Mrs Edith Chapman had grounds for divorce. However, because of her strong religious views she refused to countenance it. Thomas and Sarah, being unable to marry, now adopted the surname 'Lawrence', Sarah having been a servant to Thomas Lawrence - a surveyor employed by Lloyds of London - when she lived in Sunderland. The likelihood is, therefore, that Sarah was Thomas's illegitimate daughter. In December 1885 the Lawrences had a son, Montague Robert (known as Robert, or 'Bob').

In Ireland, the secret of the Lawrences not being man and wife would have been difficult to keep, and because of the inevitable opprobrium which would have resulted, had they been found out, this may have been the reason why the family moved to Tremadoc in North Wales. Here, on 16 August 1888, their second son Thomas Edward, or 'Ned' as he was known, was born.

Further upheavals were to follow. From Tremadoc they moved to Kirkcudbright, Scotland where, in 1889, their third son William George was born; and from there to Dinard on the Normandy coast. In 1893, in yet another place of residence, namely the Channel Island of Jersey, their fourth son Frank Helier was born and given his second name after its capital town. Finally, in 1896, the Lawrences moved to 2 Polstead Road, Oxford, where, in 1900, their fifth and last son Arnold Walter was born. Here, at last, the family were able to settle down; even though in the back of Sarah's mind was always the possibility that the secret of their 'living in sin' would be discovered – for in those days such a perceived scandal would lead to a family being ostracised by all sections of the community.

In the Polstead Road household prayers were said every day. There were frequent readings from the Bible, and three times every Sunday the family attended the Anglican church of St Aldates in the city. Sarah Lawrence objected to drink; she also made sure that young females were kept well away from her five sons.

Driven by a desire to mould the children to her own ways, Sarah disciplined the children by whipping them on their bare bottoms. (Years later she would tell Lord Astor that his horses would win races only if they were whipped). She beat Ned frequently; Frank only once; and the others, never.[1] She saw no harm in this; after all, was not the physical chastisement of children accepted as the norm throughout society in those days?

Sarah singled out Ned in particular, simply because he was naughtier and more wilful than her other sons. His grins, smirks, and laughter revealed a defiant rebelliousness which she feared might one day lead him away from that strict, religious faith and conformity which she was determined to impose upon him. And what then? What if this seemingly irresponsible youth was one day destined to bring further shame on the family? A similar shame to that which she herself had experienced: not only of being illegitimate, but also of knowingly bearing five illegitimate sons? Could her own guilt, and a fear of recidivism in her son Ned, have been what led her to whip him so often and so vigorously?

Curiously, Ned once described his mother Sarah as 'very exciting'.[2] But why? Was he excited at the prospect of his mother chastising him? This aspect of his character will be discussed further in due course. Finally, did his mother's harsh treatment of him have any longstanding adverse effects on him? This remained to be seen.

Sarah may have wondered whether young Ned 'played up' because he was, by nature, more sensitive than his brothers and, in consequence, felt disorientated and insecure by the family's constant moving of house. Or was it that he felt inferior to them on account of his shortness of stature? At 5 feet 6 inches he was now fully grown. Perhaps he envied them, felt left out, and therefore resorted to misbehaviour as an attention-seeking device.

By contrast, Robert, the eldest sibling, had, to Sarah's satisfaction, undergone a religious conversion at the local Church of St Aldate's. Having graduated from St John's College, he would serve in the First World War on the Western Front, then qualify as a doctor, and one day accompany his mother to China as a medical missionary. Then came Ned, and after Ned, William, who was tall and handsome, and excelled at athletics. He would study history at St John's College; only to be killed in the First World War. Frank, the fourth son, organised the Church Lads' Brigade (of which Ned was also a member), and like Ned, went up to Jesus College. Frank would also be killed in the war. As for Arnold, the youngest, Ned was forever championing his cause and getting into trouble for it. Nevertheless, the desire to support the underdog was a characteristic that would remain with Ned for the rest of his life, and which one day would have huge implications on the world stage. Arnold was awarded a place at New College. As for Sarah, in her defence, it should be said that she may have found it difficult – as she struggled to bring up her five sons – to give each one the emotional love and support that he needed.

Sometimes, a certain look in Ned's eye made Sarah wonder if he actually despised her – after all, had she not taken his father Thomas away from Thomas's wife Edith and their family? And if Ned were to guess that not only his mother but he himself was illegitimate (a fact which she had kept from him), might he not then despise her even more – even detest her – this hypocritical woman who, on the one hand professed the Christian faith, yet on the other, acted in exactly the opposite way by breaking the Biblical Commandment which said, 'Thou shalt not commit adultery'?

Sarah, for her part, did not deny possessing certain feelings of jealousy in regard to Ned's warm relationship with his father. For example, as far as the mutual interest in archaeology and history shared by father and son were concerned, she would always be an outsider. Not for her the delights of those long bicycle rides to distant and interesting places, which they took together. And yet, her disapproval of Ned was by no means total; for despite his rebelliousness, he was not entirely untouched by his puritanical upbringing, some aspects of which he readily embraced. For example, he abhorred smoking and drinking and became a vegetarian. He viewed physical pleasures as an impediment to intellectual thought. Generous to his friends, he himself preferred a simple, austere life, and had no interest in the world of materialism.

It was now 1905 and Sarah Lawrence chuckled as she read the latest letter from her son Ned, now aged seventeen, who was travelling further and further afield.

This one described 'a stuffed group' including 'a boa constrictor strangling a tiger' which he had seen in the Norwich Museum. 'Kindly take heaps of love from me for yourself,' he wrote, 'and when you've had enough, divide the remainder into three portions, and give them to the three worms [i.e. his brothers] you have with you'.[3] Whether his brothers would find it amusing to be described as 'worms', Sarah rather doubted.

Two years later Ned was at Caerphilly in Wales, looking at the 'magnificent castle'.

> The Horn-work (outer fortification) is most interesting, and the outworks could not be excelled, either for preservation or attractiveness. There are no good photos to be obtained, and there have been none at any time or at any castle I have visited. The conviction has been continually growing stronger upon me, that I must tour round this part again with a camera.[4]

Sarah wondered if Ned's enthusiasm for such ancient artefacts would lead him to venture even further afield. Sure enough, it did, for in the same year, 1907, he wrote to her from Mont St Michel in Northern France:

> The stars are out most beautifully, and the moon is, they say, just about to rise. The phosphorescence in the water interests me especially: I have only seen it once or twice before, and never so well as tonight![5]

And from Chartres Cathedral the following year:

> What I found I cannot describe - it is absolutely untouched & unspoilt, in superb preservation, & the noblest building (for Beauvais is only half a one) that I have ever seen, or expect to see.[6]

All this talk of the past – of castles and cathedrals – thought Sarah; it was his father who had put these silly notions into Ned's head; told him of how his ancestors the Fetherstonhaughs and the Chapmans, once inhabited great castles in Ireland. Perhaps her son dreamed that one day, he too would perform heroic deeds like the knights of yore – perhaps even own a castle of his own! His admiration for the knights was obvious, and he visited churches throughout Oxfordshire in order to take brass rubbings (the reproduction on paper of monumental brasses) of them.

According to Lawrence's mother Sarah,

> when he got older he made long journeys on his cycle to every place in England which had famous brasses of Knights; he covered the walls of his bedroom with them, and they made a wonderful show, especially by firelight: some of them were over life size.[7]

> Furthermore, Cyril F.C. Beeson, a contemporary of his at Oxford High School, stated Sir John d'Abernon and Roger de Trumpington, a crusader, had 'pride of place'.[8]

Lawrence was an avid reader, particularly of French medieval literature, such as *Chanson de geste* - 'Song of heroic deeds' - featuring in verse, legendary incidents from French history during the 8th, 9th, and 10th Centuries. Among the three books which Lawrence made a point of taking with him wherever he went. was Thomas Malory's *Morte d'Arthur* - King Arthur being the semi-legendary sixth Century King of the Britons.

Chivalry is defined as 'the medieval knightly system with its religious, moral, and social code: the combination of qualities expected of an ideal knight, namely courage, honour, courtesy, justice'. [9] King Arthur was said to embody all the qualities of the aforesaid ideal Christian knight. However, the Middle East had an even longer tradition of chivalry, which was later embraced into Islam with the advent of that religion in the seventh century.

As a youth, Lawrence declared that he had read 'nearly every manual of chivalry'.[10] This being the case, and from what is known of him since, it is more than likely that he adopted the chivalric code of the medieval knights as his own – even though he rejected the Christian religion with which it was associated.

Why could her son Ned not live in the present, thought Sarah; become a missionary and save souls, which is what she had always wanted him to do?

It was now 1915, the year that Ned's brother Frank, was killed whilst fighting in France. Sarah had written to Ned, who was now working at the Military Intelligence Office in Cairo, and here was Ned's reply. It did not please her:

> I got your letter this morning, and it has grieved me very much. You will never understand any of us after we are grown up a little. Don't you ever feel that we love you without our telling you so? I feel such a contemptible worm for having to write this way about things. If you only knew that if one thinks deeply about anything one would rather die than say anything about it.[11]

The inference of it was clear. Sarah was a person who longed for demonstrable affection, to a degree which Ned – who was by nature reserved – felt unwilling and unable to give. Sarah folded up the letter and replaced it in the envelope. There seemed to be a huge, unbridgeable gulf between herself and her sons; between her emotional requirements, and their ability to fulfil them.

Chapter 2

His Father, Thomas

Equally, one may imagine Thomas Robert Tighe Chapman sinking back into his armchair and reflecting, wistfully, on his former life. Born in 1846, Thomas, on the death of his elder brother Benjamin in 1870, inherited his late father's estate of South Hill in County Westmeath. From where he now sat, he could see his son Ned out in the back garden polishing the new, 3-speed drop-handlebar bicycle which he had recently purchased for him. They had just returned from East Anglia, and on the final leg of the journey, ridden over a hundred miles in a single day.

The Chapmans understood that their estates in Ireland had been granted to them in Elizabethan times, through the influence of their distant relative Sir Walter Raleigh. Accordingly, the family had retained their English Protestant origins, married into their own circle, and mixed little with their Catholic, Irish neighbours. Thomas had told Ned of the 'Raleigh' connection, and the boy vowed that he would one day visit Ireland and buy a few acres of land in Westmeath, which he would keep in the family in honour of the great man. Also, Ned was thrilled to hear tales of his ancestors the Fetherstonhaughs, whose seat was Bracklyn Castle; and of the Chapmans of Killua Castle – both in County Westmeath – since when, his fascination with medieval life had known no bounds.

Thomas remembered how his wife Lady Edith, whom he had married in 1873 and by whom he had had four daughters, had been nicknamed variously by the Catholic priests as 'The Holy Viper', or 'The Vinegar Queen'. Her 'crime', in their eyes was that she had attempted to convert the local Catholics to her own Protestant persuasion.

Because Edith was adamant that she would not permit a divorce, Thomas and Sarah could never marry. So there was to be no more shooting, gambling, riding, or hard drinking. That was all in the past, and not only for financial reasons; for his wife Sarah had imposed upon him the strict ways of the Scottish Presbyterian Church, and there would be no going back. She had remodelled him: forcing him to become a teetotaller and a domestic man who was careful with his shillings and pence. His old life and all his friends had gone forever. Now, the couple never went calling or socialising, lest anyone discover that they were living in sin.

So here was Thomas, living in comparatively reduced circumstances in middle-class North Oxford under the strict, puritanical influence of his common-law wife Sarah; having been made to give up his horse for a bicycle. And yet, he enjoyed his rides with Ned and would continue to go with him for as long as he was able.

Then Ned's school friend, Cyril 'Scroggs' Beeson, would have to take over. Ned had also expressed an interest in photography and carpentry – subjects in which his father was able to instruct him. However, one thing which Thomas and Sarah had in common was a respect for books. They filled the house to overflowing, for she, like all good Puritans, knew the value of learning.

In 1888, Thomas assigned his life interest in the family estates in Ireland to his younger brother Francis, in exchange for receiving an annuity of £200 for the remainder of his life.[1]

All five of Sarah and Thomas's sons, having first been taught by a governess, were enrolled as day pupils at the City of Oxford High School for Boys, where, to the couple's delight, they did well. What Ned lacked in height he made up for in fitness and determination, winning prizes for English Language and Literature, History, Divinity, and Greek, and performing well at cricket, gymnastics, and cross-country running. In 1907 he won the mile race. However, there was a downside. He told his father how he had been thrashed for tipping the head boy's straw hat down over his nose, as he considered the boy a swank. When asked to apologise, Ned had refused. However, whilst he was being thrashed, he said that he had kicked the head boy up the behind, and so hard that his spectacles fell off!

A curious event occurred in the spring of 1906 which caused his father some anxiety at the time, but was soon put right. For reasons unknown to his father, Ned decided to enlist in the Artillery as a private soldier. Was this to avoid being bullied at school? And if so, could the reason have been that the secret of his illegitimacy had somehow leaked out? No, it is unlikely that Ned was bullied, for few boys were as strong as he, and none was fitter. However, the notion of military service was quickly dispelled, and soon Ned was back in France again, sending his parents accounts of his adventures, and telling them of the new challenges that he was setting himself:

> At Erquy when returning from bathing, I rode a measured half-kilo on the sand in forty seconds exactly. There was a gale behind me, and the sands were perfectly level and very fast, but still thirty miles per hour was distinctly good.[2]

However, his greatest cycling feat was to come in 1908, when he travelled 2,000 miles through France and made delightful and detailed drawings of fortresses, such as Coucy near Compèigne, and Cahors further to the south, near Toulouse. And yet, he was still not satisfied. Said he:

> All the glorious East; Greece, Carthage, Egypt, Tyre, Syria, Italy, Spain, Sicily, Crete… Oh, I must get down here… I would accept a passage for Greece tomorrow.[3]

Sure enough, in July 1909, Thomas received a letter from Syria. 'This is a glorious country for Wandering in, for hospitality is something more than a name.' Ned was equally enthusiastic about the people he met there, 'each one ready to receive one for a night and allow me to share in their meals: and, without a thought of payment from a traveller on foot'. This was Ned's first visit to the Middle East.[4]

In 1914, on the death in Ireland of his cousin Sir Benjamin Rupert Chapman, 6th Baronet, of Killua Castle, County Westmeath, Thomas inherited the baronetcy. And when Thomas's younger brother Francis died in 1915, the former inherited £25,000 from the Chapman estate (which was valued at £120,296).[5] In March 1916, Thomas gave money to his three surviving sons; stipulating that if Will (who had officially been declared missing in action) should prove to be alive, then the other three should give back part of their gift so that he might have an equal share. Subsequently, it was confirmed that Will had, indeed died.

Ned, with typical generosity, gave £3,000 of the £5,000 his father had given him to Janet Laurie, a friend of the family. It was to this lady that Ned had once proposed, quite out of the blue, and without going through the preliminaries of courting her. The surprised Janet, naturally, turned down the offer, and the matter was never referred to again. She, subsequently, became attached to Ned's younger brother Will, and the couple planned to marry. Ned gave another £1,000 to a friend and the last £1,000 he spent on picture illustrations for a book that he was writing.

Thomas, from his armchair, could see through the window that Ned had, by now, finished cleaning the bicycle, but instead of coming inside to rest, he was now doing press-ups on the lawn. The lad was forever on the go. He was shortly to commence at Jesus College, Oxford, where he had been elected to a Meyricke Exhibition to read History. But after that, what occupation or profession could possibly satisfy one with such prodigious energy and diverse interests and talent, his father did not know. But Thomas felt certain that whatever it was, it would be nothing conventional. The answer would not be long in coming.

Chapter 3

Doctor Hogarth and Syria

From his study on the first floor of Oxford's Ashmolean Museum, Dr David G. Hogarth, the museum's keeper since 1908, could see a youth, short, and of stocky build, running swiftly towards the main entrance. Within seconds that youth would arrive, breathless, at his door, having taken the stairs two, three, or even four at a time. Whereupon the youth would produce from his pocket the inevitable piece of medieval glass or pottery – purchased for a few pence from workmen excavating foundations for new buildings in the city centre - which he would expect Dr Hogarth to identify.

Ned – who from now on will be called Lawrence – was still at school when he first met Dr Hogarth (then the Ashmolean's assistant keeper), who set the youngster to work, helping to identify and catalogue medieval pottery fragments in his spare time. And now the boy was maturing into a man.

Having already studied the castles of England, Wales, and France, Lawrence decided that in order to complete his degree thesis entitled 'The Influence of the Crusades on European Military Architecture – to the end of the XII Century', it was necessary for him to visit Syria and Palestine – and he told Hogarth as much. Hogarth, scholar, archaeologist, and author, was twenty-six years Lawrence's senior, and he himself had travelled widely throughout the Middle East. Also, he had performed archaeological excavations in Cyprus and Egypt, under the direction of Sir Flinders Petrie – generally regarded as the originator of scientific archaeological methods – who in 1881 had surveyed the Pyramids.

To this end, Hogarth put Lawrence in touch with Charles Doughty, the Arabian explorer, who tried to dissuade him, as the voyage was likely to be 'wearisome, hazardous to health and even disappointing'.[1] Ignoring this advice, Lawrence set out in the summer vacation of 1909 on the SS *Mongolia* – travelling through the Straits of Gibraltar to Port Said and his destination, the Syrian capital Beirut.

Since the early sixteenth century, Syria, together with Iraq, Jordan, Lebanon, Palestine, and the Arabian province of Hejaz on the Red Sea (which included the holy cities of Mecca and Medina, together with Jeddah), had all been part of the Turkish Ottoman Empire. The same applied to Egypt. However, a nationalist revolt in 1879 against the ruling Khedive was put down following British intervention in 1882, and that country became a British Protectorate.

Armed with a camera and Mauser pistol, and having only a smattering of Arabic, Lawrence commenced an eleven-week trek, during which time he walked 1,100 miles, suffered from flea bites, survived an assassination attempt, and contracted malaria. However, he was able to visit no less than thirty-six out of a possible fifty castles, including the famous Crac des Chevaliers at Hosn, and bring back the photographs, plans, and drawings which would enable him to complete the thesis for the Honours Degree which he was awarded, first class, in June 1910, in the School of Modern History. Lawrence, subsequently, made three visits to France to look at churches and cathedrals. He also made a study of the origins of medieval pottery for the Ashmolean Museum.

On the recommendation of Hogarth, the British Museum applied for, and obtained, permission from the Ottoman authorities to reopen excavations at Carchemish, an ancient Hittite city built around 1500 BC on the banks of the upper Euphrates, just inside the Turkish border with Syria. Hogarth, who had taken Lawrence under his wing, had recently obtained for him from his former Oxford college, Magdalen, a four-year, £100-a-year demyship (scholarship), so thus enabling his enthusiastic young protégé to participate with him in the above project.

At Christmas time 1910, Lawrence was to be found learning Arabic at the American Mission School at Jebail in the Lebanon. He had quickly learned that the Arabs were more likely to welcome a person into their group who knew even a few words of their language. This command of the language which he had now acquired was later to stand him in good stead.

In February 1910, Hogarth joined Lawrence, bringing with him what else but supplies of jam, tea, and a collection of volumes of classical literature! They now travelled together by way of Haifa, Deraa, and Damascus (capital of Syria) to Carchemish, where Hogarth was to supervise the archaeological dig. Part of the journey was by train: on the Hejaz Railway which ran from Medina northwards, all the way to Damascus, Aleppo, and finally, Constantinople. Plans to extend this railway to the holy city of Mecca were abandoned, after opposition from patrons of the camel caravans, who feared loss of business during the time of the annual pilgrimage to celebrate the birth of the prophet Mohammed. Lawrence could not have known at the time, but soon he was to find himself attacking this railway, rather than travelling along it. In the meantime, he was in his element. To his mother, in April 1911, he wrote:

> Digging is tremendous fun, and most exciting and interesting. The results so far are not nearly enough to justify a second season but the thing is like Pandora's Box, with Hope in the last spit of earth. I have had some good pottery lately.[2]

Said Sheikh Hamoudi, chief foreman of excavations at Carchemish (1911-1914):

> Even while the dig was on, he [Lawrence] seldom slept in his bed, preferring often to lie at the bottom of some newly opened trench or

> on the mound beside the river. Whenever there was discomfort or hardship there he would thrust himself.[3]

It was as if Lawrence was toughening himself up, for some great purpose that he had in mind.

Hogarth, whom Lawrence described as 'a most splendid man', was to stay in Carchemish for only two months – March and April – after which he returned to England to supervise the excavation from there.

Hogarth realised that there were those who suspected that his visits to a sensitive area like the Middle East might not be all they seemed; that his interest might not be solely academic. Some had even suspected him of being a British spy! Could this be true? The Middle East was a region of great strategic significance – that was undeniable, and it would be all the more so, were a global conflict ever to break out.

As a schoolboy, Hogarth had been at Winchester College public school with Lord Grey, the current British Foreign Secretary, with whom he had kept in close touch. And now, as director of the dig, he and his staff, naturally, kept their eyes and ears open. As far as suggestions that he regularly briefed the Foreign Office about the activities of the Turks and Germans in Syria were concerned, well.... Hogarth allowed himself the luxury of a smile.

Chapter 4

Dahoum

Lawrence spent the digging season of 1911 at Carchemish, and it was here that he met a youth called Dahoum (meaning 'the dark one'), who was to change his life. Lawrence could not help but notice him. He was looking after the donkeys. He was of slender build, and his eyes, which were large and brown, followed Lawrence wherever he went. Lawrence, equally curious about the boy, summoned him to come and look at an ancient, newly-excavated wall: one which, for centuries, had lain beneath the all-pervading sand that was the desert. The 'donkey boy', Lawrence told his mother,

> is an interesting character: he can read a few words of Arabic, and altogether has more intelligence than the rank & file. He talks of going into Aleppo to school with the money he had made out of us. I will try to keep an eye on him, to see what happens.[1]

By all accounts, Dahoum was a handsome fellow and a good wrestler. Lawrence had him pose for a sculpture, which he himself carved in limestone in the manner of the ancient Greeks, and displayed in front of his house. From his appearance, Lawrence guessed he was a mixture of Hittite (the ancient civilisation of northern Syria which included the area where they now were – Carchemish) and Arab.

There was an immediate affinity between the two, and over the weeks Lawrence was able to find out more about Dahoum, who now took on the extra task of being his servant and companion. He spoke of going to Aleppo to school; that was when he had made sufficient money from his work as a donkey boy, ferrying people to and from the site of the excavations. Meanwhile, Lawrence decided to ask Miss Fareedah, a local teacher, to help the boy with his reading and writing, and to loan him a few simple books with which to commence an education. In the same way that his own father Thomas had taught him various skills, so Lawrence taught Dahoum photography, and made him his laboratory assistant. However, perhaps remembering his resentment at his own mother's efforts to mould him to her will in matters of religion, Lawrence insisted that he remain a Moslem. He would respect Dahoum's faith, and there was to be no question of him being evangelised.

One day, the two rode out over the plains of northern Syria to visit a Roman palace. The clay of which the building was made had, originally, been kneaded with the oils of flowers whose aroma had persisted right up until the present time.

The guides led Lawrence from room to room saying, 'This is jessamine, this violet, this rose,' when suddenly, Dahoum said, 'Come and smell the very sweetest scent of all!' It was the desert, which they 'drank with open mouths'. This, the Arabs told Lawrence, 'is the best: it has no taste.'[2] It was then that Lawrence began to understand the soul of the Arab.

Lawrence had a great admiration for the Bedouin – the nomadic tribe who have inhabited the Arabian desert for centuries, travelling with their camels, sheep, and goats from oasis to oasis. He himself had adopted their attire, gone barefoot, and learned to live rough and go for long periods without a wash, or a change of clothes. He had eaten their food of camels' milk and cheese, bread, grapes, and figs.

'World-worthlessness' was 'the common base of all the Semitic creeds (relating to the family of languages which includes Hebrew and Arabic), and it was this which led them to preach 'bareness, renunciation, poverty'.[3] There was a 'homeliness' about the 'Arab God' of the Bedouin who was 'their eating and their fighting and their lusting, the commonest of all their thoughts, their familiar resource and companion.' Lawrence contrasted this with 'those whose God is so wistfully veiled from them by despair of their carnal unworthiness of Him, and by the decorum of formal worship.'[4]

In the summer of 1913, when Lawrence made a return visit to Oxford, he took Dahoum and his site foreman Sheikh Hamoudi, with him. All three stayed in the bungalow which his father had constructed at the bottom of the garden at Polstead Road, owing to the lack of space in the main building. The three drew glances, as they rode around the city on bicycles wearing their Arab costumes (Lawrence included), and when Lawrence took them to London and showed them the underground railway, Dahoum and Hamoudi were astonished. C. F. Bell of the Ashmolean Museum commissioned the distinguished artist Francis Dodd to paint several portraits of Dahoum: Lawrence describing the first, with the erstwhile donkey boy sitting down, as being 'splendid'; the second as 'almost a failure'; and the third as 'glorious'.[5]

In June 1914, Lawrence returned to England, leaving Dahoum behind at Carchemish. When war broke out in August, the Turks appointed the latter to be guardian of the site, which exempted him from service in the Turkish army. Lawrence was never to see Dahoum again, for a tragedy was to befall the youth which no one could have foreseen.

Chapter 5

Lord Kitchener

Herbert Horatio Kitchener looked up from his desk at the fresh-faced, tousle-haired apparition which stood before him; its khaki shirt creased, and its tie at half-mast. No one could ever accuse T. E. Lawrence of sartorial elegance! Yet the great man noticed that this 25-year-old seemed in no way overawed by his presence.

Born in 1850, Kitchener was already on his way to becoming a British institution. A soldier through and through, he had served in the French army in the Franco-Prussian War whilst still a cadet at the Royal Military Academy, Woolwich. As an engineer officer who knew Hebrew and Arabic, he had worked in Palestine and Cyprus, and from 1882 onwards, in Egypt as an intelligence officer. Following the siege of Khartoum, capital of the Sudan, by Sudanese revolutionary leader Mahdi Mohammed Ahmed in 1885, and the death of British General Charles Gordon, who was killed fighting the Mahdi's forces, Kitchener was appointed to lead the Anglo-Egyptian force whose object was to regain Khartoum and avenge General Gordon's death. In 1898, in the Battle of Omdurman, the Khalifa, successor of the Mahdi, was defeated.

In 1900, during the Boer War, Kitchener was appointed Chief of Staff to Lord Roberts. From 1902 to 1909 he was Commander-in-Chief in India. In 1911, by which time he was a Field Marshal, he returned to Egypt as British Agent and Consul General. During the First World War, as Secretary of State for War, he would raise three million volunteers for the British army.

Kitchener listened patiently, as Lawrence expressed his fears about the extent of German penetration into Syria. The earnest young man declared that he was worried because he foresaw a possible takeover by the Germans of the southern Turkish port of Alexandretta. Kitchener agreed, being aware that, if war came, then a clash with the Turks might well ensue. In this case, Egypt's Sinai Peninsula would be a vital buffer zone against any threatened invasion of that country and thus the seizure of the Suez Canal by the enemy. Events were to prove Lawrence right because, in 1915, the Turks did attack, whereupon it was the Indian army's Bikanir Camel Corps who were the first to confront them). Accordingly, Kitchener ordered a topographical survey of the area to be conducted, ostensibly under the auspices of the 'Palestine Exploration Fund'. In reality, this was to be a spying mission for which the Turks – who controlled the area around Aqaba (or Akaba) and Petra – surprisingly, gave their permission.[1]

Captain Stewart Newcombe of the Royal Engineers led the operation, and towards the end of 1913 he was joined in the project by Lawrence and Leonard Woolley, formerly director of the excavations at Carchemish. Lawrence's letter to his mother showed that he was well aware of the real purpose of his mission. 'We are obviously only meant as red herrings', he told her, 'to give an archaeological colour to a political job.'[2]

Chapter 6

Emir Abdullah

Abdullah, with a wavy beard, moustache, and mournful eyes, peered at the map. He was the second son of Ali bin Hussein bin Ali al-Hashimi, Grand Sherif of Mecca; the title 'Sherif' implying that he was a direct descendant of the prophet Mohammed. His family had ruled for nine hundred years.

In Arabia, different rulers held sway over different regions. Hussein ruled the desert area of the south, known as the Hejaz, within which territory lay the holy cities of Mecca and Medina. It bordered on the Red Sea, and its people were the Ateibehs. To the east was Ibn Saud and his Wahhabi people; to the north, Ibn Rashid and the Shammar. Persia lay to the east, and Egypt and the Sudan to the west. But it was to Turkey and the Ottoman Empire that the whole of Arabia deferred.

Abdullah frowned. The idea had come to him that if the various tribes of Arabia combined, they might rise up and revolt against their Ottoman rulers. He also believed that with the help of British and Allied forces, the Hejaz could withstand an attack by the Turks. Abdullah, therefore, decided to approach Lord Kitchener, British Secretary of State for War, to gauge his reaction. It was February 1914.

At first, Kitchener was unable to give the assurances that Abdullah required. However, both men were to be overtaken by events. On 4 August 1914, Britain declared war on Germany and two months later, Egypt was declared a British Protectorate. Then, on 30 October 1914, Britain declared war on Turkey. Kitchener now informed both Abdullah and his father the Sherif:

> Till now we have defended and befriended Islam in the person of the Turks. Henceforward it shall be that of the noble Arab.... It would be well if your Highness could convey to your followers and devotees who are found throughout the world in every country the good tidings of the freedom of the Arabs and the rising of the sun over Arabia.[1]

As if this letter, which anticipated the driving out of the Turks from Arab lands, were not enough, Kitchener continued, 'If Arab nation assist England in this war, England will guarantee every assistance against foreign aggression.' Abdullah smiled. He was satisfied.

Chapter 7

Lawrence's Role

Lawrence had returned to the Carchemish excavations in 1912, and again in 1913. However, he was soon to be drawn nearer to the nerve centre of Arab affairs.

When war broke out he found himself attached to the Geographical Section of the General Staff at the British War Office. This came about owing to the influence of his former mentor Dr Hogarth, who realised his value to intelligence. Lawrence now spent his time studying maps of the area of Sinai and classifying its roads and tracks. This reinforced his knowledge of an area through which he had already travelled extensively; an exercise that would shortly stand him in good stead.

On 1 November 1914, the Ottoman Empire declared war on the Allies, and soon afterwards Lawrence was commissioned as an officer and ordered to proceed to Cairo to join the Intelligence Section attached to General Headquarters, which was under the directorship of Sir Gilbert Clayton.

Lawrence was passionately in favour of Abdullah's idea for an Arab revolt. In fact, Lionel Curtis, Fellow of All Souls College, Oxford, stated that Lawrence,

> once told me that as a child he conceived the dream of freeing the Arab people from the Turkish yoke. This was why he learned Arabic. He could learn a language in a fraction of the time that an ordinary mortal would take. Lawrence himself also told me that he spent some of his vacations tramping Syria and thinking out the campaigns of Saladin. When the war broke out his strategic thinking was already done.[1]

Such a revolt would be not only a means of attacking the enemy Turkey but also, as Lawrence told Hogarth, a means to 'biff the French out of all hope of Syria'. Meanwhile, he brought his organisational skills into play by suggesting that a summary of news and information from the various theatres of war in the Middle East be published at regular intervals. The idea was put into effect in the shape of the *Arab Bulletin*, a periodical newspaper designed to keep the Foreign Office and High Commands in India, Egypt, the Sudan, and Mesopotamia fully informed of developments in Arabia. The first copy appeared on 6 June 1916, and Dr Hogarth was its first editor.

The Arab Bureau, which became the intelligence office for the Arab Campaign, was established in February 1916 by soldier and diplomat Sir Mark Sykes (who would subsequently become co-author of the Sykes Picot Treaty.) It was housed in Cairo's Savoy Hotel and staffed by experts on Arabia and the Arabs. Dr Hogarth, now lieutenant commander, was appointed its director, and Kinahan Cornwallis, a former civil servant and now an army intelligence officer, his deputy. Lawrence joined the Bureau that November: so once again, he and Hogarth were united. Hogarth later gave Lawrence credit for his part in the negotiations which had led to the Arab Revolt, and also for the role that he played in the organisation of the Arab Bureau.

Chapter 8

Gertrude Bell

Lawrence was sitting beneath a canopy, resting from the heat of the noonday sun with Dr Hogarth's deputy Reginald Campbell-Thompson. This was Carchemish in May 1911. Also present was a single lady in early middle-age named Gertrude Bell, whom Lawrence described as 'pleasant: about thirty-six' (in fact she was forty-three), but 'not beautiful - except with a veil on, perhaps'.

Born in 1868, Gertrude Bell was the granddaughter of Sir Isaac Bell, ironmaster of a foundry situated on the River Tees in County Durham. She had the distinction of being the first woman to reach the required standard for a first-class honours degree at Oxford University – though the degree was not awarded as in those times women were not permitted to be members of the university. She had been drawn to a study of the Middle East by the fact that she had relatives there, and had commenced her travels to the region when she was still in her teens.

In her book *The Desert and the Sown*, published in 1907, Miss Bell described her exploration of the Syrian interior. Here, she came across the greatest and most famous of the crusader castles, Crac de Chevaliers, which Lawrence was subsequently to visit in 1910, prior to the submission of his thesis for his university degree.

Miss Bell had irritated Lawrence on their first meeting at Carchemish in late May 1911, by telling Thompson that his ideas of digging were 'prehistoric'. She made matters worse by her fulsome praise for some German archaeologists whom she had just visited at Qualat Surgar, and in particular, for their attempts to 'reconstruct' the buildings they had uncovered. Lawrence therefore decided to give her chapter and verse on his knowledge of the Hittite civilisation, the remains of which they were currently excavating. Whereupon, she became, said he, 'more respectful' and on leaving,

> told Thompson that he had done wonders in his digging in the time, and that she thought *we* had got everything out of the place that could possibly have been got....

Having shown each other all their finds, they parted with 'mutual expressions of esteem', wrote Lawrence to his mother.[1]

In May 1911, Miss Bell described how she had met 'a young man called Lawrence (an interesting boy, he is going to make a traveller)'.[2]

Because of her extensive knowledge of the Middle East, Miss Bell was sent to Basra as the Arab Bureau's temporary agent in Iraq (whilst Philip Graves – journalist and writer – attended to Turkish affairs and A. B. Fforde represented the interests of India). Bell and Lawrence were to meet again in the near future.

A serious setback to the Allied cause occurred in the Spring of 1916 when the 6th Indian Division, under the command of Major General Charles Townshend, which had previously been successful at Ctesiphon, was cut off at Kut-el-Amara in Mesopotamia, having sustained heavy losses. General Sir George Gorringe's column, which was sent to relieve it, managed to approach to within 20 miles, but was unable to penetrate the Turkish cordon. The men were debilitated by the intense winter cold and lack of supplies, and the Moslem and Hindu soldiers of the Indian detachments preferred to starve, rather than eat horse meat (this being the only alternative), as it was against their religion. An attempt by Royal Navy river steamers to break the blockade failed and one of the ships, the *Junlar*, was captured. British aeroplanes made desperate attempts to supply the besieged division, but the quantity of food delivered was insufficient. A last-ditch attempt to save General Towshend and his men was devised by General Sir William Robertson, Chief of the Imperial General Staff.

This was the desperate situation faced by Lawrence when he was sent to Basra to meet Reginald Campbell-Thompson, his former colleague from Carchemish, and Gertrude Bell. He arrived there on 5 April; his purpose being to explore the possibility of bribing the Turks, in particular Jemal Pasha, commander of the Turkish Fourth Army, with a sum not exceeding one million pounds. In return for taking his troops out of the war, Pasha would be recognized by Britain as ruler of Syria.

Referring to this meeting, Miss Bell wrote, somewhat tongue in cheek:

> This week has been greatly enlivened by the appearance of Mr Lawrence sent out as liaison officer from Egypt. We have had great talks and made vast schemes for the government of the universe.[3]

One suspects that she was not averse to teasing her younger colleague! The attempt to bribe the Turks failed, and on 29 April 1916, 9,000 troops of the Indian Expeditionary Force - which consisted of both British and Indian Army units - laid down their arms to Turkish General Khalil Pasha.

Colonel Percy Cox, Secretary to the Government of India, was appointed Chief Political Officer with the Indian Expeditionary Force. However, he was distrustful of the Arab Bureau and feared that the sponsoring of Arab nationalism might harm Indian interests in Iraq. Nevertheless, Lawrence persuaded Cox, despite the latter's misgivings, to take Gertrude Bell onto his staff as the Bureau's 'Liaison Officer, Correspondent to Cairo'.

Gertrude Bell believed in the notion of Britain governing indirectly through local princes, and she saw no reason why this principle should not be applied as successfully in the Middle East as it had been in India. For Lawrence, however, as far as the Arabs were concerned, nothing short of complete independence would suffice.

Chapter 9

Sherif Hussein

Now elderly, with a long white beard and side whiskers, Sherif Hussein of Mecca was described by Lawrence as 'conceited to a degree, greedy and stupid', but most importantly from the British point of view, 'very friendly, and protests devotion to our interests'.

> Reason is entirely wasted on him since he believes himself all-wise and all-competent, and is flattered by his entourage in every idiotic thing he does.[1]

The Sherif had, in December 1913, received assurances from the British High Commissioner in Egypt, Sir Henry McMahon, that he might,

> rest assured that Great Britain has no intention of concluding any peace in terms of which the freedom of the Arab people from German and Turkish domination does not form an essential condition.[2]

The Sherif had no cause to love the Turks. When the Hejaz came under Ottoman Turkish suzerainty in 1517, his predecessors, the Hashemite sheriffs of Mecca, had been permitted to maintain a nominal rule. However, now using the Hejaz railway which they had built as their supply line, the Turks had gradually encroached southwards and had garrisoned the two holy cities of Mecca and Medina with their troops. In a further insult to the Sherif, they took him back to Constantinople to be held there in 'honourable captivity', as Lawrence put it, for nearly eighteen years of his life.[3] Finally, the Sherif was released by the revolutionary Young Turks, who succeeded the Turkish Sultan Abdul Hamid in 1908.

Turkey, when that country entered the war, attempted to persuade the Sherif's second son, Abdullah, to join her in a 'jihad' or holy war, against the Allies. The Sherif would have none of it, and buoyed up by McMahon's assurance that the British would support him, began to make his plans.

Upon learning that senior Arab officers serving in the Turkish army were in favour of the idea of a revolt, the Sherif sent Feisal, his third son, to Damascus to make contact with the Arab Nationalist secret societies. However, Feisal found the Arabs there were sceptical about the motives of European powers in the area, and rightly so.

Atrocities committed by the Turks in Syria – a country which they had occupied almost continuously since the year 1516 – and political executions there, together with the reinforcement of their garrison in Medina, prompted the Sherif to order Feisal to Mecca, in order that the Revolt could begin. In early June, Arab Bureau members Ronald Storrs, Dr Hogarth, and Captain Kinahan Cornwallis, met with Zeid, the Sherif's twenty-year-old youngest son, on an Arabian beach to work out its final details.

The Revolt began on 10 June 1916, when the elderly Sherif Hussein staggered out onto the balcony of his palace in Mecca bearing a heavy rifle, and fired a token shot at the nearby Turkish barracks. During the following weeks, with the Sherif's sons Ali, Abdullah, Feisal, and Zeid acting as field commanders, Mecca was cleared of Turkish troops. There followed a desperate, but unsuccessful assault on Medina, where the Turks terrified and demoralized the Arabs with their artillery, and failed to respect the Arab code of warfare by raping and butchering their people; firing houses and throwing living and dead alike into the flames. The Arabs were forced to retreat to the hills.

Ali went to the Red Sea port of Rabegh to find out why supplies provided by the British were not forthcoming, only to discover that they were being misappropriated by the local chieftain. When Ali's half-brother, Zeid, joined him and the stolen stores were discovered, the two of them decided to opt for a life of plenty and leave Feisal, who was up country, to battle on alone. However, the supply of obsolete British guns to Feisal's forces failed to make a difference, and he was forced to withdraw his troops. The start had not been a propitious one.

Chapter 10

Emir Feisal

He, Feisal, was wearing

> long white silk robes and his brown head-cloth bound with a brilliant scarlet and gold cord. I greeted him. He made way for me into the room, and sat down on his carpet near the door. As my eyes grew accustomed to the shade, they saw that the little room held many silent figures, looking at me or at Feisal steadily. He remained staring down at his hands, which were twisting slowly about his dagger.[1]

This was Lawrence's description of his first meeting with Emir Feisal on 23 October 1916; the name Feisal meaning 'the sword flashing downward in the stroke', and Emir, meaning 'chieftain and descendant of Mohammed'.

'And how do you like our place here in Wadi Safra?' Feisal enquired. 'Well; but it is far from Damascus,' Lawrence replied. The implication in his words was clear, and everyone sensed it. As he himself said:

> The word had fallen like a sword in their midst. There was a quiver. Then everybody present stiffened where he sat, and held his breath for a silent minute. Some, perhaps, were dreaming of far off success....
>
> I felt at first glance that this was the man I had come to Arabia to seek - the leader who would bring the Arab Revolt to full glory.[2]

As for the other contenders for leadership, Lawrence had previously dismissed the Sherif himself as being 'too aged'; his other sons Ali, Abdullah, and Zeid respectively, as being 'too clean', 'too clever', and 'too cool'.[3]

The meeting between Feisal and Lawrence had come about when the latter had sought the help of Brigadier General Clayton, Director of the Arab Bureau in Cairo, to allow him to transfer to it from Army Intelligence. Lawrence, it seems, was seeking a more stimulating environment from which to direct his boundless energy and talents. In the meantime, when he learned that Ronald Storrs, the Oriental Secretary to the British Agency in Egypt, planned to visit Jeddah, the port of Mecca on the Red Sea, Lawrence asked if he might accompany him. Storr's intention was to meet with Abdullah and discuss the progress of the Revolt.

Whilst they were there, Abdullah agreed that Lawrence might meet once again with his brother Feisal. As Storrs later recollected:

> I can still see Lawrence on the shore at Rabegh waving grateful hands as we left him there to return ourselves to Egypt. Long before we met again he had already begun to write his page, brilliant as a Persian miniature, in the History of England.[4]

This was a reference to Lawrence's forthcoming book *Seven Pillars of Wisdom.*

In the Arab Bulletin of November 1916, Lawrence gave a more detailed description of Feisal, the man he considered to be 'the leader with the necessary fire, and yet with reason to give effect to our science.' He was,

> tall, graceful, vigorous, almost regal in appearance… Very quick, and restless in movement. Is as clear skinned as a pure Circassian, with dark hair, vivid black eyes set a little sloping in his face, strong nose, short chin. [Also] hot-tempered, proud, impatient, sometimes unreasonable, and runs off easily at tangents. Obviously very clever, perhaps not over-scrupulous. Possesses far more personal magnetism and life than his brothers, but less prudence.
>
> A popular idol, and ambitious; full of dreams, and the capacity to realize them, with keen personal insight, and a very efficient man of business.[5]

Feisal complained that although his force of tribesmen received £30,000 per month from his father the Sherif, there were 'few rifles, insufficient ammunition, no machine guns, no mountain guns, no technical help, no information'. Lawrence replied that he was there 'expressly to learn what they lacked and to report it'. Feisal then briefed Lawrence about the history of the Revolt.[6]

From what he had been told and observed, Lawrence concluded that 'the tribesmen were good for defence only', and their keenness on booty 'whetted them to tear up railways, plunder caravans, and steal camels; but they were too free-minded to endure command, or to fight in a team'.[7] The only way 'their moral confidence was to be restored' after the setback at Medina was 'by having guns, useful or useless, but noisy, on their side'.[8]

Lawrence promised to do his best for Feisal, by creating a base at the Red Sea port of Yenbo where the stores, supplies, and armaments he needed would be 'put ashore for his exclusive use'.[9] He then sailed for Egypt where controversy was raging as to whether a brigade of British troops should be sent to the Hejaz. Lawrence argued vehemently against it, saying that the tribes 'would certainly scatter to their tents again as soon as they heard of the landing of foreigners in force'.[10] When he returned to Yenbo, Lawrence found Herbert Garland, Major in the Egyptian army and a demolition expert who could also speak Arabic, instructing Feisal's tribesmen in 'how to blow up railways with dynamite'.[11]

When Turkish aeroplanes appeared over Rabegh in November, four aircraft from the British side were sent to intercept them. Lawrence then set out to impress upon Feisal the need to attack Wejh, a port a further 200 miles up the coast. Again, the pageantry and drama of the occasion did not escape him. Feisal was sitting on his carpet.

> In front of him knelt a secretary taking down an order, and beyond him another reading reports aloud by the light of a silvered lamp which a slave was holding.

Feisal then informed Lawrence that the Turks had managed to slip 'round the head of the Arab barrier forces in Wadi Safra by a side road in the hills and had cut their retreat'. Whereupon the Harb – local tribesmen who formed part of Feisal's army – fled, as did the nearby force commanded by the Sherif's youngest son Zeid. 'The road to Yenbo was laid open to the Turks,' and Feisal had to rush down to Nakl Mubarak and protect it with 5,000 men until 'something properly defensive could be arranged'.[12] Following another Turkish attack, Zeid and Feisal had no choice but to fall back on Yenbo.

When Feisal suggested to Lawrence that he should wear Arab clothes, the latter, finding Army uniform 'abominable when camel-riding or when sitting about on the ground', readily agreed. He was accordingly fitted out in 'splendid white silk and gold-embroidered wedding garments which had been sent to Feisal lately by his great-aunt in Mecca'.[13] Colonel Pierce Joyce, who met Lawrence in Arabia during the war, and was later to broadcast for the BBC, suggested that it was 'not merely personal vanity' which led Lawrence to adopt Arab costume.

> Arabs have a respect for fine raiment, which they associate with riches and power. It made him an outstanding figure among them, excited their curiosity, and therefore increased his authority when dealing with them.[14]

The growing strength of the relationship between Lawrence and Feisal enhanced the ability of Arabs and British to co-operate with one another. It now remained to be seen whether their combined efforts would be strong enough to defeat their common enemy, the Turks.

Chapter 11

The Arab Campaign

'Feisal's stand at Nakl Mubarak' had only been 'a pause' and Lawrence was obliged to return to Yenbo, 'to think seriously about our amphibious defence of this port'.[1] An attack by the Turks was repulsed with difficulty. Meanwhile, the tribesmen kept up attacks on the enemy lines of communication, until five Royal Navy ships arrived with the purpose of raking any Turkish advance with their guns. The threat succeeded; the blazing searchlights of the ships deterred the Turks from making a night attack, and the crisis passed.

The plan, now, was to capture the town of Medina, and for Feisal to seize the port of Wejh from which further attacks could be made against the Medina-Damascus railway. Feisal's force, now 10,000 strong, was to be a 'many-tribed' one; the hope being, in Lawrence's words, that 'there would be no more silly defections and jealousies of clans behind us in future, to cripple us with family politics in the middle of our fighting'.[2]

Wejh fell to Feisal in January 1917, with the co-operation of Captain Boyle of the Royal Navy who attacked simultaneously by sea with a force of six ships – the fifty guns of which were directed by a seaplane. The Navy also put ashore an Arab landing party of several hundred men at an undefended place north of the town. With the fall of Wejh, the Turks abandoned their advance on Mecca and fell back to defend Medina and the railway, which was their vital lifeline. The tide was beginning to turn!

Lawrence was not slow to realize the beneficial effect that such a victory would have on the morale of his forces. Feisal, he wrote,

> was proud, for the advance on Wejh of the Juheina [tribe] was the biggest moral achievement of the new Hejaz government. For the first time the entire manhood of a tribe, complete with its transport and food for a 200 mile march, has left its own diva (homeland), and proceeded into the territory of another tribe with a detached military aim.[3]

From Wejh, Feisal was now able to make contact with the other nomadic tribes in the region and obtain assurances of their loyalty in oaths sworn to him on the *Koran.* Lawrence left Feisal's headquarters at Wejh on 10 March 1917 at Clayton's request, to visit Abdullah at Wadi Ais.

Troops under the Turkish commander in the Hejaz were now ordered to abandon Medina and retire northwards, using the railway to transport themselves, their guns, and their stores. By this time the British had crossed the Suez Canal and were making their thrust towards Gaza and Beersheba. With the prospect of these 25,000 Ottoman troops arriving to confront the British line, it was, therefore, decided that Abdullah should perform a pre-emptive strike against the Turkish forces. In the event, however, the Turks remained at Medina. This gave Lawrence, who was incapacitated at Wadi Ais for a month with malaria, the opportunity to rethink the campaign and achieve Clayton's aim of persuading Abdullah to concentrate on disrupting the railway.

On 9 May 1917, Lawrence was sent northwards to Maan, in enemy-occupied southern Palestine, to raise the tribes in the area. Clayton reported on this as follows:

> Captain Lawrence has arrived after a journey through enemy country which is little short of marvellous. I attach a rough sketch illustrating his route. He started from Wejh on 9th May with 36 Arabs and marched via Jauf to Nebk (near Kaf), about 140 miles north-east. of Maan, crossing and dynamiting the Hejaz railway en route. There he met Auda Abu Tayi of the Hueitat Tribe, whom he left at Nebk with instructions to raise men for a raid in the Maan-Akaba neighbourhood. Lawrence himself then rode on with only two men through, very dangerous country to a place near Tadmur where he interviewed Aneizeh Sheikhs.

He went on to destroy a small bridge at Baalbek, visited Druse chiefs at Salkhad, and then 'returned to Nebk where he found Abu Tayi had collected his force of tribesmen'. They then moved to Bair, where Lawrence left the Arab force and journeyed west, and then north. Having reached the southern shores of Lake Tiberias 'he inspected the bridges of the Yarmuk Valley'. He returned to Bair having 'destroyed the (railway) line in various places and derailed a train'.

> From Bair the Arab force (some 2,000 strong) swept the whole country down to Akaba, leaving Maan, but annihilating all the smaller posts including in one place, a whole Turkish battalion of some 500 men. The Arabs are now in occupation of Akaba where they have 600 prisoners, including 20 officers and a German N.C.O., and Lawrence estimates the Turkish losses in killed at about 700.

A minor inconvenience for Lawrence was when, in an encounter with the Turks at Abu el Lissan, he inadvertently shot the camel on which he was riding – through the head! A replacement, presumably, was provided; for Clayton subsequently recorded Lawrence's exhaustion after he had travelled 1,300 miles on a camel in only thirty days.[4]

On the strength of Clayton's report, Lawrence was recommended for the Victoria Cross by Sir Reginald Wingate, the High Commissioner for Egypt. Instead, however, he was, soon afterwards, promoted to the rank of Major and awarded the Distinguished Service Order (DSO) and made Companion of the Most Honourable Order of the Bath (CB). It was on the strength of this invaluable intelligence gathering by Lawrence, that Clayton sent him to meet General Sir Edmund Allenby 'to submit his suggestions to the Commander-in-Chief Egyptian Expeditionary Force and give the latter all information obtained.'[5]

Chapter 12

General Allenby

With the capture of the Red Sea port of Akaba in July 1917, Feisal and his Arab armies came under the command of General Edmund Allenby who had commanded the 3rd Army in France from 1915 and had subsequently been given command of the expeditionary force based in Egypt to oppose the Turks. Akaba was, thereafter, made into an 'unassailable base, from which to hinder the Hejaz Railway.'[1]

Lawrence described his first meeting with Allenby, and one may picture the scene: the commander-in-chief trying hard to know what to make of this young army lieutenant with startlingly blue eyes and a permanent grin on his face:

> Allenby was physically large and confident, and morally so great that the comprehension of our littleness came slow to him. He sat in his chair looking at me – not straight, as his custom was, but sideways, puzzled. He was newly from France, where for years he had been a tooth of the great machine grinding the enemy. He was full of Western ideas of gun power and weight – the worst training for our war – but, as a cavalryman, was already half persuaded to throw up the new school, in this different world of Asia…

When Lawrence proposed that the Arab forces could form the right, or eastern, flank of Allenby's armies in the advance through Palestine, the latter reacted favourably to his suggestion. In the end, said Lawrence, 'he put up his chin and said quite directly, "Well, I will do for you what I can," and that ended it'.[2]

As Lawrence told his friend Mrs Charlotte Shaw, wife of celebrated Irish dramatist and critic George Bernard Shaw, some ten years later:

> All he [Allenby] required of us was a turn-over of native opinion from the Turk to the British: and I took advantage of that need of his, to make him the step-father of the Arab national movement: a movement which he did not understand, and for whose success his instinct had little sympathy. He is a very large, downright and splendid person, and being publicly yoked with a counter-jumping opportunist like me must often gall him deeply.[3]

To Alan Dawnay, another of Allenby's officers, Lawrence wrote, 'I love him [Allenby] as Petrie [Flinders Petrie, the Egyptologist] loves a pyramid – not madly, but in proportion.'[4]

Lawrence then travelled to Jeddah to meet Sherif Hussein who agreed that his son Feisal, should become an army commander of the Allied expedition under Allenby. Allenby, for his part, summed up the relationship between himself and Lawrence – who now acted as Feisal's liaison officer - by saying, 'After acquainting him with my strategic plan, I gave him a free hand.'[5]

Whilst Allenby sent 'rifles, guns, high explosives, food and money to Akaba', Lawrence busied himself settling the Howeitat tribe, which he had discovered were in treasonable contact with the Turks. He did this by offering to advance their leader a proportion of a cash reward – 'something of the great gift Feisal would make him, personally, when he arrived'.[6] He also called for an air attack on the Turkish-held town of Maan, and with the help of British Army sappers, prepared himself for the mining of a train. This feat was successfully accomplished just outside the town of Hallat Ammar, when the Turks were swept off the railway carriage rooftops by machine-gun fire like 'bales of cotton',[7] and the triumphant Arabs looted and loaded up their camels with booty consisting of,

> mattresses and flowered quilts; blankets in heaps, clothes for men and women in full variety; clocks, cooking-pots, food, ornaments and weapons.[8]

Another train was mined near Maan, and it was here that Lawrence sustained a flesh wound to his hip – caused by a Turkish colonel firing at him from a window with a Mauser pistol.[9] Lawrence's 'pupils' became so expert at this type of operation that from one such mined train they captured £20,000 'in gold and precious trophies'.[10] As for the dispositions of the enemy, Lawrence stated, with typical thoroughness and attention to detail, 'we knew them exactly; each single unit, and every man they moved'.[11]

By November 1917, Allenby was poised to open a general offensive against the Turks, whilst Lawrence employed the Arabs to attack the Yarmuk Valley railway, and thence hinder their retreat. In Lawrence's words:

> Allenby's coming had re-made the English. His breadth of personality swept away the mist of private or departmental jealousies behind which [Sir Archibald] Murray [Allenby's predecessor] and his men had worked.[12]

Lawrence's admiration for his chief knew no bounds. Allenby was 'the man the men worked for, the image we worshipped'.[13]

The River Yarmuk passes through 'a narrow and precipitous gorge', and Lawrence decided that to cut either of the two railway bridges which crossed the river below would

> isolate the Turkish army in Palestine, for one fortnight, from its base in Damascus, and destroy its power of escaping from Allenby's advance.[14]

However, although two locomotives and three carriages were blown up, Lawrence's party, faced by determined Turkish defenders, failed to achieve its objective.

Meanwhile, Hogarth wrote to his wife Laura, expressing his concern for Lawrence.

> He… is away now on a very risky venture, and I'll be more than glad to see him out of it.… I only hope and trust TEL will get back safe. He is out and up against it at this moment. If he comes through its a V.C. [Victoria Cross] – if not – well, I don't care to think about it![15]

In the event, Hogarth's fears were justified for it was shortly after this that Lawrence was captured by the Turks, following an expedition that he undertook in order to reconnoitre the area around the town of Deraa. The abuse and humiliation which he suffered at their hands would change his life forever.

Chapter 13

Disillusionment

As he became more and more involved, both politically and militarily on the side of the Arabs, so doubts began to form in Lawrence's mind about the promises that Britain had made to them, promises that he suspected had been made more out of expediency than sincerity, and in this, he was absolutely right.

Sir Henry McMahon, the British High Commissioner in Egypt, had given a pledge that freedom for the Arab people would be an essential condition of any peace terms concluded with the enemy when hostilities ceased. Yet within a few months, secret negotiations were being conducted between Britain – represented by Sir Mark Sykes; France – represented by Georges Picot; and Russia. This was to culminate in the Sykes-Picot Agreement by which Syria, then a larger country than it is today, was to be divided into British and French spheres of influence, apart from its coastal region which would come under the control of the French.

Although Lawrence claimed to have had no prior knowledge of the McMahon pledges nor of the Sykes-Picot Agreement, which had been framed by wartime branches of the Foreign Office, he,

> not being a perfect fool… could see that if we won the war the promises to the Arabs were dead paper. Had I been an honourable adviser I would have sent my men home, and not let them risk their lives for such stuff. Yet the Arab inspiration was our main tool in winning the Eastern war. So I assured them that England kept her word in letter and spirit. In this comfort they performed their fine things: but, of course, instead of being proud of what we did together, I was continually and bitterly ashamed.[1]

Lawrence was to write of his 'agony of mind'; 'resentment at my false place', and 'internal perplexities'. Said he, in a note written, but not sent to Brigadier General Clayton:

> I've decided to go off alone to Damascus, hoping to get killed on the way: for all sakes try and clear up this show up before it goes further. We are calling them [the Arabs] to fight for us on a lie, and I can't stand it.[2]

Chapter 14

Degradation

Suddenly, a hand grabbed Lawrence's arm and he found himself surrounded by Turkish soldiers. Then, their sergeant spoke to him gruffly in broken Arabic (Although the Turkish language is based on Arabic, it would normally have been unintelligible to an Arab): 'The Bey wants you' – 'Bey' being the Turkish word for governor, and the bey in question here being the Governor of Deraa, Hajim Bey. They ignored Faris, the elderly peasant who had accompanied Lawrence on his reconnaissance mission to Deraa. The two had already located German stores, rudiments of trenches, and Turkish troops and their tents. Also, an aerodrome and sheds containing Albatross aircraft (biplane fighters, used by the Imperial German Army Air Force).

Lawrence replied in Arabic to the officer who had now arrived on the scene and pretended to him that he was 'a Circassian [a people from the north-west Caucasus] from Kuneitra [in south-western Syria]'. The Turks responded to this by accusing him of being a deserter. Lawrence countered by pointing out that Circassians are not required to perform military service. Finally, the officer said he did not believe him, and told him he was to be enrolled in the Turkish militia.

That evening, after being fed and washed, Lawrence stated that he was taken to the bedroom of the Hajim Bey: a 'bulky man' who 'sat on the bed in a night-gown, trembling and sweating as though with fever'. (In *Seven Pillars*, Lawrence refers to the bey – meaning 'lord' – as 'Nahi'. Subsequently, he uses the Governor of Deraa's correct name, 'Hajim Bey'.) Suddenly, the bey pulled Lawrence down onto the bed and a wrestling match took place in which Lawrence, despite his small stature, gave a good account of himself. When the bey offered to make him his orderly, and even pay him wages if he, Lawrence, 'would love him', the latter refused and pushed him away. The bey cursed 'with horrible threats' and began to paw Lawrence, whereupon the latter jerked his knee into him. Four soldiers appeared, and whilst they held Lawrence down, the bey hit him repeatedly in the face with his slipper.

Lawrence's clothes were torn off, whereupon the bey noticed 'half-healed places where the bullets [from a previous campaign] had flicked through my skin a little while ago'. The bey then took a bayonet, 'pulled up a fold of flesh over my ribs, worked the point through… and gave the blade a half-turn'. 'You must understand that I know: and it will be easier if you do as I wish,' he said. At first, Lawrence was dumbfounded, for he thought that this meant that the bey had guessed his identity.

On reflection, he decided to put it down to 'a chance shot, by which he himself [the bey] did not, or would not, mean what I feared' – i.e. that the bey had recognised him. Lawrence was then stretched over a bench whilst the corporal flogged him with,

> a whip of the Circassian sort, a thong of supple black hide, rounded, and tapering from the thickness of a thumb at the grip down to a hard point finer than a pencil.

Lawrence refused to cry out. When, eventually, he was forced to, he used only Arabic so as not to give himself away. Finally, he said, 'a merciful sickness choked my utterance'. Then, as he was being kicked, he stated that 'a delicious warmth, probably sexual, was swelling through me…'. After more kicking and beating:

> I next knew that I was being dragged about by two men, each disputing over a leg as though to split me apart: while a third man rode me astride. It was momentarily better than more flogging.

Then, Nahi (the bey) called, and Lawrence was cleaned up, but he was now rejected as being, 'too torn and bloody for his bed'. He was then taken to another room, where his wounds were washed and bandaged.

The following morning Lawrence, to his surprise, had no pain. Donning the 'suit of shoddy clothes' which hung on a door, he climbed out of the window and 'went shaking down the road towards the village'. He made his escape through a hidden valley of which he had previously made a mental note, because he believed (correctly) that it might later be used to advantage by his forces to 'attain Deraa town secretly and surprise the Turks'.

'In Deraa that night', wrote Lawrence, 'the citadel of my integrity had been irrevocably lost.'[1]

Chapter 15

Was Lawrence Recognised by the Turks? Was he Betrayed?

A letter from Lawrence to Major Stirling of 28 June 1919, indicates that Lawrence had changed his mind, and now believed that the Turks *had* recognised him and that it was 'by virtue of Abd el Kadir's [or Kader] descriptions of me', that the Turks were able, successfully, to apprehend him at Deraa. Lawrence also stated that he had 'learnt all about his [Kader's] treachery from Hajim's [the bey's] conversation, and from my guards [at Deraa]'.[1] Here, it should be mentioned that Lawrence had a working knowledge of the Turkish language.

A letter from Brigadier General Gilbert Clayton to Captain George Lloyd, dated 25 October 1917, indicates that the British had been aware, for some time, that there might be a spy operating against the Arabs:

> There seems little doubt that Feisal has a traitor in his councils and one who is well informed, as the enemy seem to get excellent information on Arab plans.[2] The traitor was therefore probably al-Qadir [or Kader], who, as Lawrence informed Stirling, with his brother Said, had been under surveillance by the British since 1915.

El Kadir was an Algerian who, together with fellow Algerian exiles, occupied villages on the north side of the Yarmuk Valley. When he joined Lawrence prior to the attacks on the Yarmuk Valley railway, the latter described him as 'an unexpected ally'.[3] Others, however, were not so sure.

Referring to a telegram received from Colonel Edouard Brèmond of the French Military Mission in Jeddah, 'warning us that Abd el Kader was a spy in the pay of the Turks', Lawrence declared, 'It was disconcerting. We watched him narrowly, but found no proof of the charge.'[4] Shortly afterwards, Auda abu Tayi, chief of the Howeitat tribe, warned Lawrence to 'Beware of Abd el Kader'.[5] Kader duly deserted, said Lawrence, and surmised that he had 'gone up to the enemy, with information of our plans and strength'.[6]

It was from 'Xury, the Druse Emir of Salkhad', that Lawrence later learned how Kader had 'spurred down the road' to Deraa, where the Turks,

> who knew his madness of old… disbelieved even his yarn that Ali [Sharif Ali, of the Harith tribe] and I would try [to blow up] the Yarmuk bridge that night. When, however, we did, they took a graver view, and sent him under custody to Damascus.[7]

Where did the truth lie? *Had* the Turks recognized their captive as being T. E. Lawrence, despite him being disguised in 'draggled clothes'.[8] When questioned, Lawrence told the Turks that he was a Circassian.[9] This was not as implausible as it might seem, for:

> Many Circassians are blond and blue-eyed [like Lawrence], while others show a common feature of the Caucasus: very light skin coupled with black or extremely dark hair. A lithe and erect physique were favoured…[10]

It is clear from Lawrence's account in *Seven Pillars* that he and the Turks conversed in Arabic.[11] Miss Fareedah el Akle, schoolmistress at the American Mission School in Jebail, who had met him at Christmastime 1910, and taught him that language over the following three months, stated that 'he picked it up very easily and in a short time he could speak and write a little as he was extremely intelligent and a good linguist'.[12] Therefore when he said, having been tortured by the Turks, 'In my despair, I spoke',[13] he spoke in Arabic, so as not to give his real identity away.

In *Seven Pillars*, Lawrence stated that following the assault on his person, he escaped at dawn from Deraa.[14] Had the Turks known who he was, a) it is inconceivable that they would not have detained him for propaganda purposes and b) they would have put him under special guard, and almost certainly have transferred him to Damascus. Therefore, even if Kader had betrayed Lawrence to the Turks, they evidently did not take him seriously, let alone act upon the information that he gave them.

Final confirmation that the Turks had failed to recognise him was given by Lawrence himself in *Seven Pillars*, where he stated that 'Halim [one of Lawrence's bodyguards] had been up to Deraa in the night, and knew by the lack of rumour that the truth had not been discovered'.[15]

Chapter 16

Rape as a Weapon of War

Said Lawrence:

> I went in to Deraa in disguise to spy out the defences, was caught, and identified by Hajim Bey the Governor....[1]

Lawrence's situation as a prisoner of the Turks may be compared to that of a prisoner in jail – yes, even in modern times – who finds him (or her) self at the mercy of his fellow inmates, or even of the prison staff. As for the motivation of the rapist, an article published by Human Rights Watch, entitled *No Escape: Male Rape in US Prisons*, states as follows:

> In the prison context, where power and hierarchy are key, rape is an expression of power. It unequivocally establishes the aggressor's dominance, affirming his masculinity, strength, and control at the expense of the victim's.[2]

The article goes on to address a popular misconception, regarding the sexual orientation of the rapist:

> Since prisoner-on-prisoner rape is by definition homosexual, in that it involves persons of the same sex, its perpetrators are unthinkingly labelled 'predatory homosexuals'. This terminology is deceptive, however, in that it ignores the fact that the vast majority of prison rapists do not view themselves [as] gay. Rather, most such rapists view themselves as heterosexuals and see the victim as substituting for a woman. From this perspective the crucial point is not that they are having sex with a man; instead it is that they are the aggressor, as opposed to the victim – the person doing the penetration, as opposed to the one being penetrated. Indeed, if they see anyone as gay, it is the victim (even when the victim's sexual orientation is clearly heterosexual).[3]

Referring to Lawrence's rape by the Turks, John Godl, in his article 'The Disputed Sexuality of T. E. Lawrence',[4] states that:

> Rape, in time of war... in the military context... was a means of stealing a man's honour, a victorious soldier emasculating a vanquished foe in the belief that by forcibly penetrating him he lost [would lose] his manhood. The indignity was more often inflicted on members of the officer class, in the belief [that] it robbed them of their authority as a leader of men, sometimes resulting in the victim's suicide.
>
> The Ottoman Turks were infamous for inflicting it [i.e. rape] throughout the Great [First World] War on captured enemy troops, beating and gang raping enemy officers often as a matter of due course. Prisons and garrisons often had personnel who specialized in this abuse, although there was nothing homosexual about it.

(Here, it is pointed out that the Turks were not the only race to practise such atrocities.)

> The Turkish soldiers perpetrating this war crime certainly never considered themselves gay, like male rapists in prison. The act has nothing to do with the sexual orientation of the attacker or victim.

Godl quotes clinical psychologist A. Nicholas Groth who, in his book entitled *Men Who Rape, The Psychology of the Offender*, states that rape in such circumstances is,

> ...not about sexual gratification, [it is] rather a sexual aggressor using somebody else as a means of expressing their own power and control.[5]

In other words, it is wrong to assume that the perpetrator of a male-on-male rape is necessarily homosexual. Lawrence's own sexual orientation will be discussed shortly.

Was Lawrence was telling the truth about the Deraa incident, bearing in mind that his account of it as appears in *Seven Pillars* is uncorroborated? If so, did his experience at the hands of the Turks adversely affect him in his future life? This will be discussed shortly.

Chapter 17

Onward to Victory

When Lawrence flew northwards to Suez and arrived at Allenby's headquarters beyond Gaza, intending to tell him of the failed attack on the Yarmuk bridge, 'word came from Chetwode [General Sir Philip Chetwode, one of Allenby's commanders] that Jerusalem had fallen'. This, for the Allies, was wonderful news. It also meant, said Lawrence, that 'the miserable details of [his] failure [i.e. to blow up the Yarmuk river bridges] could remain concealed'. Not only that, but Allenby, 'was good enough, although I had done nothing for the success, to let [Brigadier General Gilbert] Clayton take me along as his staff officer for the day'. The 'ceremony of the Jaffa Gate [Jerusalem]' was, for Lawrence, 'the supreme moment of the war'.[1]

Following the fall of Jerusalem to the Allies on 9 December 1917, Allenby and Lawrence agreed a plan whereby, the following February, the former would advance towards Jericho, whilst the latter would organise a thrust by the Arabs towards the Dead Sea. All being well, the two forces would then meet and join together in the Jordan Valley at the end of March. However, on 21 March there began a German onslaught on the Western Front, as a result of which troops were removed from Allenby's theatre of operations to be sent to Flanders to stem the enemy's advance there. Allenby was now ordered to go on the defensive, and the attack would have to be postponed whilst his army was rebuilt with Indian troops and Indian divisions from Mesopotamia. 'For the moment', he told Lawrence, 'we must both just hold on.'[2]

When the Imperial Camel Brigade in Sinai was disbanded Lawrence, now Lieutenant Colonel, asked Allenby if he might have their 2,000 camels 'to put a thousand men into Deraa any day you please'. Allenby smiled and the wish was granted.[3]

In Lawrence's words, Allenby's army,

> marched and fought nearly to a standstill, in the ledged and precipitous hills, shell-shocked and bullet-spattered, amid which they wrestled with the Turks along a line from Ramleh to Jerusalem.

Meanwhile, Feisal's Arab armies supported its right flank.[4]

The arrival of British armoured cars, driven by British crews, gave the Allies a hitherto undreamt of mobility. The cars were not used for close encounters. Instead, they stood off and softened up their targets by firing from a distance before the Camel Corps moved in to finish the job.

Lawrence paid his men £6 per month, but provided each of them with his own camel so that their money was 'clear income'.[5] However, such was the enmity between the men of the thirty tribes involved, that 'nearly sixty of them died', or in other words, murdered one another, whilst in Lawrence's service.[6]

Whilst Allenby's forces were taking Jericho, Lawrence's were halted when money to pay Feisal's army of 40,000 men was diverted by Sherif Hussein's son Zeid, who had been influenced by dishonest advisors. Whereupon, a dejected Lawrence left Tafileh and rode the eight miles to Beersheba to acquaint Dr Hogarth with the bad tidings. He took full responsibility and told Hogarth that he had 'made a mess of things'. He proposed to ask General Allenby to find him 'some smaller part elsewhere'. 'My will had gone', he wrote, 'and I feared to be alone, lest the winds of circumstance, or power, or lust, blow my empty soul away.'[7]

Dr Hogarth himself was aware of Arab deficiencies; of 'the nomad's acute distaste for sustained action and winter campaigning.' Said he:

> Nowhere as yet, have the Arabs held on for more than three days, at the outside, to any [railway] station or other point captured on the line, nor have they wrecked any of the larger bridges.

As for Zeid, said Hogarth, he was,

> deterred partly by the continued cold, partly by nervousness about operating in a new country under conditions unlike those of Arabia proper, but most of all by the natural inertia and weakness of purpose which he shares with some of his brothers.[8]

Clayton, however, impressed upon Hogarth Allenby's continuing need for the support of Arab forces. Therefore, in Lawrence's words, 'There was no escape for me. I must take up again my mantle of fraud in the East.'[9] In other words, he was aware that he was fighting under false pretences, in that the Allies had no intention of granting the Arab nations independence, once hostilities had ended.

Meanwhile, hit-and-run attacks against Turkish blockhouses, outposts, and telegraph and telephone lines continued, with the ever-present danger for the Allies of running into enemy patrols. Trained 'dynamiters' blew up the bridges and derailed the trains of the Hejaz railway, which deprived the Turks of vital food, arms and ammunition, and Arab forces claimed a great success when they severed the line, permanently, between Maan and Medina. This had the effect of isolating

Medina's 12,000-strong Turkish garrison and preventing it from moving against General Allenby.

For the past year and a half, Lawrence had spent his time,

> riding a thousand miles each month upon camels: with added nervous hours in crazy aeroplanes, or rushing across country in powerful cars.

Said he of his last five actions, 'I had been hit, and my body so dreaded further pain that now I had to force myself under fire.' The cold, hunger, frost, and dirt had 'poisoned my hurts into a festering mass of sores.'[10] And he continued to agonise over his part in the Arab Revolt:

> To-day it came to me with finality that my patience as regards the false position I had been led into was finished. A week, two weeks, three, and I would insist upon relief. My nerve had broken; and I would be lucky if the ruin of it could be hidden so long.[11]

As the palm trees quivered in the gentle breeze, the ground – like sand beneath his feet – was about to shift. However, despite his awareness of the impending betrayal of the Arabs by the Allies, Lawrence clung to the belief that he could help them:

> I salved myself with the hope that, by leading these Arabs madly in the final victory I would establish them, with arms in their hands, in a position so assured (if not dominant) that expediency would counsel to the Great Powers a fair settlement of their claims.[12]

And when the Arabs cut the railway out of Deraa he said of them,

> They had joined the war to win freedom, and the recovery of their own capital by force of their own arms was the sign they would best understand. Therefore, for every sensible reason, strategical, tactical, political, even moral – we were going on.[13]

And so Lawrence, despite near exhaustion, was dispatched to Akaba 'to make my new terms with Feisal' and plan for the forthcoming attack on Maan.[14] However, progress was slow, due to the strength of its Turkish garrison.

In July, Allenby, whose confidence Lawrence described as being 'like a wall',[15] was planning with the latter, an autumn offensive in which he would trick the Turks into thinking he was building up his forces in the Jordan Valley; whilst the real attack would come in Palestine, where railway communications were to be cut by the Arabs. As for Feisal, Lawrence's praise for him during these arduous and uncertain days was unbounded. For two years he had 'laboured daily', urging his men to 'compose their feuds' until,

> there was no blood feud left active in any of the districts through which he had passed; and he was Court of Appeal, ultimate and unchallenged, for western Arabia.[16]

Feisal 'laboured night and day at his politics.' He mediated and gave judgments in disputes; put down a mutiny by running barefoot into the midst of the mutineers, 'laying on with the flat of his sword like four men'.[17] As more and more volunteers and great sheikhs rode in to swear allegiance, he made them swear solemnly on the *Koran*,

> to wait while he waited, march when he marched, to yield obedience to no Turk, to deal kindly with all who spoke Arabic and to put independence above life, family and goods.

Said Lawrence:

> No Arab ever impugned his judgements or questioned his wisdom and competence in tribal business. By patiently sifting out right and wrong, by his tact, his wonderful memory, he gained authority over the nomads from Medina to Damascus and beyond.[18]

Lawrence made a comparison between the two leaders – Arab and British. Whereas Feisal 'was a brave, weak, ignorant spirit, trying to do work for which only a genius, a prophet, or a great criminal was fitted', Allenby:

> came nearest to my longings for a master, but I had to avoid him, not daring to bow down for fear lest he show feet of clay with that friendly word which must shatter my allegiance.[19]

It was on 18 September 1918 that Lawrence and the Arab armies, backed up by aeroplanes and armoured cars supplied by the British, cut the three railway lines out of Deraa where Lawrence had suffered his humiliation at the hands of the Turkish bey. At the same time, Lawrence feigned an attack in this area. The following day Allenby made his main thrust along the coast. His army comprised the Desert Mounted Corps (Anzac Mounted Division, Australian Mounted Division, Imperial Camel Corps Brigade, and British Yeomanry Mounted Division), which was commanded by Lieutenant General Sir Henry ('Harry') George Chauvel, together with 9,000 French troops, including Chausseurs d'Afrique and Spahis – Algerian cavalrymen of the French Army.

With Allenby's forces approaching from the south-west, and Lawrence's Arab forces approaching from the south, there is some debate about who entered the city of Damascus first. However, the end result was, in Lawrence's words, that the Turkish armies were 'scattered... beyond recovery'.[20] Emir Feisal arrived, as did Allenby, who parked his grey Rolls-Royce outside the Victoria Hotel. The city, says Lawrence, 'went mad with joy'.[21]

The capture of Damascus on 1 October 1918 was, to the Arabs, an event of immense significance. Not only did they regard it as the 'capital' of the desert, but as Gertrude Bell, the English traveller and authoress had written in 1907, this was a city which 'holds and remembers the greatest Arab traditions'.[22] Dr Hogarth, however, perhaps foreseeing the inevitable religious squabbles which would ensue, was more sanguine in his appraisal, and described Damascus as 'a great, but a very thorny acquisition'.[23]

Chapter 18

Discord

Lawrence described the first meeting between Emir Feisal and General Allenby when the former arrived from Deraa:

> It was fitting the two chiefs should meet for the first time in the heart of their victory; with myself acting as the interpreter between them. They were a strange contrast: Feisal, large-eyed, colourless and worn, like a fine dagger; Allenby, gigantic and red and merry, fit representative of the Power which had thrown a girdle of humour and strong dealing round the world.[1]

Feisal thanked the Commander-in-Chief 'for the trust which had made him and his movement.' However, the Australian Lieutenant General Chauvel, described what happened when Allenby, with Lawrence acting as interpreter, acquainted Feisal with the terms of the Sykes-Picot Agreement, made in secret between diplomats Sir Mark Sykes for Britain and George Picot for France, by which the Ottoman Empire was to be partitioned after the First World War. Feisal would govern Syria, with France as the protecting power, and he would make the day-to-day decisions in co-operation with a French liaison officer who would work with Lawrence. Lebanon and Palestine, however, would be controlled directly by Britain and France. Feisal objected strongly, saying he had been advised by Lawrence that the Arabs were to have sovereignty over the whole of Syria including Lebanon, but excluding Palestine.

Chauvel recorded as follows:

> The Chief [Allenby] turned to Lawrence and said, 'But did you not tell him [Feisal] that the French were to have the Protectorate over Syria?' Lawrence said, 'No sir, I know nothing about it.' The Chief then said, 'But you knew definitely that he, Feisal, was to have nothing to do with the Lebanon?' Lawrence said, 'No, sir, I did not.'

After Feisal had gone, Lawrence, seriously disillusioned by what he had heard, told Allenby that he would not work with a French liaison officer. He was due for leave, he said, and thought he had better take it now, and go off to England. To which Allenby replied, 'Yes! I think you had!' Whereupon, Lawrence left the room.[2]

However, Allenby did furnish Lawrence with a letter of introduction to King George V's equerry, and also one for the Foreign Office to enable him to expound the Arab case, once he had returned to England. And so, three days after the fall of Damascus, Lawrence returned to Cairo, and thence to England. In the meantime, the Allied forces captured Beirut, Horns, Hama, and Aleppo, and by the time the armistice was signed with the Turks on 31 October, the Allies occupied almost all of Syria and Mesopotamia.

British officer Colonel Pierce Joyce, who commanded the Egyptian troops which were supporting Sherif Hussein, and also helped train the regular forces being assembled at Rabegh, gave his opinion as to why Lawrence was such a successful leader:

> It was not, as is often supposed, by his individual leadership of hordes of Bedouin that he achieved success in daring ventures, but by the wise selection of tribal leaders and providing the essential grist to the mill in the shape of golden rewards for work well done.[3]

As for General Allenby, he was appointed British High Commissioner for Egypt in 1919, in which capacity he served until 1925.

Lawrence regarded Allenby as a professional soldier 'par excellence'. As for Allenby, once Lawrence had made it clear that he was not in sympathy with Britain's post-war strategy - *vis-a-vis* the French, the Commander-in-Chief had the wisdom a), to recognize the strength and sincerity of Lawrence's feelings; b), to grant him his wish to return to England and c), to provide him with the means to express those feelings to those that mattered, once he had returned home.

Chapter 19

Churchill and the Paris Peace Conference

Winston Churchill was born in 1874 and educated at Harrow School and at Sandhurst Royal Military Academy. Having served with the Spanish forces in Cuba he joined the British Army in India and in 1898 was sent to the Sudan, where he took part in the Battle of Omdurman. During the Boer War, as correspondent of the *Morning Post* he was captured but escaped and returned to England a hero. In 1900 he was elected to the House of Commons as Member of Parliament for Oldham, Lancashire.

From 1906, Churchill served in Campbell-Bannerman's Liberal Government in various capacities: as Under Secretary for the Colonies; President of the Board of Trade; Home Secretary, and First Lord of the Admiralty. After the disastrous Allied landings at Gallipoli in 1915 – in the planning and preparation of which he was involved – Churchill resigned, and in 1916 served in France at the Front with the Royal Scots Fusiliers.

In 1917 he was recalled to office by Prime Minister Lloyd George, and thus became Secretary of State for War and Air from 1919 to 1921, and Colonial Secretary from 1921 to 1922.

Churchill first met Lawrence early in 1919, prior to the Paris Peace Conference, when he took the opportunity to deliver a rebuke to him in the mistaken belief that he had snubbed King George V at a public ceremonial. The occasion referred to was Lawrence's refusal to accept from the King, whom he had met on Allenby's introduction the previous October, the decorations of CB and DSO. Only later did Churchill learn that, in fact, Lawrence and the King had engaged together in a private conversation in which Lawrence had begged that he might be allowed to refuse the medal and insignia. This action by Lawrence was not without precedent: other medals and honours awarded, but returned by him, being the 1914-18 Star, War Medal, Victory Medal with Oak Leaves, *Legion d'Honneur, Croix de Guerre* with Palms, and Italy Service Medal.

In an article for the *Sunday Dispatch*, entitled *Lawrence of Arabia as I Knew Him*, Churchill wrote as follows, concerning Lawrence's efforts to obtain justice for the Arabs:

> This was the only way in his [Lawrence's] power… of rousing the highest authorities in the State to a realisation of the fact that the honour of Great Britain was at stake in the faithful treatment of the Arabs. The King himself should be made aware of what was being done in his name, and he knew no other way.

Churchill also gave Lawrence credit for his action which had opened his (Churchill's) eyes 'to the passions which were seething in Arab bosoms.' Churchill went on to describe his subsequent meeting with Lawrence at the Paris Peace Conference which opened at Versailles on 18 January 1919. This, the latter attended in the role of technical advisor to the British delegation, and interpreter and link-man between the Allied powers and Emir Feisal (who arrived with his entourage from the newly independent territory of Hejaz):

> He [Lawrence] wore his Arab robes, and the full magnificence of his countenance revealed itself. The gravity of his demeanour, the precision of his opinions, the range and quality of his conversation all seemed enhanced to a remarkable degree by the splendid Arab headdress and garb. From amid the flowing draperies his noble features, his perfectly chiselled lips and flashing eyes loaded with fire and comprehension shone forth. He looked what he was – one of nature's greatest princes. We got on much better this time, and I began to form that impression of his strength and quality which since has never left me. Whether he wore the prosaic, clothes of English daily life, or afterwards in the uniform of an Air Force mechanic, I always saw him henceforward as he appears in [Welsh painter] Augustus John's brilliant pencil sketch.

Lawrence's views on what should happen in the Middle East after the war were well known. The previous autumn he had proposed to the Eastern Committee of the British War Cabinet, that the sons of the Sherif of Mecca should be made the post-war rulers of Syria and Mesopotamia; rather than the French or the Indian Governments who wished these territories to come under their respective spheres of influence. Such was his strength of feeling on the subject that he wrote articles in *The Times* newspaper publicising the role which Feisal and the Arabs had played in the war. He also spent much time promoting his ideas to American President Woodrow Wilson and his delegation, whom he met with in the hope that the Americans – regarded by him as a more benign influence than the French – might take responsibility for Syria. However, in Churchill's words:

> The idea that France, bled white in the trenches of Flanders, should emerge from the Great War without her share of conquered territories was insupportable to Clemenceau [the French Prime Minister] and would never have been tolerated by his countrymen.[1]

Also, Britain felt it necessary to make concessions to France in order to safeguard her own access to the Mesopotamian oil fields. And so, after three months of wrangling between Lloyd George and Clemenceau, it was finally agreed that the League of Nations (International organisation created in 1920) mandate for Syria and Lebanon should be awarded to France. When the Arabs resisted, the French reacted by expelling Feisal from Damascus. When Great Britain was assigned the League of Nations mandate for Iraq, this led to a tribal rebellion the following month, with much loss of life. Of this, Lawrence, the arch-proponent of Arab self-government, wrote,

> How long will we permit millions of pounds, thousands of imperial troops and tens of thousands of Arabs to be sacrificed on behalf of a colonial form of administration which can benefit nobody but its administrators?[2]

Lawrence also participated in the Allied negotiations with Zionist leader Chaim Weizmann, regarding the proposed creation of a Jewish national homeland in Palestine, and the immigration there of 80,000 Jews annually. When Felix Frankfurter, Professor of Law at Harvard who represented the Zionists, and Feisal met, it was Lawrence who was asked to draft the letter summarising Feisal's views. This letter, published in the *New York Times* on 5 March 1919, contained phrases such as 'working together for a reformed and revived Near East'; 'there is room in Syria for both of us'. Also, it was anticipated that the Jews would receive 'a most hearty welcome home.'[3] According to Frankfurter, the letter 'has ever since been treated as one of the basic documents affecting Palestinian affairs and Arab-Jewish relations.' However, its contents have ever since been a bone of contention. Feisal, who had represented his father Sherif Hussein at the Peace Conference, did not disavow its authorship. His enthusiasm for it may have been lessened, however, when the British failed to support him over Syria, to which country France was assigned the mandate, which she kept until 1946. Two years later, the independent State of Israel came into being.

On 7 April 1919, a telegram arrived for Lawrence telling him that his father was unwell. Whereupon he returned at once to England, only to find that Thomas had already died. Now, with the death of the 7th Baronet, there being no legitimate heir, the title became extinct.

Sherif Hussein's failure to agree to the terms of the Cairo Peace Settlement following the Allied victory in 1918, opened the door to Ibn Saud of Riyadh, who had always resisted the Sherif's claim to the Kingship of the Hejaz. In May 1919 the Sherif's forces were defeated by Ibn Saud's Wahhabi tribesmen. (In 1924, the Sherif was forced to flee into exile in Cyprus.) In the summer of 1920, an Arab rebellion in Mesopotamia was suppressed, with much bloodshed.

With the signing of the Treaty of Versailles (ratifying the peace between Germany and the Allied powers) on 28 June 1919, Lawrence's worst fears were realized when there was a failure to grant political freedom to the Arabs. Having previously been ruled by the Ottoman Empire, they and their lands were now placed under British and French control as League of Nations mandated territories.

Gertrude Bell (who had also attended the Paris Peace Conference) was critical of what she regarded as the misleading statements Lawrence was currently making in the press. Although aware of his support for the family of Sherif Hussein, she was especially worried by his failure to recognize the strength of his rival Ibn Saud, and cautioned him saying, 'You can't guard the Hejaz by backing Husain [Hussein] & dropping I.S.'[4] However, although she believed, rightly as it transpired, that in this respect Lawrence had misread the situation in the Hejaz, nevertheless, she was broadly in agreement with his aims for Arab self-determination.

In that same year, 1920, Hogarth referred to the Arab Revolt as follows:

> It would not have begun but for Kitchener's invitation in the first instance, and assurance of British support in the second; it could not have been sustained without the money, food-stuffs and munitions of which Great Britain provided; it might never have spread beyond the Hejaz but for the long sight and audacious action of Lawrence; and it won through to Damascus only as a flying right wing of Allenby's last drive.[5]

Chapter 20

Seven Pillars of Wisdom

In November 1919, Lawrence who, through being over generous to his friends, was in a desperately impecunious state, was elected, through the influence of Geoffrey Dawson (who was to become editor of *The Times* newspaper), to a seven-year fellowship of All Souls College, Oxford. Ostensibly, this was with the object of researching into the antiquities, ethnology, and history of the Near East. In reality, it was to enable him to complete *Seven Pillars of Wisdom* - his account of the Arab Revolt. By May 1922, he had completed the third draft, with eight volumes printed in Oxford.

Typically, Lawrence agonized over whether *Seven Pillars* was worthy of publication, and it was Gertrude Bell to whom he gave credit for encouraging him to proceed with the project. Her words, 'Wouldn't you consider publishing it for your friends?' were, according to him, what finally turned the tide.[1]

The beauty and elegance of Lawrence's style of writing in *Seven Pillars*, is complemented by his meticulous attention to detail, borne of a keenness of observation in regard to enemy encampments, troop dispositions, nature of terrain, and so forth. For example, of the mountains of Rumm he wrote:

> The crags were capped in nests of domes, less hotly red than the body of the hill; rather grey and shallow. They gave the finishing semblance of Byzantine architecture to this irresistible place: this processional way greater than imagination. The Arab armies would have been lost in the length and breadth of it, and within the walls a squadron of aeroplanes could have wheeled in formation. Our little caravan grew self-conscious, and fell dead quiet, afraid and ashamed to flaunt its smallness in the presence of the stupendous hills.[2]

Churchill was to write of *Seven Pillars* in glowing terms:

> As a narrative of war and adventure, as a portrayal of all that the Arabs mean to the world, it is unsurpassed. It ranks with the greatest books ever written in the English language. If Lawrence had never done anything except write this book as a mere work of the imagination his fame would last – to quote Macaulay's hackneyed phrase – 'as long as the English language is spoken in any corner of the globe'.

> When most of the vast literature of the Great War has been sifted and superseded by the epitomes, commentaries and histories of future generations… Lawrence's tale of the revolt in the desert will gleam with immortal fire.[3]

As for his rape by the Turks, Lawrence, in *Seven Pillars*, referred to this as 'the earned wages of revolution',[4] perhaps an indication of his underlying disillusionment over the fact that the Arab Campaign had been fought, in his words, 'on a lie' – albeit not one of his own telling.

Lawrence presented Churchill with two copies *of Seven Pillars*, for which he refused payment. One bore the inscription:

> W.S.C. [Churchill's initials] And eleven years after we set our hands to making an honest settlement, all our work still stands, and the countries having gone forward, our interests having been served, and nobody killed, either on our own side or the other. To have planned for eleven years is statesmanship. I ought to have given you two copies of this book!
>
> T.E.S.

The other bore the inscription:

> Winston Churchill, who made a happy ending to this show.
>
> T.E.S.

It was at All Souls College, Oxford that Lawrence began collecting poems by poets whom he admired. They included five by Thomas Hardy; three by Siegfried Sassoon, and others by Walter de la Mare and Robert Graves, whom he met at a college guest night in that same month of November 1919. Graves was later to introduce him to Edmund Blunden; John Masefield, the poet laureate; Robert Bridges, and the artist and sculptor Eric Kennington.

Chapter 21

Churchill Attempts to Make Amends

In the spring of 1921, Churchill was appointed Colonial Minister with responsibility for overseeing British interests in the Middle East. According to him, this,

> presented a most melancholy picture. Half a dozen very able men from the India Office, and those who had served in Iraq and Palestine during the war formed the nucleus. I resolved to add Lawrence to their number, if he could be persuaded.

Churchill duly offered Lawrence the position of his advisor, which the latter accepted. Said he:

> Accompanied by Lawrence, Hubert Young – a regular soldier fluent in Arabic whom Lawrence had first met at Carchemish, and Trenchard from the Air Ministry, I set out for Cairo. We stayed there and in Palestine for about a month.

The following proposals were now submitted to the Cabinet: proposals with which Lawrence no doubt heartily concurred. Continued Churchill:

> First we would repair the injury done to the Arabs and to the House of the Sherifs of Mecca by placing the Emir Feisal on the throne of Iraq as King, and by entrusting the Emir Abdullah [Feisal's brother] with the government of Trans-Jordania [now Jordan]. Secondly, we would remove practically all the troops from Iraq, and entrust its defence to the Royal Air Force. Thirdly we suggested an adjustment of the immediate difficulties between the Jews and Arabs in Palestine.[1]

Churchill was grateful for Lawrence's support, and he admired the way that the latter was able to 'sink his personality, to bend his imperious will, and pool his knowledge in the common stock.' This, he said, was,

> one of the proofs of the greatness of his character and the versatility of his genius. He saw the hope of redeeming, in large measure, the

> promises he had made to the Arab chiefs, and of re-establishing a tolerable degree of peace in those wide regions.
>
> One day I said to Lawrence, 'What would you like to do when all this is smoothed out? The greatest employments are open to you if you care to pursue your new career in the Colonial Service.' He smiled his bland, beaming, cryptic smile and said, 'In a few months my work here will be finished.'

'But what about you?' enquired Churchill, to which the reply came, 'All you will see of me is a cloud of dust on the horizon.'[2] So now, from being a victorious war hero who moved in the highest circles, T. E. Lawrence was to embark on a life of anonymity and self-effacement.

There was a moment of light relief, when in March 1921, at the end of the Cairo Peace Conference, Lawrence, Trenchard, Churchill, and Gertrude Bell rode on camels to the Pyramids to have their photographs taken.[3] When Churchill fell off his camel and insisted on remounting, Lawrence shook with laughter.

Even Churchill's efforts, on behalf of the Arabs, do not appear, totally, to have expunged Lawrence's sense of guilt and disgust about his part in the affair. In *Seven Pillars* he described looking back to August 1918 and his thirtieth birthday:

> It came to me queerly how, four years ago, I had meant to be a general and knighted, when thirty. Such temporal dignities (if I survived the next four weeks) were now in my grasp - only that the sense of the falsity of the Arab position had cured me of crude ambition: while it left me my craving for a good repute among men.... Here were the Arabs believing me, Allenby and Clayton trusting me, my bodyguard dying for me: and I began to wonder if all established reputations were founded, like mine, on fraud.[4]

Why did Britain and the Allies renege on their promises to the Arabs? A major factor underlying the debate over the post-war division of the Middle East was that oil had been found in Iraq and was needed in ever-increasing quantities, and it was in the national interest of both Britain and France to exercise control over it. The fact that Sir Arnold Wilson, former Deputy Chief Political Officer in Baghdad, later became the chairman of the Mesopotamian Oil Company, and that the American archaeologist William Yale was a senior member of the Standard Oil Company of California, is a measure of the commercial importance which the great powers attached to the region.

Chapter 22

Dream and Reality

Lawrence summarized his motives in choosing to play his role – a key one, as it transpired – in the Arab Revolt in a letter he sent, confidentially, to Foreign Office official G. J. Kidston on 14 November 1919, but which was only made public in 1968. They were fourfold:

> (i) Personal. I liked a particular Arab very much [this presumably was Dahoum], and I thought that freedom for the race would be an acceptable present.
> (ii) Patriotic. I wanted to help win the war, and Arab help reduced Allenby's losses by thousands.
> (iii) Intellectual curiosity. I wanted to feel what it was like to be the mainspring of a national movement, and so to have some millions of people expressing themselves through me: and being a half-poet, I don't value material things much. Sensation and mind seem to me much greater, and the ideal, such a thing as the impulse that took us into Damascus, the only thing worth doing.
> (iv) Ambition. You know how Lionel Curtis [Fellow of All Souls College, Oxford, and Lecturer in Colonial History who had corresponded constantly with Lawrence since 1923] has made his conception of the Empire – a Commonwealth of free peoples – generally accepted. I wanted to widen that idea beyond the Anglo-Saxon shape, and form a new nation of thinking people, all acclaiming our freedom, and demanding admittance into our Empire. There is, to my eyes, no other road for Egypt and India in the end, and I would have made their path easier, by creating an Arab Dominion in the Empire.
>
> I don't think there are any other reasons.

However, he went on to state that the first motive – 'Personal – had died some weeks before: so my gift was wasted, and my future doings indifferent on that count.' (This was clearly a reference to Dahoum, as will be seen.) The second – 'Patriotic – this was achieved, for Turkey was broken, and the central powers were so unified that to break one was to break all.' The third – 'Intellectual curiosity - was romantic mainly, and one never repeats a sensation. When I rode into Damascus the whole countryside was on fire with enthusiasm, and in the town a hundred thousand people shouted my name. Success always kills hope by surfeit.' And the fourth – 'Ambition – remained, but it was not strong enough to make me stay. If you want to make me work again you would have to re-create motives (ii) and (iii). As you are not God, Motive (i) is beyond your power.' And he ended, 'it isn't nice to open oneself out. I laugh at myself because giving up has made me look so futile.'[1]

In July, August and September 1921, Lawrence was in Jeddah trying, without success, to persuade Sherif Hussein of the Hejaz to accept the terms of the Cairo Peace Settlement. Lawrence himself did not find this task an easy one and described the visit as 'the beastliest trip ever I had.'[2]

In 1924, Sherif Hussein was ousted by his rival Arabian leader Ibn Saud of Riyadh, who had always resisted the Sherif's claim to be King of the Arabs, and whose Wahhabi tribesmen had invaded the Hejaz and defeated the Sherif's forces in May 1919. Ibn Saud's forces now overran Mecca, obliging the Sherif to go into exile: first to Akaba, and then to Cyprus. In 1930, when the Sherif suffered a stroke, the British Government allowed him passage to Amman, Jordan to be near his sons at the end of his days.

Emir Ali, eldest son of Sherif Hussein who succeeded his father as King of the Hejaz, reigned for only a few months before fleeing to Baghdad, where he spent the rest of his life as a pensioner of his brother Feisal. Abdullah, the second son became Emir of Transjordan (now Jordan) from 1921 to 1946, and King from 1946 (when the country became fully independent) to 1951, when he was assassinated. His son Tallal, succeeded him, briefly, until his abdication in 1952 when his son Hussein, came to the throne. King Hussein's death on 5 February 1999, marked the end of the longest reign of any Middle-Eastern monarch. As for Feisal, the Sherif's third son; when the French expelled him from Syria he became King of the British-mandated territory of Iraq, which became independent in 1932. He died in 1933 and was succeeded by his only son Ghazi, who was killed in an accident in 1939. Ghazi's son Feisal II, born in 1935, ruled under the aegis of his uncle Abdul al-Ilah until 1958. In the same year, Feisal II and his cousin King Hussein of Jordan proclaimed a federation of their two kingdoms. However, this was followed, almost immediately, by a revolutionary *coup d'etat*, led by Brigadier Kassem in which both Feisal and his Prime Minister Nuri as-Said, were murdered. Zeid, the Sherif's fourth and youngest son whose mother was Turkish, had no great interest in Arab independence. He lived for many years in London and died in 1961.

Egypt achieved nominal independence from Britain in 1922 under King Fuad I, and full independence in 1936.

Churchill, who in July 1922 finally, but reluctantly, agreed to Lawrence's discharge from the Colonial Office, admitted to a feeling of sadness when the latter left the scene, and hazarded an insightful guess at his reasons for doing so. Said he:

> I am sure, that the ordeal of watching the helplessness of his Arab friends to whom he [Lawrence] had pledged his word, and as he conceived it, the word of Britain, treated in this manner, must have been the main cause which decided his eventual renunciation of all power in great affairs.[3]

Churchill, said Lawrence, was,

> a great man, and for whom I have not merely admiration, but a very great liking. If we get out of the Middle East Mandates with credit, it will be by Winston's bridge.[4]

And in 1927 he described, 'the settlement which Winston put through in 1921 and 1922' as, 'the best possible settlement which Great Britain alone, could achieve at the time.' Nevertheless, said he:

> After June 1922 my job was done. I had repaired, so far as it lay in English power to repair it, the damage done to the Arab Movement by the signing of the Armistice in Nov. 1918.[5]

In other words, Lawrence, by that time, was reasonably, though perhaps not wholly satisfied with the outcome of events. So, was there an additional reason for his current lack of ambition?

To S.A.

> I loved you, so I drew these tides of men into my hands
> and wrote my will across the sky in stars
> To earn you Freedom, the seven pillared worthy house,
> that your eyes might be shining for me
> When we came

It was with this poem, the first verse of which is quoted above, and which was modified by his friend the poet Robert Graves, that Lawrence commenced his magnum opus *Seven Pillars of Wisdom* – the title being drawn from the Book of Proverbs, 'Wisdom hath builded a house: she hath hewn out her seven pillars'.

But who was 'S.A.', to whom *Seven Pillars* was evidently dedicated? A clue is given in the third verse:

> Love, the way-weary, groped to your body, our brief wage
> ours for the moment
> Before earth's soft hand explored your shape, and the blind
> worms grew fat upon
> Your substance.

This clearly implies that 'S.A.' was now deceased. As the greater part of *Seven Pillars* was written between February and June 1919, it appears, therefore, that 'S.A.' had died some time prior to February 1919.

In their book *The Secret Lives of Lawrence of Arabia*, Phillip Knightley and Colin Simpson described how, 'among Lawrence's papers in the Bodleian Library', they had discovered 'a copy of a note written by him in pencil on a blank page at the end of Sir Robert Vansittart's *The Singing Caravan*':

> I wrought for him freedom to lighten his sad eyes: but he had died waiting for me. So I threw my gift away and now not anywhere will I find rest and peace.[6]

Furthermore, the authors stated that Tom Beaumont, 'the British machine-gunner who served under Lawrence in the later stages of the Revolt', told them that:

> Dahoum, a grown man and past the nickname stage, was called both by Lawrence and the other Arabs by his proper name, which was not Sheik[h] Ahmed, as so many have believed, but *Salim* Ahmed. In Beaumont's own words:
>
> 'Salim was a very nice chap. He was fair-skinned; spoke some English and Turkish; and was skilled at photography and even accounts. He was not a soldier and never served as one. He was more like Lawrence's personal assistant. After he went behind Turkish lines, Lawrence would send someone to meet him, to take him money and instructions. And the messenger would come back with news of Turkish movements.
>
> 'We were at Umtaiye [20 miles south-east of Deraa] about September, 1918.[7] One day Lawrence told us, "Don't worry, I'll be away for a few days. I'm going to see Salim." When Lawrence came back I said to him, "Did you see Salim?" and he said, "He's finished. He's dying. He's got typhoid".'[8]

Dahoum and Salim Ahmed, or 'S.A.' were therefore one and the same person.

Of the deep friendship between Lawrence and Dahoum the donkey boy, there is no doubt, and it is reflected in a letter that the former wrote to R. A. M. Guy of the RAF in December 1923:

> People aren't friends till they have said all they can say, and are able to sit together, at work or rest, hour-long without speaking. We never got quite to that, but were nearer it daily… and since S.A. died I haven't experienced any risk of that's happening.[9]

When Dahoum died in September 1918, only one month before the Allies entered the city of Damascus, Lawrence's grief was akin to that of a father who has lost his son. Into Dahoum's hands, and into the hands of all the Arabs, he had dreamed of placing the gift of independence and self-determination, and now the young man had died before it had been achieved. Lawrence, to his way of thinking, had thrown his gift away. In other words, he blamed himself for Dahoum's death, however illogical this may seem. Now he was inconsolable.

So yes, the death of Dahoum may have been a factor in Lawrence's current lack of motivation. Also, Lawrence, was exhausted – as he himself admitted. 'If ever there was a man squeezed right out and dry by over-experience,' he wrote to Herbert Baker, the young architect whom he had met in Oxford (who had given him the use of a room above his London office in Barton Street, Westminster, where he could write *Seven Pillars* in peace) in 1922, 'then it's me. I refuse always to say 'ever' or 'never' of myself, or of anything alive: but I don't think that I'll ever be fit for anything again.'[10]

However, against this prediction of Lawrence's must be weighed his powers of endurance and stamina, which were legendary. For example, A. G. Prys-Jones (who was in the year below him at Jesus College, Oxford) stated that Lawrence, when on military manoeuvres with the college's Officer Training Corps,

> preferred to take his slumber outside, rather than inside the tent, but was an excellent marksman, and showed no exhaustion after any route march.

Therefore surely, after a period of rest and recuperation, this gifted man would recover and find some other great cause to espouse?

In June 1917, as already mentioned, Lawrence had declared:

> I've decided to go off alone to Damascus, hoping to get killed on the way.... We are calling them [the Arabs] to fight for us on a lie, and I can't stand it.[11]

Yes, Lawrence was extremely disappointed about the way that the Allies had treated the Arabs. But the question is, was there an even more profound reason for his change in character, his lack of motivation, and low self-esteem?

Chapter 23

Sir Hugh Trenchard and the RAF

Born in 1873, Hugh Montague Trenchard was a colonel in the Royal Scots Fusiliers, who had fought in South Africa before joining the Royal Flying Corps. During the First World War he commanded the British air forces in France. From 1918 to 1929 he was Chief of the Air Staff and in 1927 became the first marshal of the Royal Air Force.

In January 1922, Lawrence wrote to Trenchard, whom he had met at the Cairo Conference – where the latter had been present as representative of the RAF – to tell him that he would like to join that branch of the service 'in the ranks, of course.' Lawrence was aged thirty-three and in good health, and the reason put forward was that he wanted to write another book. 'I see the sort of subject I need in the beginning of your Force,' he said, admitting that it was an 'odd request'.[1]

In July 1922, after Churchill had agreed to release him, Lawrence was invited to Trenchard's home at Barnet where the latter tried, without success, to persuade him to accept a more responsible position. However, Lawrence had his way and on 30 August 1922, he finally joined the RAF as '352087 Aircraftman John Hume Ross'. (This was not the first time that he would change his name, as will be seen.) Here, during basic training at Uxbridge, and later at the RAF School of Photography at Farnborough, he gained the material to write his second literary work *The Mint.*

Lawrence gave his reasons for enlisting, in a letter which he subsequently sent to Dr Hogarth:

> The security of it first; seven years existence guaranteed. I haven't any longer the mind to fight for sustenance. As you realize I've finished with the 'Lawrence' episode. I don't like what rumour makes of him – not the sort of man I'd like to be! And the life of politics wearied me out, by worrying me over-much. I've not got a coarse-fibred enough nature for them: and have too many scruples and an uneasy conscience [i.e. to be a politician].[2]

However, Lawrence's efforts to achieve anonymity were in vain, for in December 1922, the *Daily Express* newspaper revealed, on its front page, the identity of the 'Famous War Hero'. This led, in March 1923, to Lawrence transferring to the Army.

On Lawrence's discharge from the RAF, under the heading 'Description on Leaving the Colours', under 'Identification Marks', the presence of 'Scars both buttocks' were recorded.[3]

Chapter 24

Bovington Camp and Clouds Hill

In March 1923, Lawrence was to be found as a private soldier, serving in the Royal Tank Corps Training School at Bovington, Dorset, under a new alias 'T. E. Shaw'. He selected this name, he said, not because of his association with George Bernard Shaw and his wife Charlotte, but, as he told Robert Graves, because it was the first one-syllabled name that appeared on the Army List Index.[1] However, the real reason was that he wished to discard forever, the name T. E. Lawrence because of its association with the betrayal of the Arabs in the desert campaign. Vehicles with which the corps was armed included: the Mark V tank; the Medium Mark C Hornet tank; the Vickers Medium Mark II tank, and the Rolls Royce armoured car.

Of Lawrence's 'identity change', Dr Michael Hunter, in his paper 'The Disputed Sexuality of T. E. Lawrence', stated as follows:

> Psychologists… believe Lawrence changed his name twice because he felt emasculated by his experience [the rape at Deraa] and wanted to escape the macho, action man image being forced upon him by popular culture increasingly obsessed with 'Lawrence of Arabia'. By changing his name, he took on another persona, left the wounded rape victim behind and became someone else for a period of time.[2]

This explanation is entirely plausible. The following spring Lawrence wrote again to Trenchard, saying that his main reason for staying in the Army was in 'the hope of getting back into the RAF,' which he longed to do.[3]

In 1899, the UK War Office purchased 1,000 acres of heathland in Bovington and adjacent parishes from Mrs Louisa Mary Featherstonhaugh Frampton of Moreton, who curiously enough was a distant relative of Lawrence. This was for use as a military camp.

During the First World War, an Infantry Training Camp was established at Bovington and in 1916 a tank training centre was created. The following year, this became the Tank Corps, comprising 18 battalions, 300 tanks, and tank repair workshops.

By 1919 the Tank Corp's Central Schools comprised headquarters, and Machine Gun; Tank; Signalling; Intelligence; Revolver; Anti-Gas; Bombing; Compass; and finally, Pigeon School! In 1922, an Armoured Car School was established.[4]

It was in September 1923, whilst motorcycling back to Bovington from Thomas Hardy's house at Max Gate, Dorchester, that Lawrence stopped at a small, derelict cottage set amongst rhododendrons. 'Clouds Hill' as it was called, had been built circa 1808, allegedly for one of the foresters of the nearby Moreton plantation.[5] (Clouds Hill does not refer solely to the cottage, but to the hill upon which it stands.) It was owned by the Frampton family, owners of the Moreton Estate, who were kinsmen of his, and from whom he duly agreed to rent it for the sum of half a crown per week. At this time, sculptor Eric Kennington, whom Lawrence had commissioned, amongst others, to illustrate *Seven Pillars,* noticed a deterioration in the latter's condition in that he seemed 'possessed of devils, visibly thinner, pale, scared and savage.'[6] Part of this may have been attributable to the recurrent bouts of malaria from which Lawrence was suffering at that time.

On the architrave above the front door of Clouds Hill, Lawrence carved the words *OU OPOVTIS*: the phrase deriving from a tale told by the Greek historian Herodotus about Hippocleides, suitor for the hand of the daughter of the tyrant Cleisthenes. Said Lawrence's brother Arnold:

> The Greek is not readily translated; 'no matter for thought', 'no care' are approximate equivalents'.[7]

However, to Lawrence himself, *OU OPOVTIS*,

> means that nothing in Clouds Hill is to be a care upon its habitant. While I have it there shall be nothing exquisite or unique in it. Nothing to anchor me.[8]

Yet beyond the confines of Clouds Hill, Lawrence had many cares, as Eric Kennington observed:

> One thing, I am certain of. T.E.'s malaise – it was a daylight nightmare – so obvious to me, [but which] was not seen by any of the young men [at Bovington Camp]. He joked about his Tank Town [the soldiers' nickname for Bovington Camp] troubles, so that I did not guess at his protracted torture there, but it was during his tank service that he paid us [i.e. Kennington and his wife Edith] a most strange visit, as usual without warning, and with a soldier on the pillion. There was a wall of pain between him and us.[9]

In *T. E. Lawrence by His Friends*, Kennington made frequent references to Lawrence's excessive giggling. This may have been an attempt by the latter to disguise his fear, or nervous anxiety, or to release pent-up emotions and inhibitions.

Is it the case that Lawrence's life was devoid of pleasure? No at all, for as Corporal Alec Dixon of the Royal Tank Corps recalled, of the summer of 1923:

> We had several outings together on the Brough, two favourite runs being to Salisbury and the Portland Bill. Another favourite spot of his was Corfe Castle, and he usually went there for Sunday morning breakfast if he happened to be free of church parade. Salisbury never failed to delight T. E., and he loved to wander round the Close pointing out the various periods represented in the architecture of its houses. T. E.'s conversation at such times was anything but dull, for he illuminated those architectural talks with amusing, and often ribald, asides on the habits of medieval priests and nobles. Our visits to Salisbury invariably concluded with a run to Stonehenge, particularly if there had been rain in the late afternoon. He liked to see the place just before sunset when the wet stones took on a purple tinge against the dull sky.[10]

In 1924, when the health of his beloved mentor and friend Dr Hogarth was failing, Lawrence described him to Charlotte Shaw as,

> a very kind, very wise, very loveable man. All my opportunities, all those I've wasted, came directly or indirectly, out of his trust in me.[11]

Chapter 25

John Bruce's Story

John Bruce, a Scotsman from Aberdeen, wrote an 85-page account in which he stated that 'for thirteen years I was Lawrence of Arabia's closest friend and associate, during the period of his life from 1922 to 1935'. He had delayed publication, having promised Charlotte Shaw and Edward Eliot, Lawrence's solicitor, that he 'would not write about Lawrence while Lawrence's mother was alive'. [As already mentioned, Lawrence's mother Sarah died in 1959. Bruce's account was acquired and published by the *Sunday Times* in May 1968.] Bruce stated that his account would 'serve to stop the scandalmongers who have delighted in blackening this remarkable man'.

Bruce had first met Lawrence in 1922, at the house of Edward Murray, a friend of Bruce's family doctor in Aberdeen, who worked in the City. He had come south, to London, seeking employment. Lawrence, he said,

> was broke, and unable to earn sufficient to pay his debtors, and there were many. There were vast sums outstanding, and pressure was being applied. That was the reason, why he nearly killed himself working all the hours that God sent on *The Seven Pillars of Wisdom*.
>
> What I'm looking for he [Lawrence] said, is someone like you, young, strong and alert who can be trusted with highly confidential personal matters, and to do what he is told without question. Everything will be legal and above board....

At the time, said Bruce, Lawrence was employed at the Colonial Office. However, on this occasion he looked 'very ill and worn out, so ill that I suggested he saw a doctor'. Lawrence agreed to pay Bruce,

> a retainer of three pounds a week to be on call, this was to last three months. He told me some time later that he was quite confident that the proceeds of *Seven Pillars* would meet all his debts, leaving a big margin.

Bruce was given to understand that Lawrence had made an arrangement for the publication of his book with a publisher, 'but he would need to have a guarantor as security'. It was also Bruce's understanding that Lawrence had made contact with a 'relation of wealth' to whom he had assigned the copyright for his book. Lawrence referred to the 'relation of wealth' as the 'Old Man'. In return, the relation would pay his debts, and any surplus would revert to Lawrence, 'less bank interest rates'. Edward Eliot duly drew up the contract. 'Then came the blow, which was to change his whole life. He lost his job at the Colonial Office.' The reason for this, according to Bruce, was that before joining the Colonial Office he had told Zionist leader Dr Chaim Weizmann, that 'the Anglican Mission in Jerusalem was a hotbed for anti-Jewish propaganda', to which the Anglican Bishop of Jerusalem, Dr. McInnes, 'strongly protested and wanted Lawrence to deny making such a statement'. However, Lawrence 'would neither deny nor confirm that the statement came from him'. As for the 'Old Man', said Bruce, he called Lawrence,

> a cheat, and a liar. Told him he had dragged the family name through the gutters. He had turned his back on God, he had insulted a Bishop, insulted King George at Buckingham Palace, he had ruined the life of a great Foreign Minister, referring to Lord Curzon… [Lawrence was] a 'Bastard' not fit to live amongst decent people. He was told the matter was of such a serious nature, that a meeting of the family would have to be called, to see what was to be done with him, the alternative would be to place himself in his hands unreservedly, which meant the copyrights etc.
>
> He was told, that he had borrowed money from friends under false pretences, and would probably land in court unless the monies were paid right away, bringing further disgrace on his family.

> As I write this a lump comes into my throat, I can see his face now, as if he were telling me over again, he kept on saying, 'he [the Old Man] called me a Bastard and meant it. How he must loathe us, for my father's sins'.

This was a clear reference by Lawrence to his father's infidelity in marriage, and to his own consequent illegitimacy.

In July/August 1922, Bruce spent a month in London, at Lawrence's request. Lawrence was,

> nervous and dejected, ill at ease, he didn't look kept, and he was very quiet. We had a cup of tea, with not much being said, and went straight to Barton Street. He told me something terrible had happened to him and he wanted to tell someone, but before doing so, he wanted to know what my future plans were. Have you ever thought about the services he asked; not for me, I said.

Lawrence told Bruce that what he was about to hear was 'in the utmost confidence and should be treated very seriously':

> He started off by telling me that he had agreed to 'the old man's' conditions, and there was no road back until the conditions were fulfilled to the entire satisfaction of the 'old man' which could take years. He had the option of being sent to Siberia or joining the Army as a private soldier, his business affairs to be controlled for him – this also applied to money matters – his discipline to be controlled by the 'old man' personally; any breach of these conditions would only prolong the length of time.
>
> He was told he must not visit his [the old man's] house again, unless asked to do so, but he would be required to submit a report about his activities once a month until further notice.

Said Lawrence to Bruce:

> I feel safe with you, safer than I have been for a long time.' By agreeing to the 'old man' the slate will be clean, [and] while I am in his hands, I shall have the satisfaction of knowing he won't turn his wrath on any other members of my family. Now do you understand why I agreed to his demands? I had to agree with him, and said, I have my mother to consider, and she comes first, whatever happens to me.
>
> Have I not made it clear to you, I'm on the edge of a precipice crying for help, and you can help. I am sure of that. The reason it's you, and not one of my friends is easy to answer. They can't be trusted. Most of them would be willing to help, for their own personal gain, and I know you would not have that in mind.

The 'Old Man', Lawrence told Bruce,

> 'has mentioned that my physique requires attention and training would be necessary, he will make me do everything I hate to do, and where you fit into things, depends entirely on him. I was made to swear over a bible by the old man that I would respect his every wish, and that's how it's going to be, there must be no half measures regarding his instructions'. [Said Bruce] Corporal punishment was mentioned, but that will be resisted, in what manner this was meant was never mentioned.
>
> [Continued Lawrence] 'When I go into the Army you will return to Aberdeen, a telegram at mid-day will bring you south early next day when needed, but you must not tie yourself to any job from which you can't get away'.
>
> The night before his enlistment, was spent at Barton Street, he walked the floor most of the night, and was in a heck of a state. We parted company after breakfast, I did not see him again until

> November. Several letters passed between us. He hinted on several occasions that the 'old man' was not satisfied, with the easy life he was leading in the Royal Air Force and had told him he had no right to be there at all, as it had been arranged that he join the Army, and he had disobeyed his instructions.

At Lawrence's request, Bruce travelled to Farnborough to meet him,

> as there were things that needed to be discussed. I got there two days later and found him most distressed, he told me a birch had arrived, there was a small note with it, saying further instructions would follow. We agreed I'd get digs in town and wait developments. I told him then, he had to put his foot down right away.

Lawrence, however, refused:

> I've already told you, I agreed to his conditions without reserve and if I kick now, this hellish life could go on indefinitely. I'm fit enough now to take a few over the buttocks, and if that's what he wants, that's what he will get, anyway this is the penalty for cheating.

This was evidently a reference to the fact that Lawrence had disobeyed the Old Man's instructions, by joining the RAF instead of the Army.

Said Bruce, 'The next I heard of him was in the press, who gave full cover about his being thrown out of the Royal Air Force.' Whereupon Bruce returned to London to search for him:

> It was now about the end of January 1923. I got a job the following day in London as Bouncer at a night club in Sussex Gardens in Paddington. Then early one morning when the club was closing up, I went outside to get a cab for a club client, there he was. When I saw him, my eyes filled with tears, not at seeing him, but the mess he was in, he looked ragged, worn out and dirty. It was to hell with the cab and the clients. I got him downstairs to a back room, the first thing he said was 'Oh Jock, I'm ashamed'. He put both hands over his face and cried like a child. I got him something to eat, while he got cleaned up, and we went back to my digs in Preeb Street, where he had a hot bath. I sent him straight to bed, and slept in a chair for the rest of the morning. He woke about mid-day. I was to be told, that for the past two weeks, he had had a bed in a Salvation Army hostel at a shilling a night, and that he had no more shillings left.

Bruce suggested that Lawrence should 'confide in his family', which,

> he flatly refused to do. 'The "old man" is the only one who can help now, and I must see him' which he did. I was never told what took place at that meeting. All he said was, it has got to be the Tank Corps, nothing else.
>
> The significance of this lies in the fact, that the 'Blood Relations' were large landowners in Dorsetshire especially around Bovington Camp, the Tank Corps Depot, where all tank recruits were sent for their training period, and that Clouds Hill, which was to be his cottage later on, was on their land.
>
> I came to the conclusion that he was so alone and frightened, not of people, but things, because he was so vulnerable for which fact, he would submit to most things without much resistance, in case he was found out [i.e. in case his fear and vulnerability were discovered]. Lawrence admitted that what I had said, was exactly his fears, adding, I'll be found out anyway, sooner or later, what then I asked, the same thing all over again. Would you feel safer if I joined with you? He said 'Oh Jock, would you do that for me? I'm not worth it, but honestly, I wanted to ask if you would, but daren't in case you refused.' I said to myself inwardly, my God what have I done. Now we have a Lawrence, no longer alone and afraid, confident nothing the future held, could not be surmounted.
>
> We made arrangements that I should return to Aberdeen, to straighten my personal affairs, and that I should join [the Tank Corps] in Aberdeen. We met by arrangement in Bournemouth in March. We entered the guard room together at the Royal Tank Corps Depot, Bovington Camp, Wool, and were put into Hut 12 in 'B' Company.

While he and Lawrence were serving in the Tank Corps, said Bruce,

> we never knew it then, but his every move had been watched and noted by a private eye, who was reporting back to the 'old man'. This fellow went about his business in a way that created no suspicion whatsoever. He was employed by a camp contractor, and by carrying a pass he was allowed to roam the camp at will.
>
> One day at lunch time, he [Lawrence] told me he wanted to see me at four o'clock the same day, as he had received a letter from the 'old man' and there was one for me too; he looked furious as he walked quickly away. After duty, we walked to Bovington – on the way down, he asked if I [had] kept a record of his movements since we joined the Tanks.

Lawrence then showed Bruce the letter he had received, from the 'Old Man', and declared, 'it's perfectly clear I'm being double-crossed, and you are the only person who is in possession of such details':

> On the following Sunday evening he came to me very sheepish and said, 'I have been to see the "old man" today, and I owe you an apology, a grave injustice has been done, please forgive me. The "old man" has had a private eye on me since the first day I came here, and has collected enough misinformation to put me in bad for years to come.'
>
> Round about this time Lawrence had got himself a cottage a mile from the Camp, named Clouds Hill. I asked him, how he managed to get it, when he had no money, he told me, it belonged to a 'blood relation' and stood on their land, and he had no difficulty in getting the titles, and there were five acres thrown in, which was a half truth, something he was expert in telling.
>
> However, said Bruce
>
> I never knew of one deliberate lie crossing his lips. When he was covering things up, that was the time he was at his best in that field, half truths.
>
> You can see how the 'old man's' pattern is taking place. The paying of Lawrence's debts, in return for the copyrights of his writings, control of his finances, choice of friends, complete domination of his life to suit his pleasure.

Lawrence told Bruce that the 'Old Man' wanted to meet him at a hotel in Bournemouth. When he and Bruce arrived, Bruce was asked to go upstairs to a room which was,

> partitioned off by a screen, the old man was at one side, and Lawrence and I at the other; there was a mirror at his side by which he could see us, but we could not see him. Then something happened: the mirror was on casters, a huge floor mirror [and] instead of him seeing us, we saw him, and Lawrence went round, and put it right for the old man, but he was too late. I saw him. The next time I saw that face was in 1935, at Eliot's office, but the things he said shall be an imprint on my mind for evermore.

Lawrence subsequently gave Bruce a typed, two-page letter, which was from the 'Old Man'. It outlined,

> what was to be expected from Lawrence (referring to him by relationship) stating that Lawrence had agreed on his honour to carry out his instructions implicitly and without hinderence [sic]. I have been told of your [i.e. Bruce's] assistance to help him on his way to recovery, both he and I, are appreciative of your efforts, and wish

> it to continue, although, I understand it is your desire to return to civilian life.

However, the 'Old Man' would prefer it if Bruce changed his mind. Having returned to Clouds Hill, Lawrence told Bruce that,

> the private eye was to be withdrawn on certain conditions (which I was not told). He begged me to stay on in the Tanks for awhile; at the most he said, it would only be two years, as the *Seven Pillars* would be published by then, he could square up with the 'old man', and with money that was over he could start up a [printing] press. He would need assistance with that, and he would be pleased to have me with him if I accepted, he said. Your future would most certainly be assured. I agreed to stay on these conditions. [However, said Bruce] the only thing that never crossed his mind was that the copyrights were no longer his, and that the negotiations for the publication were no longer in his hands.
>
> Lawrence really got to work now, every spare hour he was not soldiering was spent writing at the cottage. Our squad had completed its training period in August [1923]. Lawrence was transferred from 'B' Company to be storeman in 'A' Company.
>
> In the store hut he had his own bunk, and was afforded complete privacy, which gave him two places to write if he wished, and he made good use of both for that purpose. Because he worked all hours in the hut, sometimes until daybreak, he ate little, and never went to the dining room nor the canteen, an apple kept him going for a long stretch, he never went to the weekly pay parades, leaving his wages for weeks on end.
>
> Time had again come round for a visit to the 'old man', and there was a letter for me, with some questions to answer, in which he made it clear, my answers had to be direct and honest, I was not to show his (....)[1] any correspondence which past [sic] between us.

When Bruce was in Scotland on leave, he was summoned back by Lawrence, who,

> said he would be in London for a week straightening up his affairs and intended disappearing for good as he could no longer go on. He told me the 'old man' knew everything he had done since his last visit, and the terms which had been imposed on him, had been added to, and it was impossible to accept. Lawrence had been told by a publishing house who he had been doing translations for, that they had been informed, that any money from his work was to go to a trust – we know who the trust was! – but he had already been paid and the money spent.

> Now I knew where the money he had been spending in camp came from. I learnt from Lawrence that he had been doing translations in the storeroom, and the work on the *Seven Pillars* was being done at Clouds Hill.

Bruce suggested to Lawrence that,

> if he could borrow the money from another source, he could withdraw from the trust which he had entered, by buying it off. This would leave the *Pillars* as his property. All he said was, his [the Old Man's] obsession about my father will make that impossible.

Bruce observed,

> two blobs of froth at the side of his mouth, no doubt caused by nervous tension, and his face was grey looking, illness was upon him, and he needed attention.

The following day, said Lawrence,

> about what you told me, I've given that a lot of thought, could we talk about that again? I'll not surrender my right to live because I'm my father's son.

Lawrence, said Bruce ,

> had already told the Shaws about his financial position, and their help was there for the taking. He went and saw the 'old man' at the weekend, and I understand there were high words between them, and he lost, but the air was clearer, and he knew where he stood.

Bruce told Lawrence that,

> no man in his right senses would stand for this barbaric treatment, and if there was more that he had not told me, then this was the time to do it. 'There is more, lots more', he replied, 'do you think I would submit to this humiliation willingly, when all I have to do to rid myself of it, is to take Shaw up on his offer. If I back down he [the 'Old Man'] would ruin the Lawrence family, and that's not going to happen.

When Bruce informed Lawrence that he would after all, remain in the Army for another two years, Lawrence's,

> face lit up, and I think his eyes did too. 'Your place could never be filled', he said, 'I could trust no other.'

However, Bruce was transferred to 'C' Company and subsequently posted to Lydd in Kent. Shortly afterwards, however, he was discharged. Bruce subsequently learnt that Lawrence had arranged his (Bruce's) discharge 'on medical grounds, although I never reported sick, never was sick, and had never been sick in my life'. Bruce stated that, in writing about Lawrence, he did not 'wish to discredit him, for his weakness's [sic] in submitting to a victorian barbarian, and religious maniac of the same blood'.

Bruce now found work at a garage in Bournemouth, where he remained until Lawrence had completed *Seven Pillars*. On one occasion, when Lawrence and Bruce were attending a gymnasium in the town, Bruce,

> noticed there were marks on his legs, high above the knees, when I asked what they were, he flushed up, saying, nothing really. I was not happy about this and told him so, and insisted he should tell me how they got there. 'A birch', he said. 'Good God no, I understood you had agreed there would be none of that.' All I could get out of him was 'forget it'.
>
> There can be no doubt he was going through more than I was to know, which was having some effect on his judgement. He just couldn't care less for anything, or anyone. I was invited to Clouds Hill for the week-end, when my suspicion was confirmed. He poured out his heart to me, and told me what had been going on, saying it could not go on much longer, as he had again reached the end of his tether.

Having visited the coastal town of Poole with Lawrence on the motorcycle, and returned to Clouds Hill, Bruce declared:

> I thought that the ride would have blown away the blues, but no, intuition told me to keep alert. I knew there was a revolver in a chest in the box-room opposite to where we were, also kept there were the sleeping bags. As the evening wore on, I said I would get the bags ready, I went to get them, and at the same time, I looked to see if the gun was still there. It was, but loaded. This never used to be. I took the bullets out, and took the box with the rest of them, put the gun back, and the cartridges I put into my sleeping bag. There was no lavatory in the house, and before retiring one had to go outside, I went outside first, and when I came back he went.
>
> As soon as he was safely out of the door, I looked in the chest, the gun had gone, I took six cartridges and went down to the door. He had obviously gone further than was the custom, and was away

> longer than usual. In the still of the night I heard a click. When he did get to the door, I asked if he had been looking for something, he said 'no', I asked 'not even these', holding out the cartridges in my hand, and in the half light I could see his eyes popping out of his head, then he said, 'Give them to me', and tried to snatch them from me. 'No you give me that right now', I said, and a little scuffle took place, he trying to get the cartridges, and I trying to get the gun. I bashed his head against the wall until he dropped it, then he cried like a child. I got him up the stairs, but I'm afraid there was no sleep that night. There is no doubt he was ending it, because, the next day, we destroyed eighteen letters which he had written to various people, before I had arrived. [These letters were, presumably, suicide notes.] As I have said, we talked into the early hours of the morning, and he told me how he had been double-crossed.
>
> He had been informed that only one hundred copies of the *Seven Pillars* were to be published, and that was what he had to arrange, all the protests in the world could not alter that, as the copyrights were not his. [This meant that *Seven Pillars*] would be published at a heavy loss, putting his bank account thousands in the red. He had to get a banker's advance to be secured by the royalties of an abridgement of *Revolt in the Desert*. Can you see how this works out? The copyright owner exercises his rights, the number to be published, and Lawrence is left holding the baby – moneywise. Can you wonder at him, or blame him, for attempting to take his life? I felt like putting the cartridges back into the gun, and saying 'Here, go ahead'. I know now, I was of no further use to him, there was no way I could help – he was on his own – but how could I desert him. I was his leaning post, and had seen him through to this stage, but I felt so hopeless, because there was nothing I could do.

When Bruce returned the gun and cartridges, Lawrence said 'it's all yours. Take it with you – I don't want to see it again, and you have a solid gold promise, I will never do that again, ever'.

'John Buchan managed to convince the high ups', said Bruce, and Lawrence 'was duly transferred to the RAF in 1925. Nevertheless,

> he was past caring and lived in the hope that one day, soon he would wake up and the nightmare would be gone. The old man dead – but when?

Meanwhile, Bruce returned to the North to study engineering but agreed to return 'any time I was wanted'. In late 1925, Lawrence and Bruce were reunited in Bournemouth:

> He was looking better now, and was very fit, the Royal Air Force was agreeing with him. He was also doing translation work and was making sufficient extra money to keep himself, without the old man's knowledge. I saw quite a lot of him until he was sent to India, in 1926. He was sure, even at that time, that 1930 in the ranks would be his lot, and his dream of a printing press would come true.
>
> It was during his Karachi days that the 'Revolt' was published, and sold like hot-cakes, and he had every good reason to be pleased. [However] The copyrights of *Revolt in the Desert* belonged to trustees, who, after clearing his debts, gave all other receipts to charity. [Lawrence] did insist however, that the charity had to be the Royal Air Force Benevolent Fund, and as far as I know they got seventeen thousand pounds.
>
> I did not see him again until 1929 when he came to Aberdeen. I was married by this time and he stayed at my home. He told me that he would now be compelled to stay in the Royal Air Force until 1935. He said he was quite happy there, as he had got accustomed to the life but was looking forward very much for the day to make his farewell. There was the possibility of an allowance of four hundred a year, with some land in Ireland if he toed the line, and that was his intention. [However, said Bruce] he did not tell me, that toeing the line meant he was still under the 'old man's' thumb. In June, he wrote and told me that he had done something which had displeased the overlord, and his leave which was due in September had to be spent with me, a letter with instructions would be following and that I should keep all of September free. He was stationed at Mount Batten at this time.

When Bruce subsequently announced that his wife was expecting a child, Lawrence volunteered to be godfather. A letter from the 'Old Man' arrived in August:

> In it he said, his (…)[2] would be spending a period of his leave with me in the North around September, and he understood there were some quiet seaside coves just north of Aberdeen in the Cruden Bay area, where safe swimming was to be had; also nearby, there were vast areas of waste land where horses could be galloped. Could I arrange to rent a cottage, in one of these places, also hire three horses and a groom for the period of his stay.
>
> The place was Colliston, sixteen miles north of Aberdeen. For Lawrence to agree to this was madness. I tried to explain to him, but he insisted on going through with it. He detested horses, and disliked riding them – as for swimming in the North sea at that time of the year, it just wasn't done, the water was freezing cold, and very rough.
>
> He arrived in Aberdeen on 13 September and went straight to Colliston. In the days that followed, I fished, while they [Lawrence

> and the groom] went riding, but when he was in the water, I was always on the jetty, just in case. Lawrence's health was causing me concern. This cold sea was having its effect and on the twenty-fourth, I took it upon myself to wind up his stay and get him back to Plymouth. I went with him as far as London; his last words before I left him was 'I'll be up for the christening, let me know in good enough time'. When he knew it was a boy, he said 'let's call him LAWRENCE Bruce'. I saw him six or seven times after that in Perth, Edinburgh, London and Aberdeen….

Of his account of his relationship with Lawrence, Bruce declared:

> The only reason I write, is to have placed on record the reason why he joined the rank and file, and endured twelve years of humiliation and degradation.

Lawrence had submitted to the 'wrath' of the 'Old Man' 'in order that his own family could live in respectability – these were the very words he used'.

Finally, Bruce elaborated on the corporal punishment, to which Lawrence had subjected himself. Not only was Lawrence 'flogged with a birch' at Colliston in 1929, this was one of nine occasions where such floggings had occurred between 1923 and 1935:

> The first was in 1923 at his cottage, Clouds Hill. A birch was used and he got twelve, over his trousers; this did not satisfy the old man, and had to be done again, the following week, bare skin this time. The second was again at Clouds Hill in 1924, again twelve, bare skin. The third was at Barton Street, London in 1926 a few days before he left for Karachi. The old man wanted his pound of flesh before he left, again twelve. Again at Barton Street in 1929, after he came back from Karachi. Twelve again. In September of the same year, at my house in Aberdeen. Twelve more. In 1931, Aberdeen again, and in 1934, at Maitland Buildings, Elm Row, Edinburgh.
>
> It is hard to understand how he willingly submitted himself to this barbaric treatment, but it is harder still for me being so involved. He was as tough as nails, and rec[k]oned it was only a temperory [sic] hurt. He said, as long as it keeps the old man's wrath from the rest of his family, he was prepared to put up with it. His real fear being his mother, his own suffering mattered not.[3]

What is to be made of this account by Bruce, who comes across as a caring person, if somewhat gullible, in that he preferred to take what Lawrence told him on trust, and without question.

In his account, Bruce stated that it was he himself, who administered the floggings, but also that Lawrence had been flogged even prior to that. As for Lawrence, he himself admitted that he had been flogged, not only by Bruce but also by 'G', whose identity is unknown.

Further light was shed on the beatings by Professor Mack, who stated as follows:

> Diary jottings of Lawrence found after his death at Clouds Hill suggest five incidents of flogging between June and October 1933. Lawrence had noted, for example, 'Saturday 23rd June, 30 from Jock (Bruce's nickname). All of the other floggings were also by 'Jock' (with numbers from thirty to seventy-five indicating, presumably, the number of lashes) except four by 'G'.[4]
>
> I will now turn… to the independent observations of a service companion (i.e. of Lawrence's, who is unidentified) and to material left at Clouds Hill by Lawrence himself.
>
> Lawrence approached this companion in 1931 in great distress, explaining that he had stolen £150 from an 'uncle,' or 'old man,' who came to be known to the companion as 'R'. The Old Man had allegedly threatened to reveal to the world that Lawrence was illegitimate unless he either returned the money, which he was not in a position to do, or submitted to severe floggings. The companion's role was to witness the beatings, and report to 'R' in order to assure that 'R''s instructions were being properly carried out. The presence of the witness seems also to have served the purpose of providing a restraint to any excesses of Bruce's in carrying out the floggings.
>
> The companion observed three beatings with a metal whip between 1931 and 1934. They were brutal, delivered on the bare buttocks, and a precise number of lashes was required. Lawrence submitted to them 'like a schoolboy,' registered obvious fear and agony, but did not scream or cry out. He required that the beatings be severe enough to produce a seminal emission.

This latter comment is of great significance because it indicates that there was a masochistic dimension to the proceedings.

> Three letters, purporting to be from 'R' to the companion, and returned to him by Lawrence, have survived. In addition to the other instructions… the letters seem also to be attempts to deal, through the companion, with the possibility that the beatings might become too severe.[5]

It was Mack's opinion, that the letters were written by Lawrence himself. One of them, dated 26 October 1934, reads as follows:

> I am very obliged to you for the long and careful report you have sent me on your visit to Scotland with Ted [Lawrence], and for your kindness in agreeing to go there with the lad and look after him while he got his deserts.
>
> Did his face remain pale to the end of his punishment, and after it? Does he take his whipping as something he has earned? Is he sorry after it? Does he feel justly treated?[6]

The similarity between what Lawrence told Bruce and what he told the companion – i.e. that he had created a misdemeanour, thereby incurring the wrath and displeasure of the 'Old Man' and 'R' respectively, who therefore demanded that he be punished by flogging – lends further weight to the notion that both these characters and scenarios were inventions of Lawrence.

As for the account of the 'Old Man' and his demands, as told to Bruce by Lawrence, Bruce did not question its authenticity. Lawrence's brother Arnold, however,

> realized that my brother had invented a living uncle and that the 'nephew,' who was to be punished by beating and other trials, was T. E. himself.[7]

As to the identity of the person whom Lawrence arranged to impersonate the 'Old Man', when he and Bruce travelled to Bournemouth together, this remains a mystery.

Lawrence gave Bruce the impression that the 'Old Man' was a relative of his from nearby Moreton. Did Lawrence actually pay any visits to his kinsmen and women at Moreton, and did they ever visit him at Clouds Hill? Not as far as is known. However, Lawrence is known to have visited his cousin Teresa Charlotte Fetherstonhaugh (1856-1939):

> Riding his famous motorcycle, Lawrence made special journeys from Wool [i.e. Clouds Hill], Dorset, to her home at Brook House, Upwey, Weymouth. Lawrence allowed nothing to interfere with his visits to Upwey. Miss Frampton [i.e. Fetherstonhaugh] was one of the few people to whom he presented an autographed copy of his *Seven Pillars of Wisdom*.[8]

Also, in an undated letter to Lawrence, Teresa said, 'You haven't been to see us for a long time. I expect you are very busy.' And she expressed the desire to 'see the blinds at Clouds Hill' (presumably window blinds) and, on 8 April 1933, gave him advice about the planting of rhododendrons, which indicates that a warm relationship existed between them.[9]

Despite what Lawrence told Bruce, the former *did not* assign the copyrights for his books to the 'Old Man'. The copyright of *Revolt in the Desert* [an abridgment of *Seven Pillars*] was assigned to a charitable trust in 1926.[8] The copyright of *Seven Pillars* was owned by Lawrence until his death in 1935 when it too was assigned to a charitable trust. Nevertheless, Lawrence had refused to profit from the sales of *Seven Pillars*. 'It's part of my atonement for the crime of swindling the Arabs to continue to lose money over my share of the adventure.'[10]

Why had Lawrence gone to such lengths to concoct the complicated story of the 'Old Man', and to convince Bruce and at least one other to punish him? Was it because of guilt or masochism, on his part, or the need for sexual gratification? This will be discussed shortly.

Chapter 26

A Return to the RAF

In February 1925, Lawrence was desperate to return to the RAF. He wrote to Trenchard to enquire: 'Have I no chance of re-enlistment in the RAF, or transfer?'[1] He begged Trenchard not to turn him down again 'just because you did so last year and the year before.' However, it was not until August 1925 that, after representations to Prime Minister Stanley Baldwin by Bernard Shaw and John Buchan (author and Director of Intelligence at the Ministry of Information), his wish was granted.

Prior to his reinstatement, Lawrence, whilst staying with Trenchard, had threatened to take his own life. Whereupon, the latter, who in reality was attached to him and cared greatly about his welfare, made a joke of it and said, 'All right, but please go into the garden. I don't want my carpets ruined.'[2]

Having enrolled as 'Ordinary Aircraftman Shaw', Lawrence was sent to the Cadet College at Cranwell in Lincolnshire. He remained in the service until his retirement in 1935. Six months later, in January 1927, he was to be found in India, having told Trenchard that 'neither good-will on the part of those above me, nor correct behaviour on my part can prevent my being a nuisance in any camp where the daily press can get at me.'[3] He had, therefore, requested this present posting the previous year, as he was anxious to avoid the inevitable publicity which he knew would ensue with the publication of Jonathan Cape's unlimited edition of his book *Seven Pillars of Wisdom.*

From Drigh Road Air Station near Karachi (now Pakistan), Lawrence wrote to Trenchard to tell him about *The Mint,* a volume of 170 pages: a 'worm's eye view of the RAF – a scrappy uncomfortable thing' and so-called, 'because we were all being stamped after your [i.e. Trenchard's] image and superscription.' He admitted that 'The general public might be puzzled, and think I didn't like the RAF' whereas, in fact, he found it, 'the only life worth living for its own sake.'[4]

In March 1927, Lawrence's book *Revolt in the Desert* was published. It would make a sizeable profit and enable him, not only to clear his debts – for he was in financial difficulty – but also to make substantial donations to the RAF Memorial Fund, and also to help his fellow airmen and friends. The consequence of his generosity, however, was to leave him malnourished and virtually destitute.

In August 1927, Lawrence made his change of name to 'Shaw' official by Deed Poll. In that same month, he wrote to American businessman and friend Lieutenant

Colonel Ralph H. Isham, who had served with the British Army during the First World War, to say:

> Did I tell you that I consider what I did in Arabia morally indefensible. So, I refused pay & decorations while it lasted, and will not take any personal profit out of it: neither from a book about it; nor will I take any position which depends on my war-reputation.[5]

Here, then, was the explanation for Lawrence refusing to accept the medals that had been awarded to him during and subsequent to the First World War. In October 1927, he was promoted, by reason of his length of service, to Aircraftman Grade 1 (from Grade 2).

Following the death of Hogarth on 6 November 1927, Lawrence wrote to Charlotte Shaw in glowing terms about his late mentor, inspiration, and friend, and of the debt that he owed him. 'Hogarth sponsored my first tramps in Syria – then put me on the staff for Carchemish, which was a golden place….'[6] To C. F. Bell he wrote, 'The death of D. G. H. seems to have flattened me out, rather. He was like a reserve, always there behind me; if I got flustered or puzzled. And now I have no confidence.[7] And to Edward Garnett:

> I saw little of him in the last five years; but the knowledge of that tower of understanding fellowship was [a] reserve to me, and I felt orphaned in his going…. Hogarth carried his rareness in his mouth and eyes – and he is wholly lost.[8] [Hogarth was] the parent I could trust, without qualification, to understand what bothered me.[9]

And, said Lawrence to William Rothenstein, Hogarth was 'humane, and knew the length and breadth of human nature, and understood always, without judging.'[10] Lawrence would mourn the death of Hogarth for the remainder of his days.

In July 1928, Trenchard, who had read *The Mint,* expressed his concern to Lawrence that the book might be misunderstood, and therefore damage the RAF if its contents were to be made public.

Lawrence, having seen RAF life 'from the ground,' as he put it, suggested some reforms to the way in which the service was run. Trenchard, for his part, was not unsympathetic, having himself recognised that certain changes needed to be made. His overall aim, however, was to develop air power as a means of preventing unnecessary killings and casualties in war.

In the event, Lawrence had the satisfaction of seeing some of his proposed reforms implemented whilst he was a serving aircraftman; other suggestions of his being adopted subsequent to his having retired. Amongst them were: the abolition of compulsory church parades; an acknowledgment of the desirability of posting servicemen, where possible, to RAF stations near to their homes; the elimination of swagger sticks; the granting of permission to a serviceman to leave the service if he so wished, and the abolition of the death penalty for desertion and cowardice in the face of the enemy.

On 21 December 1928, Lawrence wrote to Trenchard to congratulate him on his resignation from the RAF. This was despite the fact that Lawrence acknowledged him as being the father of the service; the one who in ten years created it 'from the ground up'.[11] On the 27th Lawrence wrote again on the same theme, and notwithstanding his lowly position as an aircraftman, couched his letter in familiar terms. 'I'm a believer in the parent bird getting out when the chick's done his first solo,' he said, and compared his chief's action with his own when he got,

> right out of the Arab business, so [i.e. as] soon as it seemed a going concern. Arab nationality was as much my creation as the RAF was yours.[12]

Unfortunately for Lawrence, on 8 January 1929, after only two years in India, the authorities were obliged to send him back to England from his second posting at Miranshah in the northwest. This followed rumours in the press, which was always hard on Lawrence's heels, that he was actively involved in a rebellion in nearby Afghanistan – the border of which was a mere ten miles distant. Said Ralph H. Isham,

> I know there were times when he longed to go back and lose himself in the Desert, but he told me that the Government would not let him, that they so restricted him that even when the Air Force recalled him from India the boat was picketed against his leaving it for a moment at Port Said.[13]

In that year, he purchased the freehold of Clouds Hill from his kinsman Henry Fetherstonhaugh Frampton for the sum of £450. On the opposite side of Tank Park Road, which led to Bovington Camp, was a chalet, occupied by his neighbour Staff Sergeant Arthur Knowles, who had fought in the Boer War and in the First World War, winning the Military Cross, his wife Henrietta, and their family. Adjacent to the garden of the chalet, Lawrence constructed a 'water pool', to serve a), as a source of available water in the event of a heath fire and b), as a bathing pool. This he named 'Shaw's Puddle', after his friend, George Bernard Shaw.[14]

Chapter 27

The Mint

When, in August 1922, Lawrence joined the RAF under the name of 'John Hume Ross', and three years later, in 1925, re-enlisted in the same service after a spell in the Army at Bovington, he made the notes which were to be the basis of his book *The Mint*. It is from the pages of this volume that an insight into the state of his mind at this period of his life may be gained.

At first, he was in a state of panic and described 'the melting of the bowels before a crisis,' and his nerves which were 'like a rabbit.' When the doctor who performed the medical examination, prior to his enlistment, having asked him to bend over, suddenly said, 'Hullo, what the hell's those marks? Punishment?' Lawrence replied, 'No, Sir, more like persuasion, Sir, I think.' The doctor then noticed 'Two parallel scars on ribs,' and asked, 'What were they, boy?' Lawrence was evasive. 'Superficial wounds, Sir.' The doctor insisted: 'Answer my question.' To this, Lawrence replied, 'A barbed-wire tear, over a fence.'

Presumably, the 'marks' on his buttocks referred to above – which were visible to the doctor when Lawrence bent down (and which, as already mentioned, had been recorded by the RAF when he left that service for the first time) – were the legacy of his flogging by the attendants of the Turkish bey at Deraa almost five years previously, in November 1917. As for the scars, these presumably, were the legacy of the entrance and exit wounds, caused by the knife wielded by the Turkish bey himself, when he deliberately stabbed Lawrence.

'Since April I've been taking off my friends what meals I dared,' said Lawrence, hoping in vain that the doctor would not notice how thin he was. However, having been told that he had passed the medical, Lawrence was relieved to think it would be 'Seven years now before I think of winning a meal', or in other words, not have to worry about where the next meal is coming from.[1]

He lay 'sickly' on his 'allotted bed', his 'bedfellow… perfect fear', and as the men indulged in horseplay he wondered, 'how we [as new recruits] should bear the freedom of this fellowship.' He thought living might be worse than death. 'Only for survivors is there an after-pain.'[2]

Upon being required to swear the oath of allegiance to His Majesty the King, Lawrence spoke of a quite different, 'unformulated loyalty… obscurely grown' which he had discovered, 'while walking the streets or lanes of our own country,' and he believed this to be an 'ideal' which, unlike the King, 'cannot have legs and a hat. A man's enlisting is his acknowledgement of defeat by life.'[3] Such was

Lawrence's despair, but from whence did it originate? He now hints that it may have had its origin in the recent past:

> Amongst a hundred serving men you will not find one whole and happy. Each has a lesion, open or concealed in his late history. [Nevertheless] Every man in the hut [barracks], bar me, tries shamelessly or shamefully to sing and hum and whistle.[4]

He himself, however, did not join in. He cursed the stick, the 'slip of black cane with a silver knob' which the men were obliged to carry as they walked – the rule being that it was held 'parallel with the ground', the hand going back as the foot went forward,' and admitted, 'that fear is with us when we break that rule.'[5]

His shyness, modesty, and desire for anonymity was apparent when he conveyed 'slyly to the ever-open incinerator', a small picture of himself which hung in the canteen alongside those of King George, Trenchard, Beatty, Haig, some 'land-girls', and 'a destroyer at speed.'[6] And when his commendation from the King fell, accidentally, onto the floor from his notebook, Lawrence hid it from his friend Parker, and pretended it was his birth certificate.

It was a point of honour with Lawrence that, even when he was exhausted from shovelling 'pig-shit' into a lorry, he did not 'fall down and fail in a job' because 'with my pound note accent' he believed 'they'd have taken it for granted I was too soft for man's work.'[7] Lawrence described his body as being 'unpleasantly taut', and he was prone to accidents: such as when he fell onto wet tarmac and broke a little finger; or sprained an instep whilst carrying a sack of flour.[8]

Lawrence's determination to subject himself to the will of those in authority over him, however unpleasant this experience may have been, was apparent in his attitude to Corporal Abner. He suspected Abner of 'resenting much that he had to make us undergo, and of seeing the futility of most routine,' and observed, 'Routine is too often an easy way of saving thought.'[9] And as for the RAF:

> We are its ridden beasts; and of our officers and NCOs some will be bad riders. We must acquire the stolidity to carry on and like the work too well to let it suffer, however they mishandle or punish us, ignorantly. The RAF is bigger than itself.

Lawrence's hatred of bullying was revealed when he described Corporal Raper, 'who assumed great licence in the camp' because he had won the VC, 'degrading himself and his species' by making one of the men, Clarke, who had taken off his boot to remove a nail, run up and down the alley of the hut with one boot off and the other on.[10] Lawrence's support for the underdog had previously manifested itself in his championing of the Arabs in their struggle against Turkish domination.

Likewise, when he found himself having to witness his commandant humiliating one of the men by flinging the latter's cap to the ground, his emotions almost exploded:

> I found myself trembling with clenched fists, repeating to myself, 'I must hit him, I must,' and the next moment trying not to cry for shame that an officer should play the public cad.[11]

Sergeant Pearson, he described as, 'our worst tormentor'. At question time, 'he made a fool of me, as is too easy for an instructor with a stammering recruit. Some sense of discipline ties me, tongue-ties me.' However, despite the sergeant's foul and hurtful names 'I hung there, more curiously miserable than indignant.' Lawrence's failure to look the sergeant in the eye inflamed the latter even more:

> 'Look at me!' he yells: But I can't. If I am angry, I can outface a man; but when this hyaena curses me I sicken with shame wondering if my authority, in the past, so deflowered myself and those under me.[12]

The sensation of touch, he said, is the one that 'I fear and shun… most, of my senses.' He had never indulged in 'venery (sexual intercourse)… never having been tempted so to peril my mortal soul…', advice given to him years ago at Oxford by the select preacher at evening service.[13] If the 'Perfect partnership, indulgence with a living body, is as brief as the solitary act, then the climax [achieved during sexual intercourse] is indeed no more than a convulsion', lasting, as the preacher was '*credibly informed*' for 'less than one and three-quarter minutes,' then 'the temptation flickers out into the indifference of tired disgust once a blue moon, when nature compels it.'

Speaking of sodomy he declared, 'anyone listening in to a hut of airmen would think it a den of infamy. Yet we are too intimate, too bodily soiled, to attract one another.' However, he admitted that,

> in the four large camps of my sojourning there have been five fellows actively beastly [homosexual]. Doubtless their natures tempted others: but they fight its expression as the normal airman fights his desire for women, out of care for physical fitness.

By this, he was presumably referring to the danger of venereal disease.[14]

Of Lawrence's concern for his fellow aircraftmen, there is no doubt, as he provides his readers with vivid descriptions of horseplay between the men, and of the basic language which is their stock in trade. This includes the men having affectionate nicknames for each other:

> Nobby is miserable. We keep him company, afraid that he wishes to destroy himself. Lofty talks of being bought out (of the service), for

> he is too physically loose to control his arms and legs in drill and so is always under punishment. Enter White with tea and shortcake biscuit for Sailor, who took them, clapped biscuit over cup and inverted it successfully crying, 'Elementary fucking science!'[15]

Later, in *The Mint*, he contrasted life at the 'Depot' (the Royal Tank Corps Depot, Bovington) – 'a savage place' – with the new life which he had begun at Cranwell Cadet College, which he described as 'different' and 'humane'. He was always 'a slow starter, always unfavourably impressed' whenever he was 'dropped into a hut-full of strangers'. Yet he displayed tolerance and also patience when he said it is 'only after their [i.e. the men's] crudities have been well learned and forgiven that the more interesting core appears.' The beds were so hard that the airmen 'sleep very restlessly', constantly shifting, groaning, muttering, dreaming, and sometimes saying 'beast-like things in their sleep.'[16] Gradually, however, a happier and more contented Lawrence emerged; one who rushed out in breeches, puttees, and gauntlets, for a ride on his motorcycle after a day's work. Its,

> first glad roar at being alive again nightly jarred the huts of Cadet College into life. 'There he goes, the noisy bugger,' someone would say enviously in every flight. It is part of an airman's profession to be knowing with engines: and a thoroughbred engine is our undying satisfaction. The camp wore the virtue of my Brough [motorcycle] like a flower in its cap. Tonight Tug and Dusty came to the step of our hut to see me off. 'Running down to Smoke, perhaps?' jeered Dusty: hitting at my regular game of London and back for tea on fine Wednesday afternoons![17]

'The habit of "belonging to something or other" induces in us a sense of being one part of many things,' said Lawrence – thus dispelling any notion that he was a 'loner' – and described himself and the men 'sighing in happy excess of relaxation' as they lay out in the warm sunshine, waiting for a 'kite' [aeroplane] to return. When they put on their working dress, 'oil, water, mud, paint, all such hazardous things, are instantly our friends.' And when they dived into the swimming pool whose 'elastic water… fits our bodies closely as a skin: – we belong to that too. Everywhere a relationship: no loneliness any more.' And he ended *The Mint* by saying, 'I can't write "Finis" to this book while I am still serving. I hope, sometimes, that I will never write it,' which implies that he wished this happy state of affairs to continue forever.[18]

Lawrence had reassured Trenchard that he would refrain from publishing *The Mint* until at least the year 1950. However, in November 1933 the *British Legion Journal* printed the last three chapters; the document having been presumably leaked by one of the many people to whom Lawrence had loaned it. For this, Lawrence 'got into awful trouble with the Air Ministry' and thought he, 'may be in civvy street next week because of it.'[19] Fortunately for him, this was not to be the case. *The Mint* was finally published in 1955.

And so, at last, Lawrence found, in the RAF, a kind of contentment where he was no longer lonely or hungry. He had friends, all of whom he knew by nickname, and was free to go off in his spare time on his beloved motorcycle 'Boanerges'. And he scotched, once and for all, any notion that he was homosexual.

In 1931, Lawrence declared to Henry T. Russell the United Press correspondent:

> As for the Arab business, I had a hateful war: and after it two and a half years of a dog-fight with the British Cabinet to secure the fulfilment of the promises to which they had made me an unwilling and post-facto accessory. When Winston Churchill fulfilled all that was humanly attainable of those promises I was free to quit events and return to the class and mode of life that I belong to and feel happy in.[20]

In December 1932, King Feisal wrote as follows to Lawrence: 'As a sincere friend of us who has ever been our valuable support, I wish you pleasant long life', and he ended the letter, 'I close by reiterating my wishes for your everlasting prosperity and happy days. Your friend Feisal'.[21]

A measure of the affection in which Lawrence was held, is indicated by the fact that numerous friends and acquaintances proffered him an open invitation to their homes. Among them were Wilfred S. Blunt, Robert Bridges, Winston S. Churchill, Noel Coward, R. B. Cunninghame Graham, Charles M. Doughty, Sir Edward Elgar, James Elroy Flecker, David Garnett, Harley Granville-Barker, D. G. Hogarth, Augustus John, Rudyard Kipling, Frederick Manning, Ezra Pound, George Bernard Shaw and his wife Charlotte, Lord Stamfordham, and Sir Hugh Trenchard. And it is to their great credit that they did not abandon him when he joined the lower ranks of the armed forces.[22]

Chapter 28

E. M. Forster

Running parallel to Lawrence's service life was another of a totally different nature, brought about by his love of literature, music, and the arts, which led him to seek out and cultivate the eminent practitioners of the day. Such a man was the novelist Edward Morgan Forster. Born in 1879 and educated at Cambridge, Forster lived from 1904 to 1907, mainly in Italy and Greece, where he gleaned material for his first two novels: *Where Angels Fear to Tread* and *The Longest Journey* – both of which are about the nature of human relationships. There followed *A Room with a View* in 1908, and *Howards End* in 1910. Before the First World War, Forster spent time in India and, during the war, served in the Royal Welsh Fusiliers in the trenches in France. He returned to India in 1921 as secretary to the Maharajah of Dewas. The outcome of this was his final novel, *A Passage to India.*

Lawrence first met Forster in February 1920 at a lunch held in London at a Mayfair hotel for Emir Feisal. In February 1924 he wrote to Forster in the familiar self-deprecatory terms, describing himself as an 'imitator' rather than an active writer. He explained how he had struggled with the book *Seven Pillars of Wisdom*, for four years 'till I was nearly blind and mad.' He had felt 'profoundly dejected over it all' and 'the failure of it was mainly what broke my nerve, and sent me into the RAF' (Forster had been lent a copy of *Seven Pillars* by his and Lawrence's mutual friend, the poet Siegfried Sassoon). But for all his self-doubt, Lawrence confessed to having 'a longing to hear what men say of it.'

Lawrence had earned a mere £11 from his writing since 1914, and 'a scruple' had prevented him taking his pay whilst out east (in India), and also from 'taking profits on any part of the record of the adventure.' He was grateful to Forster for bothering 'to write to me whole pages about my effort' (i.e. *Seven Pillars*), at a time when the former was endeavouring to finish *A Passage to India.*

To be in the Army, which was his 'assured bread & butter' was clearly a relief to Lawrence and better than 'a gamble outside.'[1]

Lawrence told Forster how much he and fellow private soldiers in the Royal Tank Corps at Bovington (whom he was in the habit of inviting to Clouds Hill for rest, relaxation, and an introduction to classical music, particularly that of Bach, Beethoven and Elgar, played on his Columbia gramophone) had gained from Forster's recent visit there, and how the latter was always,

> ...extremely welcome. Any stranger is, almost: but men who write and draw come nearer to my taste than others.[2]

Forster described Clouds Hill as follows: 'In those days the two bottom rooms were full of firewood and lumber. We lived upstairs.' There was a,

> leathered covered settee... here we talked, played Beethoven symphonies, ate and drank. We drank water only, or tea – no alcohol ever entered Clouds Hill. We drank out of pretty cups of black pottery. T. E. always laid in a stock of tinned dainties for his guests. There were no fixed hours for meals and no one sat down. To think of Clouds Hill as T. E.'s home is to get the wrong idea of it. It wasn't his home; it was rather his pied-a-terre – the place where his feet touched the earth for a moment, and found rest.[3]

Ernest H.R. Altounyan begged to differ. He had first met Lawrence at Carchemish in 1911 whilst an undergraduate at Cambridge, since when the two had kept in touch by letter. Altounyan subsequently became a physician and founded a hospital at Aleppo. Of Clouds Hill said Altounyan, Lawrence 'was completely in love with it'.[4] As for alcohol, said Ralph H. Isham, 'Others have remarked that he never took alcohol, but when we dined together he drank wine of various sorts freely'.[5]

In June 1925, Lawrence wrote to Forster in regard to a book entitled *With Lawrence in Arabia* by Lowell Thomas (the American official correspondent who had visited Aqaba for ten days in 1918), in which he had discovered a number of errors. 'My family isn't Irish from Galway,' said Lawrence, but was 'an Elizabethan plantation from Leicester [England] in Meath without a drop of Irish blood in us, ever.' Also, his height was actually 5 feet 5½ inches, and his weight 10 stone.[6]

However, it is from Lawrence's comments on Forster's novel *Dr Woolacott*, which is about homosexuality (Forster was himself homosexual), that further insight is gained into the former's character. Lawrence wrote of the novel to Forster in December 1927, shortly after the death of his former mentor Dr Hogarth, 'for whom I had long cared very greatly.'

> There is a strange cleansing beauty about the whole piece of writing. So passionate, of course; so indecent, some people might say: but I must confess that it has made me change my point of view.

Referring to the episode in Deraa when he was raped, Lawrence said:

> The Turks, as you probably know did it to me, by force: and since then I have gone about whimpering to myself 'Unclean, unclean'. Now I don't know. Perhaps there is another side, your side, to the story. I couldn't ever do it, I believe: the impulse strong enough to make me touch another creature has not yet been born in me: but

> perhaps in surrender to such a figure as your Death there might be a greater realisation – and thereby a more final destruction – of the body than any loneliness can reach.[7]

These words of Lawrence's make it clear that he never, voluntarily, participated in, or for that matter desired to participate in, any physical relationship whatsoever, let alone one of a homosexual nature.

In August 1928, Lawrence was concerned about his book *The Mint*. He believed Trenchard 'over-estimates the harm which *The Mint* would do the RAF,' but the main reason he had decided to hold back from publication at least until the year 1950, was 'the horror the fellows with me in the force would feel at my giving them away' or, in other words, portraying them when they were relaxing and off guard.[8] Forster's opinion was that:

> *The Mint* is not as great a work as *The Seven Pillars* either in colour or form; but it is more new, more startling and more heartening than either *The S. P.* [*Seven Pillars*] or anything else I've read.[9]

Lawrence's correspondence with Forster continued until 1929, by which time he was happily installed at RAF Cattewater, Plymouth, 'a decent little camp, quiet and easy. Very beautifully placed in Plymouth Sound.'[10] And finally, in October 1932 he apologized for being unable to afford to send Forster a copy of his translation of *The Odyssey*, which 'cost twelve guineas'.[11]

Lawrence's gatherings at Clouds Hill – a somewhat spartan little cottage with no electricity and only two decent-sized rooms: one on the ground floor which he used as a bedroom-cum-library, and the other on the first floor which served as a music room-cum-sitting room – demonstrates one of the most engaging features of his personality: namely, that despite his abject poverty, he could enjoy the company of, and share cultural experiences with, all manner of people from whatever station in life.

Chapter 29

George Bernard Shaw

Another of Lawrence's friends was George Bernard Shaw. Born in Ireland in 1856, Shaw moved to London in 1876 and was one of the first to join the socialist Fabian Society in 1884. He became a music critic and journalist and in the 1890s wrote his *Plays Pleasant*, including *Arms and the Man* (1894) and *The Devil's Disciple* (1896). Further plays followed (often written by him for famous actors and actresses of the day) including *Captain Brassbound's Conversion*, *Man and Superman*, *Pygmalion*, and *St Joan*. His often flippant and irreverent style had the purpose of provoking people into making them think. His books included *The Intelligent Woman's Guide to Socialism and Capitalism* published in 1928.

Lawrence first met Shaw in March 1922, having been introduced to him by Sydney Cockerell, curator of the Fitzwilliam Museum, Cambridge. Ever anxious for literary criticism of his work, Lawrence, on the strength of this brief encounter, asked Shaw if he would 'read, or try to read, a book which I have written,' – in other words *Seven Pillars*.[1] Shaw, then aged 67, replied on 1 December to the effect that it was a great book, but confessed that though his wife Charlotte had 'ploughed through it,'[2] he had not actually read it yet. Charlotte, whose marriage to Shaw was alleged to be platonic and based on companionship only, shared with Lawrence the fact that she too had suffered in her childhood from having a dominating mother.

Aware that Shaw did not believe that he had a serious purpose in joining the lower ranks of the armed services, Lawrence wrote to him in 1923 saying:

> People come into the army often, not because it is brutal and licentious, but because they haven't done very well in the fight of daily living and want to be spared the responsibility of ordering for themselves their homes and food and clothes and work.... Regard it as an asylum for the little-spirited.[3]

Shaw however, who thought the idea 'a maddening masquerade,' was impatient and said that if he did not know Lawrence better, he might conclude that he was 'a depressed mechanic oiling up fuselages for profanely abusive pilots.' When the story of Lawrence's enlistment in the RAF broke in the press, Shaw wrote:

> Like all heroes, and, I must add, all idiots, you greatly exaggerate your power of moulding the universe to your personal convictions.

> You have just had a crushing demonstration of the utter impossibility of hiding or disguising the monster you have created. It is useless to protest that Lawrence is not your real name. That will not save you. Lawrence may be as great a nuisance to you sometimes as G. B. S. is to me, or as Frankenstein found the man he had manufactured; but you created him, and must put up with him as best you can.[4]

On 21 May 1923, Shaw sent Prime Minister Stanley Baldwin a private memorandum. Referring to Lawrence, he declared, 'the private soldier business is a shocking tomfoolery', and he urged Baldwin to provide the former with a pension.[5] However, although Baldwin left Shaw with the impression that the pension would be granted, it never was. Finally, Shaw failed to understand why Lawrence steadfastly refused to take any profit from his book *Seven Pillars*.

In October 1924, Shaw returned the manuscript of *Seven Pillars* to Lawrence, having taken a full year to criticise and proof-read it. 'Confound you and your book: you are no more to be trusted with a pen than a child with a torpedo,' he said, and proceeded to give Lawrence a lecture on punctuation and also on the law of libel, rewriting appropriate passages for him 'in terms that were not actionable.'[6]

In 1927, Shaw again attempted to persuade Prime Minister Baldwin to award Lawrence a pension in return for his past services to the nation. The following year Lawrence described Shaw, in a letter sent to his mother from India, as being 'like a tonic, and very kind. A most sensible, vigorous old man.'[7] In April 1928, Shaw wrote to Lawrence encouragingly about *The Mint*, saying 'the slightest reticence or self-consciousness about it would be misplaced and unpardonable.'[8]

In July, Lawrence was again to be found in an introspective mood and feeling inadequate. 'What I have wanted and tried to do has always come off, more or less, except when it was trying to write,' he told Shaw, 'and then despite all the good you have said of my books, I am assured of failure. Not complete failure, perhaps. A relative failure, let's call it.'[9]

In 1929, when Lawrence arrived at his new station, RAF Cattewater, it was on a new Brough motorcycle – given to him anonymously by the Shaws. Had he been in a position to purchase it himself, he said, it would have cost him 'three years of my pay'.[10] Shaw, however, mindful of Lawrence's many spills, had reservations about it. 'It was', he said, 'like handing a pistol to a would-be suicide.' Shaw again, demonstrated his concern for Lawrence when he learned that the latter could not afford to buy himself an overcoat; he kindly lent him his second one.

When in January 1932, Lawrence sent Shaw a critique of the latter's new play *Too True to be Good* – a satire on the military establishment – Shaw responded with gratitude and incorporated into it all of Lawrence's suggestions.

Lawrence's last letter to Shaw was written in January 1935, when Shaw's wife Charlotte was recovering from blood poisoning and the couple were planning a holiday abroad.

The two men had a common interest in writing and were mutually supportive of one another. Lawrence, however, was desperate for reassurance and Shaw often had to chide him – though always good-naturedly – for his lack of self-belief. However, neither Shaw nor Lawrence himself fully understood the true reason for the latter's attitude to himself. It was with Shaw's wife Charlotte that Lawrence was to form his deepest and most meaningful relationship.

Chapter 30

Charlotte Shaw

Over the twelve-year period between January 1923 and January 1935, Lawrence wrote at least 300 letters to Mrs Charlotte Shaw, wife of playwright George Bernard Shaw (GBS.); she was thirty-one years Lawrence's senior. It is from these letters that a further insight is given into the man, his relationship with Sarah his mother, and the effect his rape by the attendants of the Turkish bey in Deraa had on him.

Authors Phillip Knightley and Colin Simpson, writing in the *Sunday Times Weekly Review* of 30 June 1968, explained how 'after his wife Charlotte died [in September 1943] Bernard Shaw went through her papers. He read T. E. Lawrence's letters to her, and her letters to T. E. Lawrence....' Shaw himself told his half-cousin Georgina Musters, 'I lived with Charlotte for forty years, and I see now that there was a great deal about her that I didn't know. It has been a shock.' And to a friend Eleanor O'Connell, in 1944, 'from a diary I discovered lately, and some letters which she wrote to T. E. Lawrence, I realize that there were many parts of her character that even I did not know, for she poured out her soul to Lawrence.'[1]

It was the opinion of Simpson and Knightley that:

> Charlotte's marriage with GBS had, by agreement, been childless, and she now directed on Lawrence all the maternal affection she had suppressed for years.... It was Charlotte who first discerned the literary genius of Lawrence, who guided his energy, who encouraged him when he needed it and who, above all, allowed him to unburden himself of the guilt he had carried since Deraa.[2]

In a letter to Shaw in December 1922, following his first meeting with him and his wife Charlotte on 25 March of that year, Lawrence told how 'when I finished it I nearly burned the whole thing [i.e. *Seven Pillars*] for the third time. Is there any style in my writing at all? Anything recognizably individual?' he asked.[3] Charlotte, for her part, having confessed that she had driven her husband 'almost mad by insisting on reading him special bits when he was deep in something else...' enquired of Lawrence:

> Now is it *conceivable*, *imaginable*, that a man who could write the *Seven Pillars* can have any doubts about it? If you don't know it is a 'great book' what is the use of anyone telling you so.... I devoured

> the book from cover to cover as soon as I got hold of it. I could not stop. It is one of the most amazingly individual documents that has ever been written…[4]

What is more, over a two-year period, Charlotte corrected proofs of the manuscript, advised on cuts, and gave general encouragement, in recognition of which, Lawrence presented her with the very first copy of *Seven Pillars*. (By contrast, Shaw was critical of the punctuation in the book, and wrote at length to Lawrence about his use of colons, semi-colons, nominatives and so forth.) Charlotte was also to help him with his own book *The Mint*, and with his translations of Adrien le Corbeau's *Gigantesque*; Pierre Custot's *Sturly* – a novel about life under the sea, and Homer's *Odyssey*. (Lawrence was proficient in many languages.)

In March 1924, Lawrence wrote to Charlotte about the trial scene in Shaw's play *St Joan*, and compared Joan's plight with his rape at Deraa:

> I was thinking of her [Joan] as a person, not as a moral lesson. The pain meant more to me than the example. You instance my night in Deraa. Well, I'm always afraid of being hurt: and to me, while I live, the force of that night will lie in the agony which broke me, and made me surrender. It's the individual view. You can't share it.
>
> About that night. I shouldn't tell you, because decent men don't talk about such things. I wanted to put it plain in the book, and wrestled for days with my self-respect… which wouldn't, hasn't, let me. For fear of being hurt, or rather to earn five minutes respite from a pain which drove me mad, I gave away the only possession we are born into the world with – our bodily integrity. It's an unforgivable matter, an irrecoverable position: and it's that which has made me forswear decent living, and the exercise of my not-contemptible wits and talents.
>
> You may call this morbid: but think of the offence, and the intensity of my brooding over it for these years. It will hang about me while I live, and afterwards if our personality survives. Consider wandering among the decent ghosts hereafter, crying, 'Unclean unclean!'
>
> You speak of submissive admirers… but that hurts them and me. I'll write you pictures of the two most concerned some day, and will try to show you how far from an object of admiration I must be to them. And the contrary? Do I admire them? There's not a clean human being into whose shape I would not willingly creep. They may not have been Colonel Lawrence… but I know the reverse of that medal, and hate its false face so utterly that I struggle like a trapped rabbit to be it no longer.
>
> I dodge GBS reading part of *Joan* to me, partly because he's great and I'm worthless: partly because it's my part to shun pleasures… through lack of dessert. There's expiation to be made: and the weak

> spirit is only too ready to lunch with you, or to enjoy a book, or to hide a quiet while in a cloud-defended cottage: any alleviation of the necessary penalty of living on…[5]

So here is Lawrence, manifesting in his letters to Charlotte Shaw two of the classical symptoms of a victim of rape: overwhelming guilt, and a feeling of uncleanliness.

In June 1924, Lawrence expounded to Charlotte his views about sexuality:

> Why, if fathers and mothers took thought before bringing children into this misery of a world, only the monsters among them would dare to go through with it. The motive which brings the sexes together is 99% sexual pleasure, and only 1% the desire of children, in men, so far as I can learn. As I told you, I haven't ever been carried away in that sense, so that I'm a bad subject to treat of it.
>
> I hate and detest this animal side – and I can't find comfort in your compartmenting up our personalities… I think I'm sorry I was brought into the world. I think I'll be glad when I go: but meanwhile I can't associate myself with the process in any effort to end or mend it.[6]

In August, his theme was the relationship between himself and his fellow aircraftmen:

> The Air Force fellows are like Oxford undergraduates in their second term… buds just opening after the restraint of school and home. Their first questioning, their first doubt of an established convention or law or practice, opens a floodgate in their minds for if one thing is doubtful all things are doubtful: the world to them has been a concrete, founded, polished thing: and the first crack is portentous.
>
> So the Farnborough fellows used to come to me there… [to Clouds Hill] after 'lights out' and sit on the box by my bed, and ask questions about every rule of conduct and experience, and about mind and soul and body: and I, since I was lying on my back, could answer succinctly and with illumination. Those who seek me out down here are the keenest ones, and they have been following up the chase of the great Why themselves…[7]

In September 1925, writing to Charlotte from RAF Cranwell, Lawrence said, following a visit to Lord Winterton, Under-Secretary of State for India:

> I've changed, and the Lawrence who used to go about and be friendly and familiar with that sort of people is dead. He's worse than dead.

> He is a stranger I once knew. From henceforward my way will lie with these fellows here, degrading myself… in the hope that some day I will really feel degraded, be degraded to their level. I long for people to look down upon me and despise me, and I'm too shy to take the filthy steps which would publicly shame me, and put me into their contempt. I want to dirty myself outwardly, so that my person may properly reflect the dirtiness which it conceals… and I shrink from dirtying the outside, while I've eaten, avidly eaten, every filthy morsel which chance threw in my way.[8]

In June 1926 he explained to Charlotte why he 'backed out of the race':

> I tried (All Souls and elsewhere) to live with decent people; and couldn't. There is too much liberty up aloft. I was able to avoid others all day long: and there is no goodness in being a recluse. So I wrote myself down a failure, socially: and I believed (I still believe) that I'd failed in my ambition to become an artist, at book-writing, by taking thought. Creative work isn't achieved by dint of pains. Consequently, rather than be a half and half, a Cherry Garrard [polar explorer] or Stephens [Irish poet] or Stanley Baldwin [Prime Minister], I backed out of the race and sat down among the people who were not racing. Racing, in these modern and specialized days, is a pursuit limited to thoroughbreds and detached observers sometimes wonder whether these over-tensioned, super-charged delicate creatures are bred really to improve the race, or just give pleasure to men-fanciers.[9]

In other words, Lawrence had deliberately opted out of 'the rat race'. In February 1927 he revealed something about his attitude to Christianity which, he said,

> has handicapped itself with [i.e. in the eyes of] a growing proportion of people since [the year] 1600 by apparently assuming (i) that we exist, (ii) that man is the centre of his universe, and (iii) that God is, more or less, analogous to man. When you say 'not proven' to (i), 'impossible' to (ii) and 'ridiculous' to (iii), then you lose patience with a crowd which fusses over details like transubstantiation.[10]

In April 1927, Lawrence poured out his soul as he described the tension which existed between himself and his mother who,

> hears from me about 4 times a year, and banalities only. I would like you, if you agreed (it is to take a risk) to see her if she comes to England now that China has closed itself to her [That country was at that time being wracked by civil unrest]. Mother is rather wonderful: but very exciting. She is so set, so assured in mind. I think she 'set'

> many years ago; perhaps before I was born. I have a terror of her knowing anything about my feelings, or convictions, or way of life. If she knew they would be damaged, violated, no longer mine. You see, she would not hesitate to understand them: and I do not understand them, and do not want to. Nor has she ever seen any of us growing, because I think she has not grown since we began. She was wholly wrapped up in my father, whom she had carried away jealously from his former life and country, against great odds, and whom she kept as her trophy of power.
>
> And now two of my brothers are dead [a reference to Frank and Will who were both killed in the war], and Arnie (the youngest) and I have left her, and avoid her as our first rule of existence: while my eldest brother [Montague Robert] is hardly her peer or natural companion. It is a dreadful position for her, and yet I see no alternative. While she remains herself, and I remain myself it must happen. In all her letters she tells me she is old and lonely, and loves only us; and she begs us to love her, back again, and points us to Christ, in whom she says, is the only happiness and truth. Not that she finds happiness, herself.
>
> Of course I shouldn't tell you all this, but she makes Arnie and me profoundly unhappy. We are so helpless; we feel we would never give any other human being the pain she gives us, by her impossible demands, and yet we give her the pain, because we cannot turn on love to her in our letters, like a water-tap; and Christ to us is not a symbol, but a personality spoiled by the accretions of such believers as herself. If you saw her, you whose mind has not grown a shell-case, perhaps you could show her the other sides and things of which she does not dream. If only she would be content to loose hold of us.
>
> One of the real reasons (there are three or four) why I am in the service [RAF] is so that I may live by myself. She has given me a terror of families and inquisitions. And yet you'll understand she is my mother and an extraordinary person. Knowledge of her will prevent my ever making any woman a mother, and the cause of children. I think she suspects this: but she does not know that the inner conflict which makes me a standing civil war, is the inevitable issue of the discordant natures of herself and my father, and the inflammation of strength and weakness which followed the uprooting of their lives and principles. They should not have borne children.[11]

On 17 May 1927, Charlotte revealed to Lawrence that she too had experienced similar problems as a child:

> I had a perfectly hellish childhood and youth, after I got old enough to take things in at all. My mother was a terribly strong character – managing

> and domineering. She could not bear opposition: if it was offered she either became violent, or she cried. She felt (genuinely felt)… that we none of us loved her enough or considered her enough, or helped her enough (she would never be helped – ever) or respected her wishes sufficiently, or cared to spend our time with her.

On the other hand, Charlotte's father was 'gentle and affectionate – well-educated…. He was a marvel of patience with my mother, which was terribly bad for her'.[12] Charlotte's description of her mother would most certainly have struck a chord with Lawrence, vis-à-vis his own mother Sarah.

In August 1927, Lawrence admitted to Charlotte that

> I've not written any letters of this sort to anyone else, since I was born. No trust ever existed between my mother and myself. Each of us jealously guarded his or her own individuality, whenever we came together. I always felt she was laying siege to me, and would conquer, if I left a chink unguarded.[13]

Two months later he expressed to Charlotte a certain satisfaction over his role in the war:

> I was right to work for Arab self-government through 1919 and 1920: and my methods then, though not beyond criticism, were I think reasonably justifiable. The settlement which Winston put through in 1921 and 1922 (mainly because my advocacy supplied him with all the technical advice and arguments necessary) was, I think, the best possible settlement which Great Britain, alone, could achieve at the time. And after June 1922 my job was done. I had repaired, so far as it lay in English power to repair it, the damage done to the Arab Movement by the signing of the Armistice in Nov. 1918.[14]

In March 1928, he wrote, 'The RAF is now my very own service, and I learn to fit in, slowly: to give up my rights to personality.'[15] And in May:

> All this finishing and finishing for ten years without the faintest desire or stirring to begin anything anywhere again. I have no more notes for books in my bag: and no urge to join the boy scouts or the House of Commons. The RAF seems natural somehow, as a way of living: and no other life seems natural: or is it that no energy to attempt any new life remains? Nunc dimittis… if I had a Lord, and he were a decent fellow, he would tell his servant to go to sleep, in reward for having worked 'over-time', and very hard, for forty years [a slight exaggeration on Lawrence's part as he was currently aged

> only 39]: or I think he would. It is what his servant (if profitable) would ask as a reward.[16]

And in November 1928:

> My sympathies, in such shows, are always with the weaker side. That's partly, perhaps, why I was able to help the Arabs whole-heartedly (Was it whole-hearted? Perhaps: but often I think that it's only in trying to write that my whole heart has ever been engaged: and then not for very long).[17]

In April 1929 he told Charlotte, 'The flaw is that *John Bull* has announced that I do no work in camp, but tinker with my motor-bike and translate the *Odyssey*....'.[18] And in March 1930:

> My St Andrew's degree trouble [the university had wished to confer an honorary degree upon him] is easily over: [James Matthew] Barrie [playwright and novelist] and [John] Buchan [author and politician] played up and freed me from it. I think the public occasion would have been unbearable. A reaction from publicity, which began in me about 1919, has grown stronger since year by year. I like to see my name in the papers – no: when I see it I get a snatch of horrified interest – and I hate anybody telling me they have seen it.[19]

He told Charlotte that she was 'the solitary woman who lets me feel at ease with her, in spite of all the benefits you heap on me. [and admits] Usually I am a very grudging taker, too.'[20]

In August 1933 he learned that his idol, the composer Edward Elgar, was ill. He therefore requested of Charlotte that:

> If you see him will you present my constant pleasure in his music, whether human rendered or from my [gramophone] box? Nobody who makes sounds gets so inside my defences as he does, with his 2nd Symphony and Violin Concerto. Say if the 3rd Symphony has gone forward from those, it will be a thrill to ever so many of us. I feel more and more, as I grow older, the inclination to throw everything away and live on air. We all allow ourselves to need too much.[21]

When, in May 1934, the Shaws returned from a cruise, Lawrence indicated that he had missed them desperately:

> You will think it queer, but I have been looking and longing for this news to appear in the Papers. Your return makes England seem furnished, somehow. I so seldom call: yet my two visits to London

> while you were away found the place barren: and I came back here sooner than was necessary, just because there seemed no point in wandering about. I'm ever so glad you are here.[22]

In December 1934 he wrote from Bridlington, his final RAF posting:

> Next year [the year in which he was due to retire] I am going to draw in my ink-horns: for this year I have tried – vainly! – not to spend more than 2/- [shillings] a week on post. After February my total means will be 25/- a week, and I shall not spend more than three pence weekly upon post; After the first week, when I have to warn people that I am ceasing to write.
>
> The Brough purred smoothly, to Royston and Biggleswade and Stamford and Grantham and Bawtry and Goole and Bridlington. Even the rain ceased after a while, and I got in warm and dry. Today I have cleaned the good servant till it shines again. All the last two months it has been stored at Clouds Hill, until I felt that it had almost shared my unhappiness in our separation.

And referring to the Shaws' forthcoming visit to New Zealand (which commenced in March 1935):

> I hope you get securely and well on to your [ship] *Reina del Pacifico*, and I hope the cruise is a success. When you come back my great change will have happened. I wonder… I wonder how it will be with me. Twelve years ago I thought that the question of an 'after' to the Service would never happen: the twelve years felt as though they would be enough for me. Yet here I am still strong and trenchant-minded, but with nothing in my hand. I have learnt only the word NO in 46 years. However, I suppose myself is my own business and I should not trouble others with it. At least you will find me very different, after this.

And he concluded, 'I do hope that [the] voyage is excellent. When you come back, Time will mean nothing to me: Then we can meet and not write.'[23]

Lawrence, in his writings to his friend and soulmate Mrs Charlotte Shaw, revealed the classical symptoms of what in modern parlance is described as, 'Rape Trauma Syndrome'. He feels shame and a sense of worthlessness. He feels dirty and despicable in other men's eyes and desires that they perceive him in that light. He also shows a lack of purpose and self-determination; all in stark contrast to the energetic and enthusiastic Lawrence of old. In addition, resentments within him, concerning his parents' 'discordant natures' and the 'uprooting of their lives and principles', also resurface and demonstrate the long-lasting traumatic effect this had on him in his formative years. He comes across as an intensely private individual; disturbed by her frightening sense of certainty and desperate to avoid being sucked dry by his mother's limitless emotional demands. Her treatment of him has made him forever terrified of ever marrying or having children.

Nevertheless, his spirit is not entirely vanquished, in that he finds pleasure in intelligent conversation with his fellows and in music, especially that of Elgar; and when the Shaws go away he finds himself eagerly anticipating their return. And always, shining through like a bright beacon is his asceticism, epitomised by his assertion, 'We all allow ourselves to need too much.' Eric Kennington shed further light on this lifestyle of self-imposed frugality. Lawrence, he said:

> considered himself fallen from his sublime standard and made the rest of his life an intermittent struggle to reclaim or recreate his soul, by altruistic labour, self-denial and penance. By turns he gained and lost ground, his humble R.A.F. service granted him periods of purification and with them happiness, but never steady strength.[24]

As for those who pursue a life of materialism, said Ralph H. Isham:

> 'Once, when we were talking of man's greed, he [Lawrence] said, 'The fools don't realize that their possessions, in time, come to possess them'.[25]

However, long before the Arab Campaign, Fareedeh el Akle, who had taught him Arabic in the early months of 1911, had observed that 'the material things of life had no attraction for him, and money he only valued for its convenience'.[26]

Chapter 31

Thomas Hardy

The literary figure whom Lawrence revered, perhaps more than any other, was Thomas Hardy. Born in 1840 at Higher Bockhampton near Dorchester, in Dorsetshire; the son of a stonemason and amateur musician, Hardy was articled to an architect and spent time as a restorer of churches, before writing the first of fourteen novels *Desperate Remedies*, which was published in 1871. This was followed, in 1872, by *Under the Greenwood Tree.*

In 1874, the year he wrote *Far from the Madding Crowd*, Hardy married Emma Louisa Gifford, whom he had met in Cornwall. In 1885, the couple moved into Max Gate, Dorchester: a house which he had built to his own design. There, he wrote *The Return of the Native* (1878), *The Mayor of Casterbridge* (1886), and *The Woodlanders* (1886-87): all of which were set in the West Country – referred to by the author as 'Wessex'. A favourite theme of Hardy's was the struggle of human beings against the more powerful forces of nature and the gods. The couple travelled extensively on the Continent and lived for a time in London.

The honesty with which Hardy wrote about male/female relationships, as in *Tess of the d'Urbervilles* (1891), offended Victorian sensibilities, and the further criticism which followed the publication of *Jude the Obscure* in 1895, decided him to write no more novels, apart from his final one *The Well Beloved* in 1897. Thereafter, he devoted himself to writing poetry. From 1904 to 1908 he engaged himself in creating a monumental epic drama *The Dynasts*, about the Napoleonic Wars, which he wrote in blank verse. In 1910, he was awarded the Order of Merit. In over 100 hundred poems, Hardy expressed the sorrow and remorse he felt following the death of Emma in 1913.

The year after his wife died, Hardy married Florence Emily Dugdale, a published author of children's stories who had previously assisted him with research and secretarial work over a number of years.

At a guest night held at All Souls College, Oxford, in November 1919, Lawrence had met the writer Robert Graves whom, together with Siegfried Sassoon, was numbered amongst Thomas Hardy's circle of 'war-poet' friends. In March 1923 he wrote to Graves from his London address, to enquire as to whether he thought that 'old Hardy would let me take a look at him?' as he, Lawrence, considered Hardy to be 'a proper poet and a fair novelist…'[1] The Hardys' home was only 10 miles from Bovington where Lawrence was stationed.

When the answer came back in the affirmative from Florence (who undertook most of the correspondence at Max Gate, and saw it as her duty to protect her elderly and distinguished husband from the unwanted attention of the outside world), Lawrence wrote directly to her, admitting that his seeking out the meeting,

> feels rather barefaced, because I haven't any qualifications to justify my seeing Mr Hardy: only I'd very much like to. *The Dynasts* and the other poems are so wholly good to my taste.[2]

To sculptor Eric Kennington, whom Lawrence had met following an exhibition of the former's paintings in London in 1920, Lawrence described his first meeting with Hardy, whom he visited from 'Tank-town' (Bovington) on 29 March 1923, saying, 'it was worth it, and I'm going again, if ever he asks me.' However, Lawrence was not uncritical of Hardy's books, about which he wrote:

> His weakness in character-drawing is a reflection of himself. A very sensitive little man: faded now: with hope yet that mankind will give up warfare. He felt incredibly old to me.[3] [Hardy was in fact eighty-two years old at that time].

Lawrence, by this comment, showed that he had underestimated the strengths of Hardy's fictional characters, such as: Gabriel Oak, Bathsheba Everdene, Clym Yeobright, Michael Henchard, Tess d'Urberville, Sergeant Troy, Fanny Robin, Angel Clare, Dick Dewy, and countless more whose names are now household words, not only in his native land, but also throughout the world. However, Lawrence described Hardy's poems as being 'so wholly good to my taste',[4] and he held *The Dynasts*, in particular, in great esteem. (A leather-bound copy of the book, inscribed to 'Colonel Lawrence from Thomas Hardy' was found amongst the collection in Lawrence's possession at the time of his death). For his part, Hardy read *Seven Pillars*, and Lawrence was 'very proud with what he said of it.'[5]

On 8 September, Lawrence, in a letter to Robert Graves, contrasted Hardy 'so pale, so quiet, so refined into an essence' with Bovington Camp, which was 'such a hurly-burly.' There was, he said,

> an unbelievable dignity and ripeness about Hardy: he is waiting so tranquilly for death, without a desire or ambition left in his spirit, as far as I can feel it: and yet he entertains so many illusions, and hopes for the world, things which I, in my disillusioned middle-age, feel to be illusory. They used to call this man a pessimist, while really he is full of fancy expectations. And the standards of the man! He feels interest in everyone, and veneration for no-one. I've not found in him any bowing-down, moral or material or spiritual.

This latter quality of Hardy's struck a chord with Lawrence:

> Max Gate is a place apart: and I feel it all the more poignantly for the contrast of life in this squalid camp. It is strange to pass from the noise and thoughtlessness of sergeants' company into a peace so secure that in it not even Mrs Hardy's tea-cups rattle on the tray: and from a barrack of hollow senseless bustle to the cheerful calm of T. H. [Hardy] thinking aloud about life to two or three of us.[6]

On 26 November 1924, Lawrence, Siegfried Sassoon, E. M. Forster, and Florence Hardy attended the first production of *Tess of the d'Urbervilles* at the Dorchester Corn Exchange, where the actress Gertrude Bugler, played the part of Tess. Hardy himself was not present, but joined his wife and guests afterwards.

Parlourmaid Nellie Titterington, described how Lawrence's visits always transformed the household at Max Gate:

> He had a wonderful sense of humour, at least that is how he looked to me, and I always saw and chatted with him when he came and I opened the door. When he called I always asked as a joke, 'Is it Col. Lawrence, Mr Shaw or Mr Ross today?'; he would smile and say 'Mr Shaw today'. In front of us maids Mr Hardy always referred to Lawrence as Mr Shaw, and Lawrence always called Mr Hardy T. H. when speaking to us or in front of Mr Hardy. Lawrence would come over from Bovington several times a month to talk to him. Indeed he would never pass through Dorchester without a call and a chat.

Describing Max Gate, Nellie said:

> A gloom filled the whole atmosphere. That's why Lawrence's visits were such a joy to me. He brought happiness for a few moments. Just to open the door to him was a pleasure. He also brought pleasure to Mr Hardy, as did several other of his friends… but apart from these occasions it was a house of noiseless gloom.

What a paradoxical situation, considering the inner turmoil of Lawrence's own life! Nellie also recalled Hardy's dog 'Wessex', a Caesar terrier, which she described as a 'terror' and 'a fierce, ugly-tempered beast':

> No guest [at table] could pick up a spoon or anything dropped without the probability of a nasty nip on the hand by Wessex. Hardy could do anything with the dog without any danger, while, if the dog was in a good mood, Mrs Hardy could sometimes pick up a dropped object safely. Col. Lawrence… was the only one who could safely deal with Wessex: he could pick anything up without any ill humour on its part. Wessex was very fond of Colonel Lawrence, who would pat him and speak to him and had a wonderful sense of power over him.[7]

In January 1927, Lawrence wrote to Florence from India to tell her of the 'delightful privilege' it had been for him to have known her and her husband, and to have the freedom of Max Gate and saying how much he looked forward to finding them both there when he came back. He also expressed concern for Hardy's health – Hardy was now eighty-six years of age. Wessex had died, and Lawrence said he hoped the dog had experienced 'a peaceful parting,' and he demonstrated his humanity further with the comment 'The killing of animals just because they are ill or old is not a medicine we apply to our own species.'[8] In other words, why should the same humaneness not be extended to animals, as is extended to humans?

Lawrence was not to see Hardy again, because a year later, on 11 January 1928 when he was still in India, Hardy died. His heart was buried in the churchyard at Stinsford near Dorchester and his body was cremated and the ashes interred in Westminster Abbey.

Lawrence felt that he could not be a friend of Hardy's because 'the difference in size and age and performance between us was too overwhelming.' And he blamed himself for intruding upon his presence and troubling his peace.[9] Nonetheless, he was drawn back to him time and again. 'I wish I hadn't gone overseas,' said Lawrence later. 'I was afraid, that last time, that it was the last.'[10]

Chapter 32

Florence Hardy

Lawrence found the peacefulness of Max Gate, home of Thomas and Florence Hardy, a complete contrast to the 'hurly-burly' of his life at Bovington Camp.[1] Here, Hardy had done Lawrence the honour of hanging a portrait of the latter on the wall of his study.

In December 1923, Lawrence explained why he could not come to lunch with the Hardys on Christmas Day: the reason being that someone had borrowed his Brough motorcycle without permission, 'and left her, ruined, in a ditch.'[2] As for Florence, she once confessed to a friend Louise Yearsley, that Colonel Lawrence had taken her for a ride on the back of his motorcycle along the Wareham Road. When asked how she had enjoyed it, she replied, 'I found speed exhilarating.'[3] It was manufacturer George Brough's opinion, that he never saw Lawrence 'take a single risk nor put any other rider or driver to the slightest inconvenience.'[4] The evidence, however, does not bear this out, as will shortly be seen.

The war poet and novelist Siegfried Sassoon, also a visitor to Max Gate, described the scene when he arrived there on 6 August 1924.

> Got to Max Gate at 4.45. A motor-bike leaning against some shrubs suggested T. E. L. Sure enough, there he was, grinning genially at me through the window of the sitting-room: back-view of T. H. also visible. Loud bark from Wessie [the dog Wessex] (tied up on the lawn out of sight). Mrs Hardy very smart, all in white silk, greets us in the Hall, and T. H. is close behind her, looking exactly the same, and brisk as ever.

Sassoon recorded that the conversation was mainly about archaeology and that Lawrence had 'sold his [Arabian] dagger for £120 to pay for doing up his cottage at Clouds Hill.' After tea they

> all trooped out into the garden to inspect the new half-acre of ground Mrs H. [Florence Hardy] has purchased from the Prince of Wales. On it vegetables are grown and chickens kept. We stood looking at the chickens for some time, while Wessie barked at them.

The following day, said Sassoon

> She [Florence] says she would like a small car, but T. H. is very firm against it. His young [er] brother [Henry] (aged seventy-two and stone-deaf) has lately scandalized his parish by purchasing an expensive Sunbeam which he drives furiously.[5]

In August 1925, in a letter to Florence, Lawrence explained, with regret, that his move from Bovington to the RAF Cadet College at Cranwell, Lincolnshire, was so sudden that there had been no time for farewells. Nevertheless, he showed that he still thought affectionately of his cottage and of his friends, when he said, 'Alas for Clouds Hill, and the Heath, and the people I had learned in the two years of Dorset!' He asked to be remembered to 'Mr Hardy, who is no doubt wholly taken up now in *Tess*.' (In other words the dramatized version of his novel).[6] To Florence, in November, he wrote

> Please give Mr. Hardy my very best regards. I've promised myself to call as soon as I have the chance. It's a solidity, to be sure that he will be in Max Gate whenever I can come.[7]

It was whilst Lawrence was with the RAF in Karachi, Pakistan, lying on his bed and listening to Beethoven's last quartet being played on a gramophone, that news came to him of Thomas Hardy's death. He wrote to Florence to express his sorrow, and his appreciation of the care which she had given to her husband. 'It was only you who kept him alive all these years: you to whom I, amongst so many others, owed the privilege of having known him.'[8] When Florence replied, it was to pay Lawrence the greatest tribute.

> He [Hardy] was devoted to you. Somehow I think he might have lived had you been here… You seem nearer to him, somehow, than any one else, certainly more akin.[9]

In his final letter to Florence (of December 1932), Lawrence apologised for the fact that his translation which he had sent her of the *Odyssey* had gone astray, and he promised to send another to Max Gate. The money (presumably from the sales of his book), he said, was useful, in that he was using it to have the wood beetles (which were eating the roof of Clouds Hill) 'doctored and sprayed', and the kitchen downstairs turned into 'a book-room, with shelves.' Finally, if the money lasted, he hoped to have a 'bath and hot-water boiler' installed. He was sorry that his mother Sarah and brother Bob had gone to China to continue their missionary work as 'they were happy in the cottage [Clouds Hill, which they had recently visited]. Perhaps they will come back?'[10]

As Lawrence acknowledged, it was thanks to Florence Hardy that he was granted entry to Max Gate, there to indulge in his favourite pursuit of literary conversation and criticism, and also to have a taste of home life, which as a single man he had not experienced since childhood. Florence considered Lawrence to be:

> the most marvellous human being I have ever met. It is not his exploits in Arabia that attract me, nor the fact that he is a celebrity: it is his character that is so splendid.[11]

She was sad that her husband had died whilst Lawrence was in India. On his return to England, she made him a gift of a coffin-stool, and of the great man's fountain pen.

Chapter 33

Robert Graves

Lawrence and Robert Ranke Graves, poet, novelist, and author, met at All Souls College, Oxford in 1919, and the two became friends. Graves, born in 1895, would go on to write an autobiography *Goodbye to All That* (1929, about the First World War in which he served in the Army); *I Claudius* (1934, a historical novel about Imperial Rome); and a biography of his friend, entitled *Lawrence and the Arabs*, published by Jonathan Cape in 1938. From 1929 onwards Graves lived mainly, in Majorca.

When Graves learnt that Lawrence had joined the RAF and was serving in the ranks, he attempted to intervene and invited the latter to join him and his family and go to live in Nepal. However, although the offer sounded attractive, Lawrence declined saying, 'partly I came here to eat dirt, till its taste is normal to me…'. The RAF, he said, had 'the one great merit of showing me humanity very clear & clean.'[1]

Lawrence, as already mentioned, had previously stated that he hoped 'that some day I will feel degraded', and that he longed 'for people to look down upon me and despise me.' He wanted his 'person' to 'properly reflect the dirtiness which it conceals.'[2]

What was the origin of these extraordinary sentiments which suggest that not only did Lawrence feel dirty, but that he wished others to perceive him as being dirty? Could it be that, following his rape by the Turks, he had felt unclean – perhaps contaminated might be a better word? This will be discussed shortly.

In March 1923, Lawrence informed Graves that the RAF had thrown him out because of 'too great publicity' and that he was now a recruit in the Royal Tank Corps. Following a request by Lawrence, Graves was now instrumental in effecting an introduction for him to Thomas Hardy.[3]

In 1925, Lawrence was to be found giving Graves a critique of *Poetic Unreason*, in which the latter used psychology as a tool with which to interpret poetry. In 1928, Lawrence wrote to Graves from India, thanking him for the two 'excellent letters you have given me about [Lawrence's own book] *The Mint*.'[4] 'In the main', said Graves, 'I liked it very much, better than *Seven Pillars*, because it had been written straight off, not brooded over.'[5] A propos of the last page of Graves's letter 'about fucking', Lawrence shed further light on his own sexuality:

> I haven't ever: and don't much want to. Judging from the way people talk it's transient, if 2¾ or 3¾ or 3 hours & ¾s. So I don't feel I miss much: and it must leave a dirty feeling, too.[6]

In 1929, Lawrence wrote to Graves in glowing terms about *Goodbye to All That*

> This is very good. The war is the best part and completely carries on and ups the excitement of the opening chapters. Most excellent. Your pictures of wounds & nerves are exactly as they should be: sane, decent, *right*. S. S. [Siegfried Sassoon] comes out very well. I'm glad of that, for I like him: homosex and all.[7]

This latter comment brings to mind the phrase 'warts and all' and implies that Lawrence liked Sassoon, in spite of the latter's homosexuality, rather than because of it. It also implies that although Lawrence did not consider himself to be a homosexual, he was still able to be open and frank with Graves, whom he *knew* to be homosexual.

In April 1931, Lawrence, now based at Plymouth, told Graves – now living in Majorca with American writer and divorcee Laura Riding – about his work on 'new types of marine craft for the RAF'[8] The couple were writing a book which featured an autogyro, for which Lawrence was able to provide technical information. However, *No Decency Left*, published in 1932, failed to attract the attention of Hollywood as Graves and Riding had hoped, and was a commercial failure.

In February 1935, Lawrence, now in Bridlington, Yorkshire, told Graves how he had set aside some money, and spent the rest 'on friends and books and pictures and motor-bikes and joys of sorts.' Now however, when he was less than a month away from retirement from the RAF, interest rates on investments had fallen and left him having to make up 'about £700 more.' Lawrence, who had given Graves financial assistance on a previous occasion, noted that the latter was now financially secure, having published *I Claudius* and *Claudius the God* in the previous year. However, even though the positions were now reversed, and it was Graves who now offered help to Lawrence, the latter declined the offer, except as 'a reserve, only if ever I get meshed and unable to help myself.'

Lawrence went on to tell Graves how he had recently met the producer Alexander Korda, whom he had dissuaded from making a film about him. Lawrence loathed 'the notion of being celluloided', and his rare visits to the cinema always deepened in him 'a sense of their [i.e. the films being shown] superficial falsity….'

Lawrence agreed for Graves to write his obituary for a London newspaper which had requested it, in advance, for its files – or 'morgue' – as Lawrence called it, but advised Graves as follows:

> Don't give too much importance to what I did in Arabia during the war. I feel that the Middle Eastern settlement put through by Winston Churchill and Young [Major Hubert Young who had been at Carchemish] and me in 1921 should weigh more than fighting.

He discussed his present work of designing and testing rescue boats, and declared proudly that:

> not one type of RAF boat in production is naval.... We have found, chosen, selected or derived our own sorts: they have (power for power) three times the speed of their predecessors, less weight, less cost, more room, more safety, more seaworthiness.

Lawrence did not claim sole credit for this. 'They have grown out of the joint experience, skill and imaginations of many men,' he said. Lieutenant-Commander H.E.E. Weblin, in charge of the Marine Craft Detachment, Bridlington, said of Lawrence:

> he was the greatest assistance in the detachment. His knowledge of every subject that cropped up, both technical and otherwise was astounding and could always be applied practically. This covered such diverse subjects as photography, wireless, handling of speed boats under all weather conditions and even such things as the most efficient colour for painting bombing targets. It was in each case backed by practical experience and I have yet to find an instance where it was not correct. [9]

Finally, referring to *Seven Pillars*, he reverted to his familiar role of self-deprecation. 'Well, I failed in that,' he said. When he and Graves were together at Oxford, he:

> was then trying to write; to be perhaps an artist or to be at least cerebral. By measuring myself against such people as yourself and Augustus John, I could feel that I was not made out of the same stuff. Artists excite me and attract me; seduce me. Almost I could be an artist, but there is a core that puts on the brake.

He could not pinpoint the reason for this. 'If I knew what it was I would tell you, or become one of you. Only I can't. So I changed direction, right, and went into the RAF...'

It appears that Lawrence, 'after straightening out that Eastern tangle with Winston', was now more or less satisfied with the final Arab settlement. 'How well the Middle East has done: it, more than any part of the world, has gained from that war.'

He went into the RAF, he told Graves

> ...to serve a mechanical purpose, not as leader but as a cog of the machine. I have been a mechanic since, and a good mechanic, for my self-training to become an artist has greatly widened my field of view. ...one of the benefits of being part of the machine is that one learns that one doesn't matter![10]

This brings to mind the inscription 'OU OPOVTIS', which he carved into the stone architrave above the front door of his cottage at Clouds Hill. This is a quotation from the Greek historian Herodotus, and, translated loosely, it means, 'Does not care.'

Like Shaw, Graves showed concern for Lawrence's welfare and the two men collaborated over their various literary creations. As for Lawrence, his delight in the company of artists and writers, and his enthusiasm for perfecting his rescue boats, reflects an altogether more positive frame of mind, after all the traumas of the past.

Chapter 34

Lady Astor

Lawrence arrived back in England from India in January 1929 with one suit of plain clothes, two sets of uniform, and a motorcycle. 'I see hardly anyone', he wrote, 'and don't know what to say to them when I do see them.'

There followed, in March 1929, one of his happiest postings: to the RAF Flying-Boat Station at Cattewater on Plymouth Sound. The commanding officer was Wing Commander Sydney Smith, who had previously been assigned the task of spiriting Lawrence off the liner SS *Rajputana*, to escape the attentions of the press. Lawrence soon became friends with him, his wife Clare, their daughter Maureen, and the family's retinue of dogs. They nicknamed him 'Tes' (the initials of T. E. Shaw, his adopted name).

Lawrence was later to describe the two years he was to spend here as his *Golden Reign*.[1] It is 'in a lovely place', he said, with a good camp 'comfortably laid-out', where 'we are a happy family.' He also described the magnificence of his new 'Brough' motorcycle (given to him anonymously by the Shaws), and how it had 'taken me twice to London' in a 'fastest time of four hours and forty-four minutes.'[2]

In April 1929, Lady Nancy Astor visited Cattewater (later renamed 'Mount Batten') and the two commenced a friendship. She called him 'Aircraftman' and enjoyed the occasional pillion ride on his motorcycle. He called her 'The Peeress'. They, subsequently, corresponded by copious letters and telephone calls.

The Astor family originated in Heidelberg, Germany, and John Jacob Astor, who emigrated to America, made a fortune in the fur trade and in property speculation in New York. His great-grandson, William Waldorf Astor, moved to England and was created first Viscount. Nancy Astor née Langhorne, born in Virginia, USA, in 1879, was the wife of the second Viscount, also Waldorf, and the family seat was at Cliveden in Buckinghamshire. When, on his father's death in 1919, her husband went to the House of Lords, Lady Astor succeeded him as Member of Parliament for Sutton, Plymouth. She was the first woman MP to take her seat in the House of Commons, and she held the Plymouth constituency until 1945.

In contrast, Lawrence was one of society's poorest members – though this was partly from his own volition. Nevertheless, he admired the generosity of the philanthropic Lady Astor and her husband, telling her:

> You and Waldorf are two of the rich who would very easily pass through the eye of the needle, I reckon. If only the rest of us were as unselfish with our money.[3]

Lawrence's letters to Lady Astor reveal his keen sense of humour and a refreshing facility not to be overawed by people of wealth and privilege. Referring to a forthcoming 'GBS. reading,' he said

> I will attend (probably in uniform, but I shan't mind your being differently dressed!) on the 23rd. If I do not turn up, then please blame the RAF rather than my expectant self.[4]

And describing a ride back from Cliveden when he raced 'a sports Bentley... [motor car] across the Plain.... I wished I had had a peeress or two on my flapper bracket!'[5] He made reference to his poverty. 'I cannot answer your wires, because often I have not a shilling to spare.'[6] 'I cling to camp', he said, 'because there I feel I belong. Belonging is a good feeling.'[7]

He spoke of his mother, saying

> She writes often and at length [from China] and cries out for letters as when at home she cries out for our love... as if it could be turned on in a tap.

And he advised Lady Astor

> Don't play the mother too long to your kids, please! If you are interesting enough they will keep in touch. If not – why don't wish it![8]

In March 1931, Lady Astor wrote to Aircraftman Shaw to say:

> I am arriving at Plymouth tomorrow at about three or four o'clock. This is to warn you that I shall call you up, and hope that if the weather is fine you will take me out in your boat. If it isn't fine, I should prefer pillion riding!!![9]

The boat to which she referred was the *Biscuit*, a speedboat produced by the American Purdy Company, which a wealthy friend gave Lawrence the use of. The *Biscuit* demonstrated the RAF's need for a new generation of fast and manoeuvrable air-sea rescue boats which Lawrence lobbied for, and he soon found himself involved in their development, production, and testing. He, and his commanding officer Sydney Smith, whose work involved developing fast-rescue launches, and who managed the seaplane races for the Schneider Cup (competition created by Jacques Schneider in 1911), took a keen interest in getting the *Biscuit* into good working order. On her first outing, Smith was duly impressed:

> Never have I seen such antics from a speed-boat. Tes [Lawrence] turned her round in her own length and showed her off like a small boy with an exciting toy.[10]

On 4 February 1931 there was a fatal accident in Plymouth Sound when a flying boat nosedived into the sea, and it was Lawrence who dived with the other rescuers to recover the body of her pilot and who was also involved in the rescue of six of her crew.

In 1932, when Lawrence's mother Sarah and eldest brother Bob (a medical missionary of the China Inland Mission), returned to England on holiday and stayed at Clouds Hill, Lady Astor made them a present of some rugs. When they returned to China later in the year, Lawrence made no secret of his regret.

> I wish these poor things hadn't this cast-iron sense of duty. They are not fit for life in rough places, and they were so quaint and happy in my Dorset cottage, improbable home as it is.[11]

In the event, this was to be the last time that Lawrence would see them.

Lawrence's friends were anxious about what he would do when he retired from the RAF: an event which occurred on 26 February 1935. He was certainly subdued when he wrote to Lady Astor on 5 May from Clouds Hill.

> It is quiet here now, and I feel as though I were fixed in my cottage for good. It is as I thought… something is finished with my leaving the RAF It gets worse instead of healing over.[12]

He was offered the secretaryship of the Bank of England, which he declined. Then Lady Astor invited him to Cliveden (her home in Berkshire) to meet Stanley Baldwin, who the following month would succeed Ramsay MacDonald as Prime Minister. 'I believe when the Government reorganizes', she told Lawrence on 7 May, 'you will be asked to help reorganize the Defence Forces.' However, the suggestion was in vain, for Lawrence replied:

> No: wild mares would not at present take me away from Clouds Hill. It is an earthly paradise and I am staying here till I feel qualified for it. Also there is something broken in the works, as I told you: my will, I think. In this mood I would not take on any job at all. So do not commit yourself to advocating me, lest I prove a non-starter. Am well, well-fed, full of company, laborious and innocent-customed.

> News from China [i.e. about his mother and brother] – NIL. The area is now a centre of disturbance. [Signed] TES.[13]

Lawrence could scarcely contain his joy at seeing Lady Astor (nine years his senior) when she visited, which was all too infrequently, and taking her out on his motorcycle or in his boat. The happy times spent in her company were probably as near as he was ever to come to having a fulfilling relationship with a member of the opposite sex.

Right: Lawrence's Brough motorcycle at Corfe Castle, one of his favourite places to visit. (Jonathan M. Weekly)

Below: The Bey of Deraa (centre) with his officers, January 1918. Provenance of Targan Carikli. (The Secret Lives of Lawrence of Arabia, by Colin Simpson and Phillip Knightley, Thomas Nelson & Sons Ltd, 1969)

Clouds Hill, front entrance

Above: Clouds Hill, circa 1893. The man on the left is the tenant, Edward Pride (born 1840). On his left, wearing a white apron, is his wife Elizabeth (née Kellaway, born 1842). (Courtesy of Janetta Mizen, granddaughter of Frederick James Honeybun – the tallest man – and his wife Bessie Pride – on his left)

Below left: John Bruce, 1923. Provenance of John Bruce. (The Secret Lives of Lawrence of Arabia, by Colin Simpson and Phillip Knightley, Thomas Nelson & Sons Ltd, 1971)

Below right: Lawrence as Aircraftman Shaw in his second RAF period. (Bodleian Library, University of Oxford)

Above: Clouds Hill. (Wareham Town Museum)

Below: Clouds Hill, downstairs, 1935. (Wareham Town Museum)

Above: Clouds Hill, upstairs, 1935. (Wareham Town Museum)

Below: Wool Camp, circa 1920. (Trustees of Seven Pillars of Wisdom Trust)

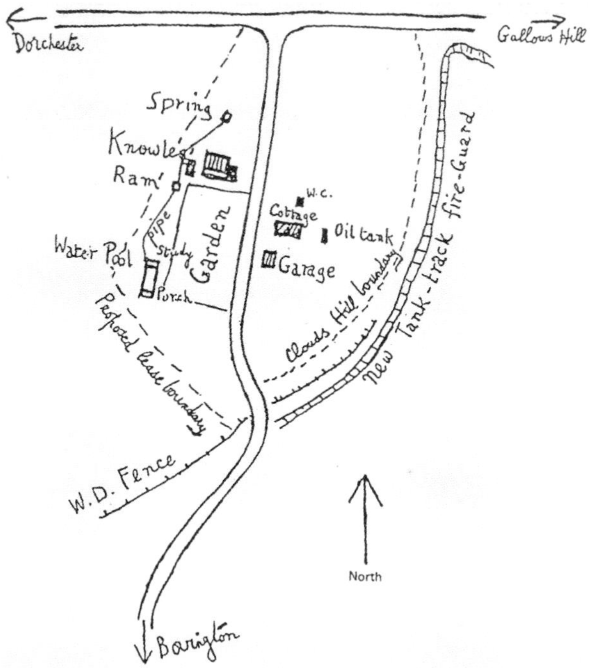

Right: Clouds Hill, sketched by Lawrence, April 1934.

Below left: Aerial photograph of Clouds Hill and vicinity, taken by the RAF in 1947. (Dorset History Centre)

Below right: Bovington/ Clouds Hill. (Google map, 2008)

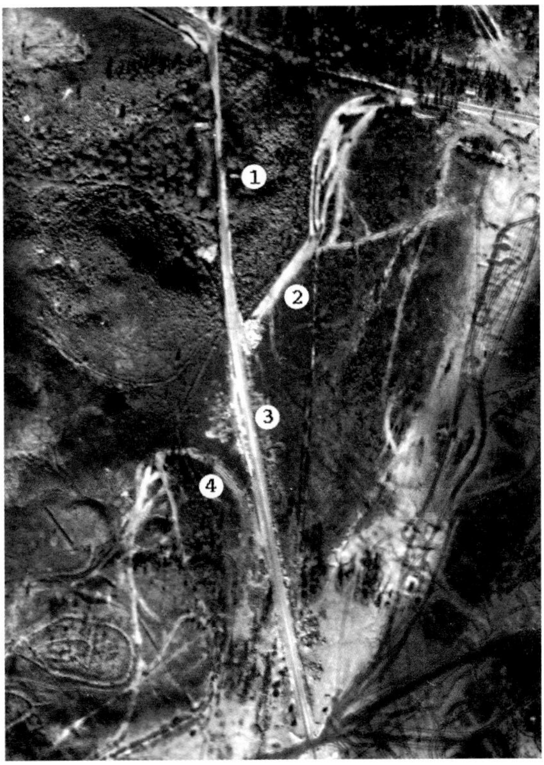

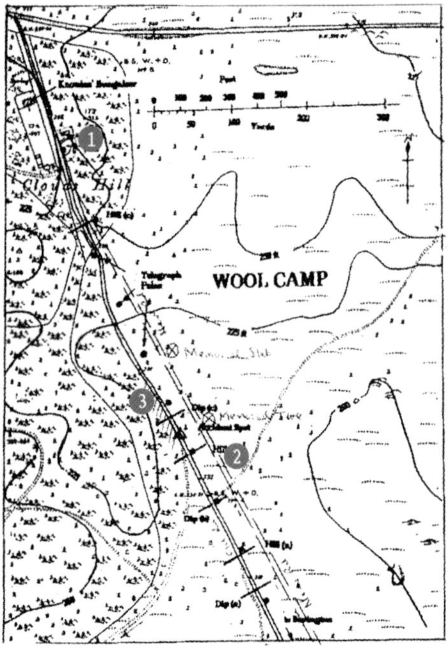

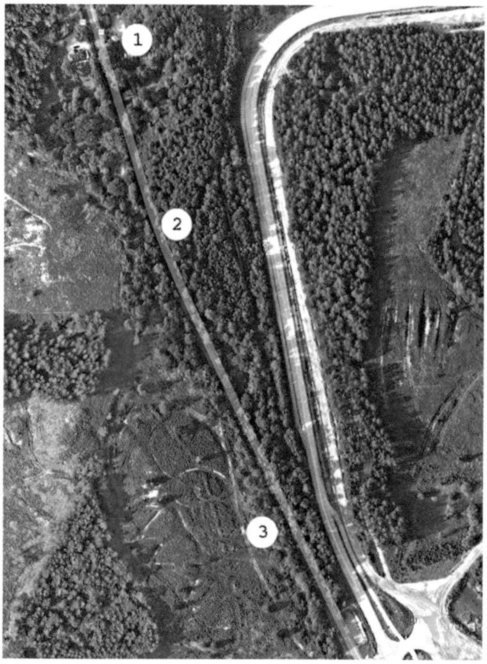

Above left: Position of King George V Road, superimposed on the 1901 Ordnance Survey map, by Andrew B. Simpson.

Above right: Clouds Hill, King George V Road, and remnants of Tank Park Road. (Google map, 2008)

Below: Tank Park Road leading northwards from Bovington, circa 1930.

From crash site looking south, 14 May 1935. (Bovington Tank Museum)

From crash site looking south, 2013.

From crash site looking north, 14 May 1935. (by an unknown photographer)

From crash site looking north, 2013. Barry King standing by what remains of a large tree on right-hand side of road.

The author and the tree stump in question, 2013.

From crash site looking north, mid-May 1935. (Joyce E. Knowles)

Above: From crash site looking north, mid-May 1935. (Joyce E. Knowles)

Below: From crash site looking north, 2013.

Left: Bank and hillock on left-hand side of road.

Below: Diagram of crash site by Paul Marriott and Yvonne Argent, after Frank Fletcher.

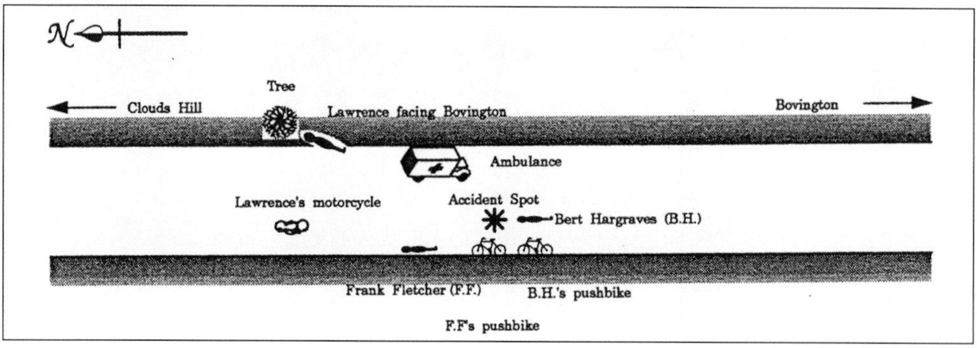

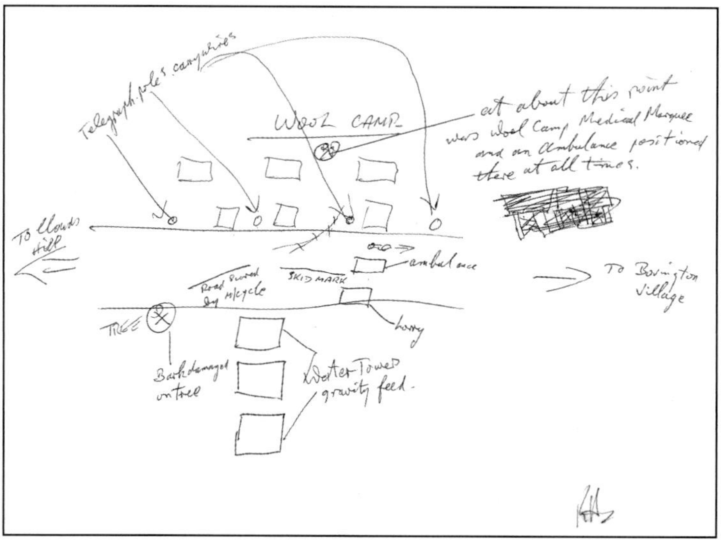

Roland A. Hammersley's diagram of the crash site, after Joan Hughes. (Wareham Town Museum)

A, B, and C. Albert Hargraves's damaged bicycle. (Bodleian Library, Oxford)

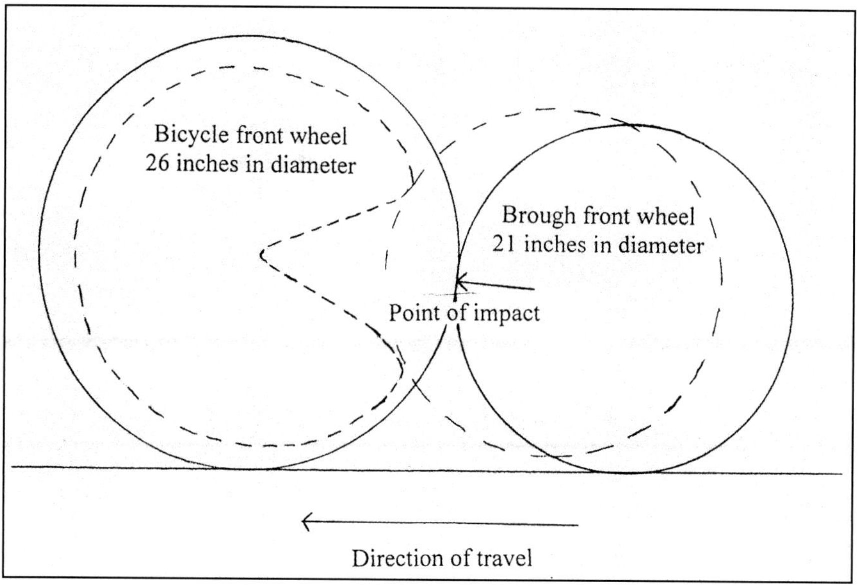

The crash: point of impact.

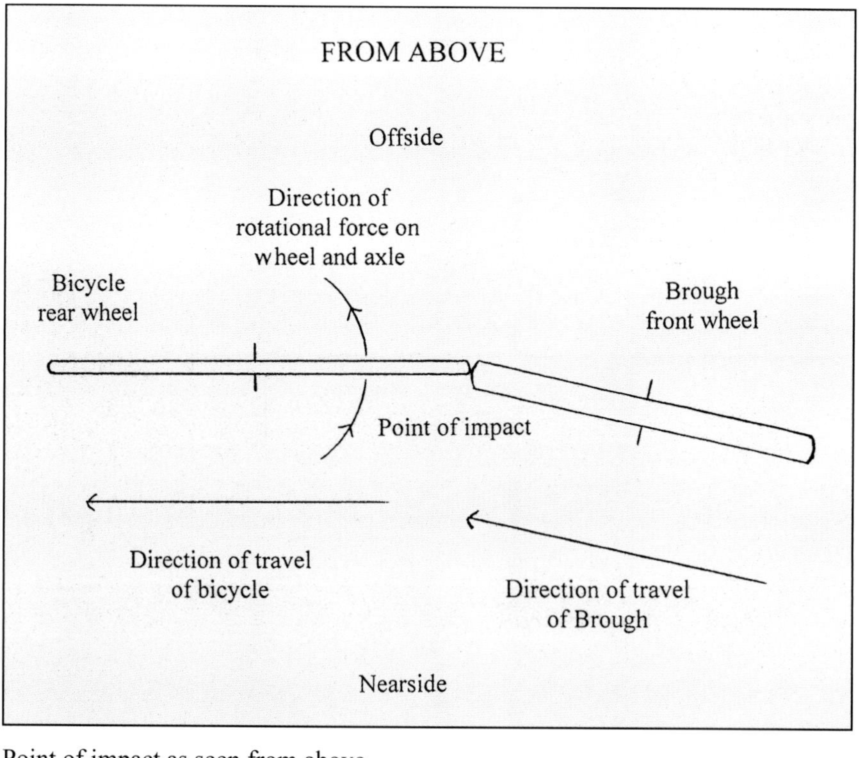

Point of impact as seen from above.

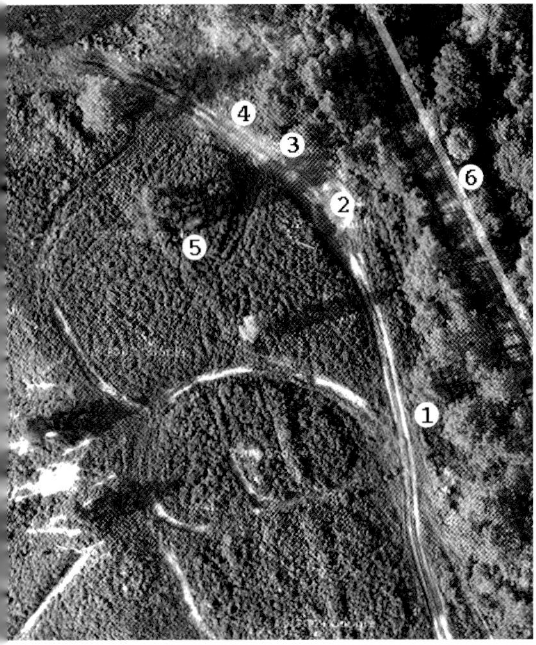

Above left: Vicinity of the crash. (Google Map 2008)

Above right: Sister Wendy Vallance, Dorset County Hospital, circa 1978.

Below: Dorchester County Hospital.

Wreckage of the Blackburn Iris Seaplane N238, Batten Bay, Plymouth, 4 February 1931. Aviation Safety Network.

Sir Hugh William Bell Cairns, circa 1945. Wikimedia Commons.

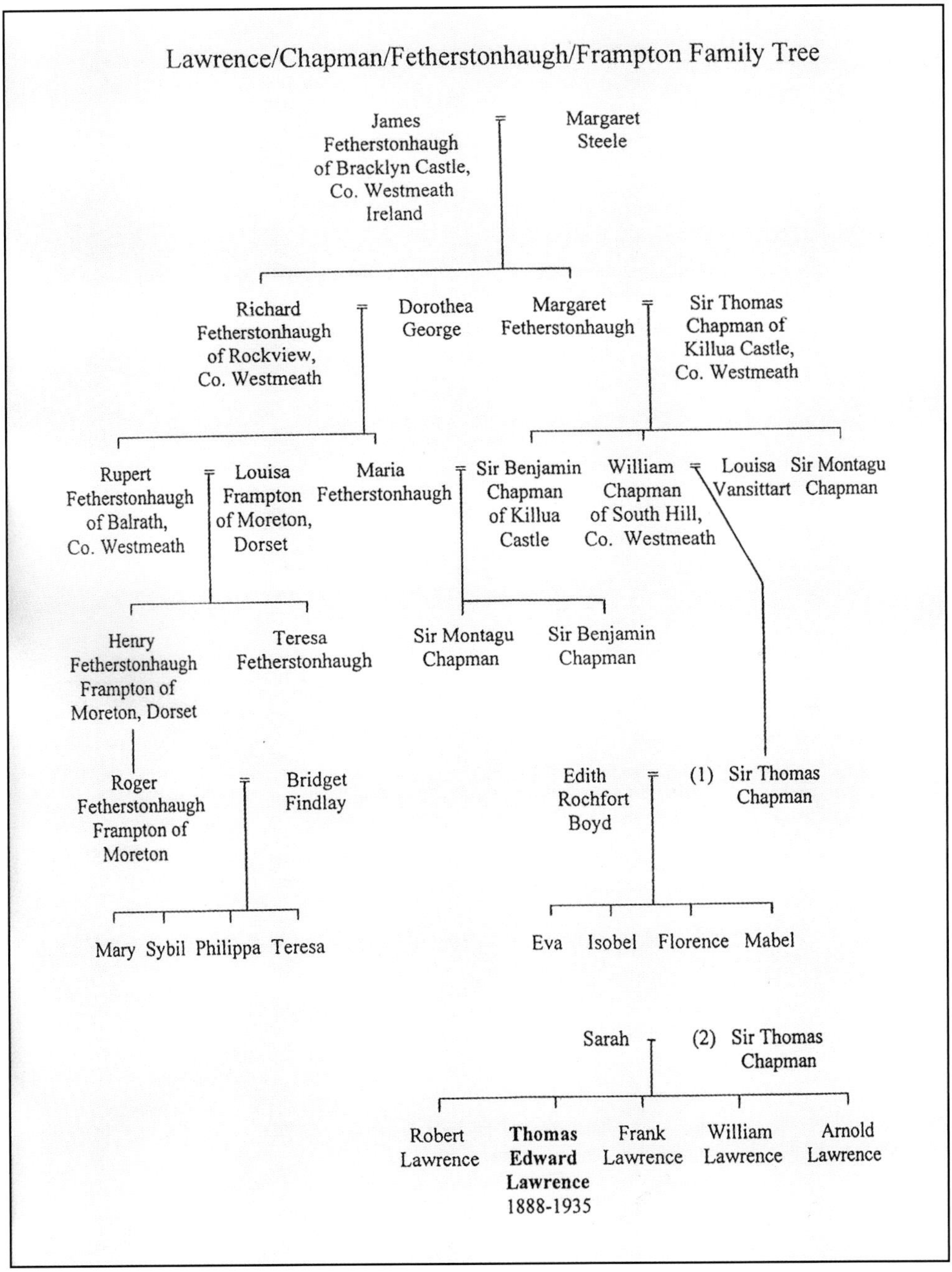

Lawrence/Fetherstonhaugh/Frampton Family Tree.

Bernard C. Burgess at Clouds Hill, 2023.

Chapter 35

Deraa and the Alleged Rape: Was Lawrence Telling the Truth?

Some have questioned whether Lawrence's account of his capture, beating, and rape by the Turks at Deraa, was a fabrication by him, or merely a figment of his imagination. After all, he had invented the 'Old Man' story, so why not the rape? Lawrence's friend George Bernard Shaw, in a note written in the flyleaf of his wife's subscribers copy of *Seven Pillars* (published in 1926),[1] stated as follows:

> One of his chapters (LXXXI) tells of a revolting sequel to his capture by the Turks and his attraction for a Turkish officer. He told me that his account of the affair is not true. I forbore to ask him what actually happened.[2]

On the other hand, to Shaw's wife Charlotte, his closest friend and confidante, Lawrence had indicated quite the opposite.

Doubts about the authenticity of Lawrence's account continue to be expressed. For example, in 2003, biographer Suleiman Mousa declared, 'I think that Deraa was an invention. It never happened, to my mind'. Whereas biographer Michael Yardley opined, 'I don't think the rape at Deraa happened in the way that Lawrence suggested it did'. Nonetheless, Yardley did not discount the possibility that Lawrence may have been raped whilst he was in Arabia.[3] In May 2006, an article by Elizabeth Day appeared in the *Telegraph* online entitled 'Lawrence of Arabia "Made Up" Sex Attack by Turk Troops':

> The supposed rape on November 20, 1917, at the Syrian fortress town at Deraa has been the subject of much speculation over the years. The most controversial incident in the colourful life of Lawrence of Arabia was made up by the celebrated hero, according to new forensic evidence.
>
> Although he recounted some detail of the attack in his 1922 memoir, *Seven Pillars of Wisdom*, the pages of Lawrence's diary covering the period when the incident is meant to have taken place have been ripped out. Until now, scholars have been unable to

> ascertain Lawrence's whereabouts during those crucial days from November 15-21, when he claimed that he had been captured by the Turkish governor, Hajim Bey, then whipped and raped by guards. Yet evidence uncovered by James Barr, author of *Setting the Desert on Fire: T. E. Lawrence and Britain's Secret War in Arabia 1916-1918*, suggests that Lawrence never went to Deraa.

In order to discern what might have been written on the missing pages, Barr submitted Lawrence's diary for electrostatic data analysis. Said he:

> The tests produced three grey transparent films which didn't look promising. When I got them home I noticed there was a faint capital letter 'A' in Lawrence's handwriting, in the entry for November 18. I realized I had found significant new evidence.
>
> The 'A' from the missing page provides strong evidence from Lawrence that he did not leave Azraq [an oasis situated some 70 miles south-east of Deraa] until November 19 at the earliest.[4]

In *Seven Pillars*, Lawrence indicated that it took him at least two days to travel from Azrak to Deraa – a distance of 70 miles. Barr is therefore implying that if his theory is correct, then given the fact that the rape occurred on 20 November, Lawrence could not have made the journey in the time stated. However, Barr's theory is based on several assumptions, which may not be correct. For example, he assumes that the 'A' stands for Azrak, whereas there are other proper nouns that begin with the letter 'A'. And even if the 'A' discovered by Barr did stand for Azrak, the presence of the word on the page cannot necessarily be taken to mean that Lawrence was present in that town on the day in question.

Lawrence's Field Diary: the missing pages

Lawrence's diary, in which he simply recorded where he was on a particular date, reads as follows:

12 [November] Kasr [palace of] Azrak [an oasis]
13 Kasr Azrak
14 Kasr Azrak

As already indicated, pages for 15 November 1917 through to 21 November 1917 inclusive, are missing. The diary then jumps forward to:

22 Azrak
23 Butum [Wadi Butum]
24 Bair [80 miles south of Azrak][5]

Seven Pillars

A difficulty with *Seven Pillars* is that Lawrence seldom included dates in the narrative. However, according to him a), he was at Azrak (where he used a partially ruined former Crusader castle as his base) from late October 1917 and b), from here, he led an attack on trains and railway bridges in the Yarmuk Valley,[6] returning to base on 12 November.[7]

The strategic significance of the town of Deraa

Lawrence alleged that his rape had occurred at the town of Deraa, then occupied by the Turks and chosen by him as a highly significant target.

> For my eyes, the centre of attraction was Deraa, the junction of the Jerusalem-Haifa-Damascus-Medina railways, the navel of the Turkish Armies in Syria, the common point of all their fronts; and, by chance, an area in which lay great untouched reserves of Arab fighting men, educated and armed by Feisal from Akaba.[8]

What more natural, therefore, than for Lawrence to embark on a reconnaissance mission prior to an attack on Deraa, in which 'we could cut it off on north and west and south, by destroying the three railways.'[9] After all, he had embarked on many similar such operations prior to this one: for example, to various locations on the Hejaz railway between March and September 1917.

Furthermore, Lawrence's description of the journey from Azrak to Deraa (with details of who accompanied him): 'the hollow land of Hauran'; 'the curving bank of the Palestine Railway' on the outskirts of Deraa; and the 'old Albatross machines in the sheds',[10] leaves little doubt that he did, in fact, make the journey which he claimed to have made.

Lawrence's correspondence with his parents

On 14 November, a week prior to the Deraa episode, Lawrence had written to his mother from Azrak to say

> I am staying here a few days, resting my camels, and then will have another fling. Last, 'fling' was two railway engines.[11] [This was a reference to the recent destruction of two locomotives on the railway, south of Deraa.][12]

Why did Lawrence not mention his proposed visit to Deraa in the letter? For security reasons, obviously. After all, he was hardly likely to reveal the fact that he was about to embark on a spying mission, even to members of his own family!

On 14 December 1917, three weeks or so after the rape, Lawrence, in another letter to his parents, stated: 'I wrote to you last from Azrak.... After that I stayed for ten days or so there, and then rode down to Akaba....'[13] In this letter, he again concealed from his parents the fact that he had visited Deraa. He also made no mention of his beating and rape.

Why did Lawrence delay, before going public about the rape?

It was on 28 June 1919, 19 months after the event had taken place, that Lawrence, in a letter to Major W. F. Stirling, Deputy Chief Political Officer, Cairo, first mentioned the Deraa incident.

> I went in to Deraa in disguise to spy out the defences, was caught, and identified by Hajim Bey the Governor.... Hajim was an ardent paederast [i.e. pederast] and took a fancy to me. So he kept me under guard till night, and then tried to have me. I was unwilling, and prevailed after some difficulty. Hajim sent me to the hospital, and I escaped before dawn, being not as hurt as he thought.[14]

From this, it is clear that Lawrence could not bring himself to admit the truth, and instead, gave the impression that it was *his*, rather than the bey's will which prevailed. As to whether or not the bey was 'an ardent pederast', this will be discussed shortly.

If, as seems likely, Lawrence was, at this relatively early stage, in denial about the rape, then this is entirely understandable, for it would have had a devastating effect upon his psyche, leaving him too shocked and ashamed to admit to it. This is borne out in a letter that he wrote on 26 December 1925 to his friend Charlotte Shaw, where he confessed that he agonized, for some time, on whether to go public about the matter in the book which he was currently writing entitled *Seven Pillars of Wisdom*.

> That is the 'bad' book [i.e. Book 6, of a total of 10 books of which *Seven Pillars of Wisdom* was composed], with the Deraa chapter. Working on it always makes me sick. The two impulses fight so upon it. Self-respect would close it: self-expression seeks to open it. It's a case in which you can't let yourself write as well as you could.[15]

Lawrence's dilemma is clear. Either he keep the matter secret, or tell all and risk further humiliation by doing so.

Lawrence's injuries

Evidence of the fact that Lawrence was, at some time in his life, brutally whipped came to light subsequently, on 12 March 1923, when he was examined by an Army doctor at the Central Recruiting Office, Whitehall, London, prior to his joining the Royal Tank Corps at Bovington, Dorset. On the enlistment document, under the heading 'Marks indicating congenital peculiarities or previous disease', the doctor wrote, 'Scars [to] both buttocks. In other words these did not look like recent scars.'[16]

Furthermore, Lawrence's Entry Examination Record Card for the Royal Air Force, which he joined in August 1922, also recorded signs of previous injury to his person: the medical officer noting 'Four superficial scars, left side. Three superficial scars, lower part of back.'[17]

Other confidantes

A letter from Lawrence to Edward Garnett (novelist, critic, and publisher's reader for Jonathan Cape) dated 22 August 1922, also revealed just how agonising it was for him to go into print about the rape.

> If that Deraa incident whose treatment you call severe and serene… had happened to yourself you would not have recorded it. I have a face of brass perhaps, but I put it into print very reluctantly, last of all the pages I sent to the press. For weeks I wanted to burn it in the manuscript: because I could not tell the story face to face with anyone, and I think I'll feel sorry, when I next meet you, that you know it.[18]

It is unlikely that Lawrence would have attempted to deceive people such as Garnett, an employee of his publisher Cape; Charlotte Shaw, his confidante, who to him became something of a mother figure, and novelist and critic E. M. Forster, whose writings he admired, and whose opinion he sought concerning his own literary efforts. Finally, Lawrence's biographer Michael Korda states that

> when the British Government finally released most of the papers and documents relating to Lawrence, almost everything he claimed was confirmed in meticulous detail.[19]

In other words, Lawrence was not in the habit of falsifying evidence.

Why did Lawrence finally decide to reveal all?

By publishing details of what had befallen him at Deraa, Lawrence risked humiliation in the eyes of the world; jeopardising his position in the military; and the possible termination of his relationship with Emir Feisal. He, more than any other, had managed to persuade the Arabs to unite together. How, if he published, could he expect to retain the credibility and influence necessary to achieve his dream – that of ensuring that the Arabs would, one day, regain sovereignty over their territories? Finally, however, 'self-expression won the day', when Lawrence decided that his ordeal was not something which he could keep to himself.

Conclusion

What possible motive could Lawrence have had for inventing the rape scenario, and going public about it, when he had so much to lose by doing so?

Chapter 36

Rape Trauma Syndrome

In Lawrence's era, rape was a taboo subject, and its victims were largely disbelieved and ignored. Nowadays, however, the adverse effects which rape may have on the victim are well recognised and well documented, and fall under the heading 'Rape Trauma Syndrome'.

A timeline for the short-term and long-term response of the victim to his or her rape has been constructed by Mary P. Koss and Mary R. Harvey, who classified the different phases sequentially as follows:

1. The anticipatory phase immediately precedes the sexual assault. Realizing that they are potentially in danger, the victim employs 'various defense mechanisms such as dissociation, suppression, and rationalization to preserve their illusion of invulnerability'.
2. The impact phase includes the duration of the assault and the immediate aftermath. The 'intense fear of death or bodily harm resulted in varying degrees of disintegration and disorganization in the ability to appraise or respond to the situation'.
3. The reconstitution phase begins with the victim attending to 'basic living considerations. Immediately after the initial impact of rape has occurred, a denial phase often is seen. Sometime between two weeks and several months later, the feelings experienced at the time of the assault return. This phase may be... lengthy and have serious debilitating effects. Common experiences at this time include specific anxiety, nightmares, and fears; depression, guilt, or shame; catastrophic fantasies; feelings of vulnerability, helplessness, dirtiness, alienation, and isolation; sexual dysfunctions and physical symptoms'.
4. The resolution phase is characterized by anger, despair, hopelessness, and shame.[1]

In 1980, A. Nicholas Groth and Ann W. Burgess published the results of a study of twenty-two subjects who had participated in male-on-male rape, of whom sixteen were perpetrators and six were victims.[2] In the victims, the following symptoms were noted:

Anger

Male victims… seemed to evidence considerable anger at having been raped, and fantasised or planned retaliation against their assailants.

Lawrence demonstrated his anger towards the bey, when he described him in June 1919 as an 'ardent paederast'.[3] (Pederasty is defined as sexual relations between a man and a boy.[4]) Previously, in September 1918 he had told his commander Zaagi at Tafas 'The best of you brings me the most Turkish dead', thus revealing his hatred of the Turks in general, and undoubtedly, of the bey in particular.[5]

A tendency to keep the matter secret

The male victims felt pressured into not reporting the rape for several reasons: 1) societal beliefs that a man is expected to be able to defend himself against sexual assault, 2) the victim's sexuality may become suspect, and 3) telling is distressing ('It's embarrassing to tell someone you've been raped').

As already mentioned, it was evidently not until 19 months after the rape, that Lawrence first made mention of it.

Fear

The authors described fear as one of the psychological reactions that could adversely affect the victim and disrupt his lifestyle.

'You instance my night in Deraa. Well, I'm always afraid of being hurt: and to me, while I live, the force of that night will lie in the agony which broke me, and made me surrender'[6]

In February 1918, Lawrence declared that he 'feared to be alone…'.[7] This may account for him subsequently joining the armed forces, where he would always have company.

The inability to eat or sleep

In 1927, Lawrence told Alan Dawnay that 'the job of proof-correcting [Seven Pillars] has made the war memories very vivid to me, so that they have been coming back as night-terrors to shorten my already few hours regular sleep'.[8] And these 'war memories' would surely have included the rape at Deraa.

Not being believed by others

Many have suggested that Lawrence concocted the Deraa rape episode, but without giving a credible explanation as to what motive he would have had for so doing.

A sexual identity crisis

A major strategy used by some offenders in the assault of males is to get the victim to ejaculate. This effort may serve several purposes. In misidentifying ejaculation with orgasm, the victim may be bewildered by his physiological response to the offense.

As far as Lawrence is concerned, it seems more likely that, during the rape, he had an orgasm, rather than a mere seminal emission – hence his words, 'a delicious warmth, probably sexual, was swelling through me…'. Whatever the truth may be, however, it is likely that a), he was initially confused by it and b), the experience reinforced his pre-existing sexual fantasies.

In an article published in 2005, Jayne Walker, John Archer, and Michelle Davies published the results of a study of forty survivors of male-on-male rape, in which the psychological functioning of the victims was compared with that of a control group.[9] The results were as follows:

Self-worth and self-esteem

The survivor group showed significantly lower self-esteem scores than the controls. There were substantial differences showing that the survivors saw themselves as lacking self-esteem regarding their general competence, their appearance, and in their social lives.

'We are social bed-rock, those unfit for life-by-competition: and each of us values the rest as cheap as he knows himself to be'.[10] *Also, Lawrence repeatedly told Charlotte Shaw that since the rape, he had felt worthless. For example, 'Good, perhaps, to feel like a prehistoric animal, extinct, and dead, and useless: but wounding also'.*[11]

Re-experiencing the rape

> The majority suffered from intrusive re-experiencing of the rape: 58% reported experiencing intrusive thoughts 'often' and 32% 'sometimes'. The experiences reported most often were: 'I thought about it when I didn't mean to' and, 'Pictures about it popped into my mind'. 80% reported having trouble falling asleep because of images and thoughts related to the rape. 75% reported experiencing dreams and nightmares. Accordingly, most survivors consciously recognized the importance of avoidance of certain ideas, feelings, and situations. 85% acknowledged that they stayed away from reminders. 68% experienced avoidance reactions 'often', and 22% 'sometimes'.

'You may call this morbid: but think of the offence [i.e. the rape], and the intensity of my brooding over it for these years. It will hang about me while I live…'.

(Lawrence to Charlotte Shaw, 1924.)[12] *The Depot is dreary.... It is a desert very like Arabia: and all sorts of haunting likenesses try to remind me of what I've been for eight years desperately fighting out of my mind'.*[13]

Anxiety and depression

> The survivors showed more somatic symptoms [relating to the body, as distinct from the mind] than controls, anxiety and insomnia, social dysfunction, and depression.

Admittedly, Lawrence was depressed a), because the Arab nations were not granted full self-government and b), because of the part that he had played in the deception. However, this in no way explains the profound level of depression which he experienced in the years after the rape. 'There is something broken in the works'.[14]

Suicide

> Some of the survivors were suffering serious consequences, including suicide ideation and attempts [at suicide].

Lawrence attempted suicide, at Christmastime 1925.

The long term sequelae of rape trauma syndrome

> These results support previous reports that male rape survivors display high levels of psychological disturbance and health problems, even years after the assault.

These symptoms, which could persist for a decade or more, included social dysfunction, depression, posttraumatic stress disorder, and suicidal ideation and attempts.

It was certainly the case with Lawrence, that his symptoms persisted for many years after the rape.

Guilt and self blame

In another study, Jayne Walker, John Archer, and Michelle Davies found that the incidence among victims of 'guilt and self-blame, e.g. for not being able to prevent the assault' was 82.5%.

'For fear of being hurt, or rather to earn five minutes respite from a pain which drove me mad, I gave away the only possession we are born into the world with - our bodily integrity. It's an unforgivable matter, an irrevocable position... '. Lawrence to Charlotte Shaw, March 1924.[15]

Feeling dirty

One of the victims stated as follows. 'Before the assault I was proud to be a homosexual; however, now I feel 'neutered'. I feel sex is dirty and disgusting and I have a real problem with my sexual orientation'.

This is not to imply that Lawrence was homosexual. However, Lawrence repeatedly told Charlotte Shaw that since the rape, he had felt unclean.

Social withdrawal

72.5% of victims demonstrated 'withdrawal from family and friends'.[19]

Lawrence's relationship with his family members does not appear to have been a close one. As for his friends, his role in the Arab Revolt and his subsequent commitment to fighting for a just settlement for the Arabs following the end of hostilities would necessarily have curtailed some of his friendships.

However, in reference to Cranwell Cadet College, his posting from 1925-6, Lawrence declared in The Mint, 'Everywhere a relationship: no loneliness any more'.[20] *And in reference to RAF Cattewater, said he, in 1929, 'I cling to camp because there I feel I belong. Belonging is a good feeling.'.*[21] *This is an indication that by now, his traumatisation as a result of the rape had diminished, and he was therefore able to make new friends.*

A loss of direction

Ritchie J. McMullen, author of *Male Rape* , stated as follows:

> Being a victim [of rape] means being powerless. It means not being able to control or direct one's body, life, or circumstances. It means lacking autonomy and the freedom to self-govern or self-regulate. It also means not having the power of self-determination....[22]

Lawrence was content to live, thereafter, in relative obscurity in the lower ranks of the armed services; where others would provide his meals, make decisions for him, and in short, absolve him of having to take responsibility for his own life, while at the same time providing him with the company for which he yearned.

Did Lawrence ever come to realize that it was the after-effects of rape which were the cause of his symptoms? Yes, undoubtedly, but perhaps only to a limited extent.

Supposing for a moment that Lawrence, for reasons best known to himself, had invented the story of the rape – in the same way that he had invented the story of the 'Old Man'. Then there is another condition which would account for many of the symptoms described above, namely Post-traumatic Stress Disorder (PSD), brought on by the scenes of carnage that he had witnessed first-hand, during the months he had served with the Arab forces.

> The essential feature of Post-traumatic Stress Disorder is the development of characteristic symptoms following exposure to an extreme traumatic stressor involving direct personal experience of an event that involves actual or threatened death or serious injury…. The characteristic symptoms resulting from the exposure to the extreme trauma include persistent re-experiencing of the traumatic event, persistent avoidance of stimuli associated with the trauma and numbing of general responsiveness and persistent symptoms of increased arousal [i.e. to anger or strong emotions]. The disturbance must cause clinically significant distress or impairment in social, occupational, or other important areas of functioning.

Furthermore, individuals with PSD 'may describe painful guilt feelings about surviving when others did not survive [e.g. Dahoum] or about the things they had to do to survive'. The duration of symptoms varied, but many had:

> persisting symptoms for longer that 12 months after the trauma. The severity, duration, and proximity of an individual's exposure to the traumatic event are the most important factors affecting the likelihood of developing this disorder.[23]

However, Arnold Lawrence, hardly a person likely to be easily hoodwinked, told Professor Mack, with whom he was personally acquainted, that 'he never questioned the factual nature of his brother's account of the Deraa experience'.[24]

Chapter 37

Lawrence's Sexual Orientation

Lawrence's sexuality has been the subject of endless speculation. In late March 1924, Forster wrote insightfully to Sassoon to say:

> Have just had four very enjoyable days with T. E. L. I can't understand his attitude towards the body, his own and other people's. He thinks the body dirty, and so disapproves of all voluntary physical contact with the bodies of others. I should like to know whether he held that view before he was tortured at Deraa.[1]

The answer to this question was given by Lawrence himself, in his letter to Forster of December 1927 where he stated that :

> The Turks, as you probably know did it to me, by force: and since then I have gone about whimpering to myself, "Unclean, unclean".[2]

However, although Lawrence had felt defiled at the hands of the Turks, he subsequently made it clear that the notion of his participating in a sexual relationship had *always* been anathema to him. In December 1927 he told Forster that 'the impulse strong enough to make me touch another creature has not yet been born in me'.[3] To Robert Graves in November 1928, Lawrence wrote, 'Fucking defeats me wholly. I haven't ever: and don't much want to. So I don't feel I miss much: and it must leave a dirty feeling, too.'[4] 'The period of enjoyment, in sex, seems to me a very doubtful one. For myself, I haven't tried it, and hope not to', he told F. L. Lucas in March 1929.[5] And to Ernest Thurtle in April 1929 he wrote:

> There is no difference that I can feel between a woman and a man. They look different, granted: but if you work with them there doesn't seem any difference at all. I can't understand all the fuss about sex.[6]

In 1933 he declared, 'I do not love anybody and have not, I think, ever – or hardly ever. Nor have [I] ever, I think, except momentarily-and-with-the-eye lusted'.[7] The sensation of touch, said Lawrence in *The Mint*, is the one 'I fear and shun… most, of my senses.' He had never indulged in 'venery (sexual intercourse)… never having been tempted so to peril my mortal soul'.[8]

Lawrence 'remained', according to his brother Arnold, 'a virgin until his death'.[9] In other words, he had a strong aversion to sexual intercourse, whether it was of a heterosexual or a homosexual nature, and this aversion clearly predated the rape. Lawrence may, therefore, be said to exhibit Sexual Aversion Disorder, the essential feature of which:

> is the aversion to and active avoidance of genital sexual contact with a sexual partner. The disturbance may cause marked distress or interpersonal difficulty. The individual reports anxiety, fear, or disgust when confronted by a sexual opportunity with a partner.

Such an aversion may be 'lifelong' – i.e. dating from the onset of sexual functioning – or 'acquired'. Possible causes of Sexual Aversion Disorder are child sexual abuse; obsessive self-consciousness with regard to body image; and rape.[10] (However, as already demonstrated, Lawrence's aversion to sex predated the [alleged] rape at Deraa.) But often, there is no discernible cause. In fact, according to Robert Graves, Lawrence had a 'morbid horror of being touched',[11] and those who knew him well were aware that he was averse even to shaking hands.[12]

Can Lawrence also be described as a masochist? Masochism[13] is defined as 'the enjoyment of an activity that appears to be painful or tedious'.[14] 'Pain of the slightest had been my obsession and secret terror, from a boy,'[15] Lawrence had declared in *Seven Pillars*. Therefore, he cannot be described as a masochist in this sense of the word. However, masochism may alternatively be defined as 'the tendency to derive sexual gratification from one's own pain or humiliation'.[16]

In the summer of 1986, Professor Mack met Bruce, now aged 64, in person, and was told by the latter that 'Lawrence seemed to get no pleasure from the beatings.' (Bruce also told Mack that, in his opinion, Lawrence was not homosexual.)[17] However, as already mentioned, Mack stated that Lawrence's service companion had told him that Lawrence 'required that the beatings be severe enough to produce a seminal emission' – an indication that *there was* a masochistic dimension to the proceedings.

At what age did Lawrence's masochistic tendencies first appear? It is known that in respect of the masochist, sexual fantasies are likely to have been present in childhood.[18] Lawrence described how, when he was a child, his mother beat him frequently on his bare buttocks. He subsequently described her as 'very exciting';[19] which suggests that the beatings may have resulted in him becoming sexually aroused.

The following is a quotation from Confessions (written in 1770 and published in 1782) by Swiss-born philosopher Jean-Jacques Rousseau (1712-1788). In this passage, Rousseau has been sent for private tuition to the home of a Protestant minister named Lambercier and his sister Miss Lambercier, who was aged about thirty:

> As Miss Lambercier felt a mother's affection, she sometimes exerted a mother's authority, even to inflicting on us when we deserved it,

> the punishment of infants. She had often threatened it, and this threat of a treatment entirely new, appeared to me extremely dreadful; but I found the reality much less terrible than the idea, and what is still more unaccountable, this punishment increased my affection for the person who had inflicted it. All this affection, aided by my natural mildness, was scarcely sufficient to prevent my seeking, by fresh offences, a return of the same chastizement; for a degree of sensuality had mingled with the smart and shame, which left more desire than fear of a repetition.
>
> This event, which, though desirable, I had not endeavoured to accelerate, arrived without my fault; I should say, without my seeking; and I profited by it with a safe conscience; but this second, was also the last time, for Miss Lambercier, who doubtless had some reason to imagine this chastizement did not produce the desired effect, declared it was too fatiguing, and that she renounced it for the future. Till now we had slept in her chamber, and during the winter, even in her bed; but two days after[wards] another room was prepared for us, and from that moment I had the honour (which I could very well have dispensed with) of being treated by her as a great boy.
>
> Who would believe this childish discipline, received at eight years old, from the hands of a woman of thirty, should influence my propensities, my desires, my passions, for the rest of my life…?[20]

In 1886, Austrian psychiatrist Richard von Krafft-Ebing (1840-1902), published his book *Psychopathia Sensualis: eine Klinisch-Forensische Studie*, in which he described the case of a 29-year-old artist:

> Sex desire arose in him at the age of seven whilst being caned on the buttocks. The wish to be flogged was ever present in his mind since he was ten years old. He claimed that flagellation was the only adequate sexual act during which he could experience really pleasurable ejaculation.[21]

According to Magnus Hirschfeld, in regard to the spanking of children, 'it is an undeniable fact that this method of chastizement… *very frequently* leads to a deflection of the child's sexual impulse'.[22] Hirschfeld cited other researchers, to demonstrate how spankings defeat their punishment purposes by providing the young victims with erotic stimulation. But he stressed that a child's inherent makeup ultimately determines whether she [or he] will become a sadist or a masochist.[23]

In 'An Essay on Flecker', which he composed in 1925,[24] Lawrence described how he met James Elroy Flecker, diplomat and poet, in August 1911 in Beirut, where the latter was British Acting Vice-Consul. The two men became friends, and Lawrence described himself and Flecker 'Carelessly flung beneath a tree talking of women, slippers, and of whippings.' From this, it may be deduced that Flecker, 'an unapologetic masochist'[25] had in mind the notion of being whipped by a woman with a slipper, and that the notion of being whipped was also of more than passing interest to Lawrence; hence him taking the trouble to record that such a conversation had taken place.

Lawrence regarded his rape by the Turks as both abhorrent and terrifying. Said he, 'Many men would take the death-sentence without a whimper to escape the life-sentence which fate carries in her other hand.'[26] Nevertheless, when he described how 'a delicious warmth, probably sexual, was swelling through me', this implies an intense degree of sexual arousal, to say the least. It is, therefore, likely that the whipping he received on that occasion served to reawaken masochistic tendencies which were already present within him. Subsequently, he sought out John Bruce and others to beat him, presumably with the object of recreating the selfsame pleasurable, orgasmic feelings. 'Sexual Masochism is usually chronic, and the person tends to repeat the same masochistic act.'[27]

The means by which flagellation stimulates sexual arousal, orgasm, and seminal emission, doubtless has a physiological basis, in which hormones, notably testosterone, probably play a significant part.

Were feelings of guilt at the heart of Lawrence's masochistic nature – about his having been complicit in the British betrayal of Arabia, for example, or for having submitted to his rape by the Turks? Probably not, for his masochism appears to have predated these events. However, it suited him to construct a 'script'[28] (blueprint or guideline) for himself, whereby such perceived misdemeanours, and the resultant requirement for punishment, were woven by him into the narrative of his masochistic fantasies – viz. John Bruce and the 'Old Man'. (A feature of masochists – and also of sadists – is that they typically construct such a 'script', in order to define the role that they are to play in their particular brand of sado-masochistic activity.)

Chapter 38

The Crash

In November 1934, Lawrence was transferred to the RAF marine-craft station at Bridlington on the Yorkshire coast, where he continued his work on rescue boats. The following month he wrote to John Buchan:

> If you meet Mr Baldwin [the former Prime Minister] in the near future, will you please tell him that the return to the Air Force secured me by him (on your initiation) has given me the only really contented years of my life?

Lawrence spoke of doing his best:

> to raise the pride and respect of the ranks, and to make them pleased with their duties.... I owe the two of you more than my twelve years work (and another twelve on top of it, were I young enough) in the sheer satisfaction it has been.[1]

And to Basil Liddell Hart (Lawrence's biographer), in anticipation of his forthcoming retirement

> For myself, I am going to taste the flavour of true leisure. For forty-six years I have worked and been worked. Remaineth twenty-three years (of expectancy). May they be like Flecker's 'a great Sunday that goes on and on'. [The correct quotation, from his friend the poet James Elroy Flecker, should read, a 'calm Sunday that goes on and on'].[2]

In January 1935, a month before his retirement from the RAF, Lawrence was to be found at Bridlington, having left his Brough motorcycle at Clouds Hill; intending to take it back to the factory, as he felt he would be unable to afford to run it on his income of 25 shillings per week. He had always been passionate about motorcycles and his latest acquisition was a 1932 SS (Super Sports) 100 model.

For this particular model, George Brough selected state-of-the-art components from several different manufacturers:

Engine – JAP 998 cc air-cooled, twin cam, overhead valve, by J. A. Prestwick of Tottenham, London

Carburettor – by AMAL

Gearbox – 3-speed, manual, by Sturmey Archer

Frame – cantilever-sprung suspension by Bentley and Draper

Brakes and wheels – by Enfield

Dynamo, headlamps and horn – by Lucas

Front forks – by Castle Brampton, from a design by Harley Davidson

Oil pump – by Pilgrim

Chain – by Coventry

Saddle – by Lycett Aero

Pillion passenger's cushion – inflatable, for greater comfort

Large alpine carrier and bags with valises

Small toolbox, fitted low down on nearside

The following additional, non-standard features were included at Lawrence's own request:

Rear wheel – 19-inch diameter, instead of a 21-inch, to suit his relatively small frame.

Petrol tank in stainless steel – by Skegness Sheet Metal Works

Speedometer – 120 mph by Jaeger

Muffler – fitted to the carburettor to prevent icing up[3]

The registration number of Lawrence's Brough, the seventh motorcycle that he had owned, was GW 2275. His collective name for them was 'Boanerges' – 'Sons of Thunder' - this being the name given by Jesus Christ to his two disciples James and John – not that Lawrence had any particular religious convictions. Eric Kennington summed up Lawrence's attitude to 'God' thus.

> 'What was his God? What I think I heard in the flow of eloquence, was a record of process without aim or end, creation followed by dissolution, rebirth, and then decay, to wonder at and to love. But not a hint of a God, and certainly not of the Christian God.'[4]

In regard to his motorcycles, each individual model he nicknamed 'George', the current one being 'George VII'. In a letter sent to George Brough after taking delivery, he described it as 'the silkiest thing I have ever ridden.'[5]

The Brough SS100, however, had a serious flaw, in that the Royal Enfield front brakes were not designed to be fitted to the Castle front forks. The outcome was that, unlike the rear brakes which were thoroughly efficient, this was not the case with the front ones.

On 26 February 1935, Lawrence, who had decided that he could no longer afford to run his Brough motorcycle, chose to bicycle all the way from Bridlington to his cottage at Clouds Hill, where he proposed to retire and pursue a career in writing. On the way south he broke his journey at Fordingbridge, Hampshire, to call on the painter Augustus John, who had completed a portrait of him in oils, and also two pencil sketches of him in charcoal. However, when he returned home and found that the press were besieging his cottage, Lawrence postponed taking up residence there until the middle of March. On 3 May he wrote to Brough, prophetically as it transpired, to tell him

> My last two long rides have been at 49 and 51 mph respectively. It looks as though I might yet break my neck on a B. S. ['Brough Superior'].[6]

On Monday 13 May, Lawrence motorcycled from Clouds Hill, southwards along Tank Park Road to Bovington Post Office, to send off a parcel of books and a telegram. The intended recipient was the author Henry Williamson, about whose book *Tarka the Otter*, Lawrence had written a long and detailed critique which Williamson had much appreciated. Williamson, who was a strong advocate of friendship between England and Germany, and who could see that 'the world was dropping down into war', hoped to enlist Lawrence's support for a meeting with the German Führer.

The telegram, which read 'Lunch Tuesday wet fine cottage 1 mile North Bovington Camp', showed Lawrence to be in a positive frame of mind. He then refilled with petrol at the Red Garage across the road. But, on his return journey, collided with one of two boy cyclists; was thrown over the handlebars, and sustained a fractured skull from which he died six days later (on Sunday 19 May), without regaining consciousness. The cyclists were Albert Hargraves or 'Bert', a butcher's errand boy whose father, also Albert, was a soldier at Bovington Camp, and Frank Fletcher his friend, who had gone along with him to keep him company.

'Private John B. Connolly, a Tank Corps soldier was having an injured knee dressed in Bovington Camp hospital that morning. Shortly after the crash a man ran in and told the medical orderly or officer that there had been a serious accident up the road involving several persons.... [7] Connolly was then detailed to drive up to the accident scene in a soft-sided, Morris Commercial 4 x 4 ambulance with Captain Geoffrey Anderton.'

'Anderson checked Lawrence over and they put him and Hargreaves onto stretchers and into the back of the vehicle, Connolly holding the door open. Captain Geoffrey Anderton, the officer he [Conolly] named as in charge, was a regular soldier of about 40 years of age.'[8]

Charles Philip Allen, a captain in the Royal Army Medical Corps, received 'Mr T. E. Shaw [i.e. Lawrence] and Hargraves' to the Bovington Military Hospital at the stated time of 'about 11.45', which was 25 minutes after the time that the accident occurred. It was the Captain who, together with neurosurgeon Hugh W. B. Cairns, performed the post-mortem examination on Lawrence. Meanwhile, Lawrence's brother Arnold, a reader in archaeology at Cambridge, who was in Spain at the time, flew back to the hospital to be briefed by the doctors. Captain Allen described

> A large, fissured fracture, nine inches long, extending from the left side of the head backwards to the middle line across the back of the skull and forward to the right side. Also small fracture of left orbital plate. The brain was severely lacerated, especially on the left side.

There was no mention of any other injuries, such as cuts, abrasions, or bruises to other parts of the body.

The cause of death was given as 'fracture of the skull and laceration of the brain, heart failure and congestion of the lungs'. Captain Allen ventured the opinion that 'had Mr Shaw lived he would have been unable to speak and would [have] lost his memory and would have been paralysed'. The coroner for East Dorset, Ralph Neville Jones, declared that

> the evidence would lead one to think that Mr Shaw must have been travelling at a very fast speed and possibly lost control of his motorcycle. I do not think there can be any other conclusion on the evidence.

The coroner's jury duly brought in a verdict of accidental death.[9]

As for errand boy Hargraves, although he was found to be 'not seriously injured', he was, nevertheless, detained in hospital for several days.[10]

Inquest into the death of T.E. Shaw, 21 May 1935. Statements from witnesses

Corporal Catchpole

One of the witnesses to the crash was Corporal Ernest Catchpole of The Royal Army Ordnance Corps, stationed at Tidworth, Wiltshire, who stated at the inquest that

> At about 11.20 a.m. on May 13th 1935 I was at Clouds Hill Camping Ground [a tented military summer camp, otherwise known and designated on Ordnance Survey maps of the time as 'Wool Camp'] and about 100 yards from the road. I heard the noise of a motorcycle

> coming from the direction of Bovington Camp. I saw the motorcycle which was going between 50 and 60 miles an hour. Just before the motorcycle got level with the camp it passed a black car – it was a private car and the motorcycle passed that safely. I then saw the motorcyclist swerve across the road to avoid two pedal cyclists going in the same direction. The motorcyclist swerved immediately after he passed the car which was going in the opposite direction. I then heard a crash and saw the motorcycle twisting and turning over and over along the road.
>
> I immediately went to the road and called for help. I found the motorcyclist lying on the right side of the road – his face was covered in blood and I sent to the [Bovington] Camp for a stretcher. An Army lorry came along and I asked them to take the injured persons to Hospital, which they did. One of the pedal cyclists was lying some distance down the road on the left side. I did not actually see the accident happen.

Said Catchpole, on cross-examination

> the car was not going very fast. I actually saw the deceased pass the car. I should say the collision occurred about 15 to 20 feet after the motorcyclist had passed the car. I do not know whether the pedal cyclists were riding one behind the other or abreast. There would have been sufficient room for the motorcyclist to pass between the car and the pedal cyclists if the motorcyclist had not been going at such a speed. I did not see the pedal-cyclists before the crash. The car was on its proper [i.e. left hand] side of the road.

In other words, according to Catchpole,[11] there was only a distance of between two and three times the length of the Brough (which was seven and a half feet long) between the car and the rearmost bicycle when the collision occurred. When the coroner recalled Catchpole to ask him if he might have been mistaken about the presence of the black car, the latter replied, 'No, sir.' He also affirmed that the vehicle was a black, four-seater saloon. 'I could not see how many people were in it. It was going about thirty miles an hour.'[12]

Frank Fletcher

Said 14-year-old Fletcher

> On 13th May 1935 at about 11.20 a.m., I was riding a pedal bicycle from Bovington Camp towards Clouds Hill and Albert Hargraves was with me. I was riding in front and Hargraves was riding at the back. I was riding on the left of the road. When

> opposite Clouds Hill Camp I heard a motorcycle coming from behind. I then heard a crash and Bert's bicycle fell on top of me and knocked me off my bicycle. I got up and saw Mr Lawrence go over the handlebars of the motorcycle and fall about five yards in front. I went to Bert who gave me the butcher's [account] book & I saw three pennies lying on the road. He [Hargraves] then seemed to fall asleep. I saw a lot of men running over from the tents. I was riding close to the left-hand side – between one and two yards. There were no cars on the road then. I did not pass a car from the time I left Bovington Camp and the accident. We did not leave the road at all.
>
> When the crash occurred the other boy was not at my side. I do not know what part of the road the motorcyclist was on at the time of the accident. After Bert's bicycle struck me I looked up and saw the motorcycle about five yards in front in the direction in which I was going and the rider going over the handlebars. We had been riding one behind the other for about 100 yards.[13]

On 15 May 1935, six days prior to the inquest, Fletcher had told Bournemouth's *Daily Echo* that

> The man [Lawrence] who had gone over the handlebars had landed with his feet about 5 yards in front of the motor cycle which was about five yards in front of where I fell.[14]

Albert ('Bert') Hargraves

Said Hargraves, the butcher's errand boy, who like his companion Fletcher was also aged fourteen:

> On 13 May 1935, I was cycling from Bovington Camp to Warwick Cross, Tonnerspuddle [Turner's Puddle] and Frank Fletcher was with me for company. Opposite Clouds Hill Camp I was riding four to five feet behind Fletcher and on the left-hand side of the road. I heard the sound of a motorcycle coming from behind. No motor car passed me about this time nor any traffic of any sort. I do not remember any more until I found myself in Hospital.
>
> We were riding at a normal pace with both hands on the handlebars. We changed position because of the noise of the motorcycle. We had been riding in single file for about eighty yards. When we left Bovington Camp we were riding abreast. I slowed up and got behind Frank. I did not wobble at all.[15]

George Brough

Manufacturer George Brough examined the motorcycle subsequently and found no structural or mechanical failure. However, Private Arthur Russell of the Royal Tank Corps, who had collected both the Brough and Hargraves' bicycle from the crash site and taken them to the Inquest, noticed that the front brake cable had snapped – presumably as a result of Lawrence's final frantic efforts to slow down and avoid the boy cyclists.[16]

Albert Hargraves, 1982

In 1982, Hargraves declared

> Apparently we both [he and Lawrence] went up in the air. I was in Wool Military Hospital for 11 days. I've got deep, brown gravel scars on my arms and back which have been with me ever since.[17]

However, Hargraves' mother Agnes, said that her son was in hospital for 9 days only.[18]

Frank Fletcher, 1985

In early 1985, Fletcher stated as follows, to a reporter from Bournemouth's *Daily Echo*.

> You've got the straight bit of road first of all and then it dipped down a bend a wee bit more than up again. The second dip we were above [i.e. beyond] that – a few yards along, he wouldn't have seen us like.[19]

On 18 May 1985, Fletcher, now a resident of Wandsworth, was again quoted in Bournemouth's *Daily Echo*.

> My mate heard the motorbike coming up behind us. We were riding side by side at the time then I moved in. And then we only went along another twenty yards or so when – wooff – it hit the back of my mate's bike and then that hit mine (though there was no damage to mine) and I went over to one side.
>
> The motorbike itself skidded along the road – I thought it was going to explode – I straightened myself up and looked round. I saw my mate unconscious. Then I looked across the road. I saw Mr Lawrence go over the handlebars and the bike skid across the road. It wasn't a very wide road, more like a track then, and he was sitting up against a tree facing Bovington Camp. So I went across

> to him and saw this blood on his face. The next thing I knew the soldiers came and an ambulance, which must have come from the camp....

Fletcher was adamant that at the time of the crash, 'Bert was definitely behind me - because he was the one that told me to get to the side of the road in front of me [i.e. get to the nearside]'.[20]

Frank Gordon, 1985

On 25 May 1985, Lance Corporal Frank Gordon was interviewed by architect and writer Andrew R. B. Simpson. Gordon was on duty at Bovington Camp and actually saw Lawrence leave the Red Garage on his Brough, for that last, fateful journey. He described Wool Camp's Casualty Clearing Station (where troops who were injured on manoeuvres were taken, and from there transferred to hospital if the need arose). 'The Casualty Clearing Station was just in sight of it [the accident] and they [the soldiers] saw it happen.'[21]

Margaret Montague, 1985

On 5 September 1985 the following letter was published in Bournemouth's *Daily Echo.*

> Sir – as I was clearing away some old *Echos* I saw an article about Lawrence of Arabia and it stated: 'There was no car' [i.e. a reference to the black car which Corporal Catchpole said he saw]. I can assure you there definitely was a car, and it was a black one. It was a Hillman. The registration number was COW 41, and I know who was driving it. The driver and Lawrence waved at each other as they passed.

The letter was signed Margaret Montague.[22]

In November 1985, Margaret was interviewed by Andrew Simpson. She told him that

> when Lionel Montague [her husband, who was manager of an insurance company[23]] arrived in Sandford Garage, north of Wareham, having passed through Wareham, Mr. Douglas Hope, the then owner of the garage, or one of his employees, told Montague that Lawrence had had an accident. Montague replied (in the vein of) he didn't believe it as he had just waved to him on the road near Clouds Hill.

The car, said Margaret, was a black Hillman 10.[24]

Joan Hughes, 1986

Interviewed on 10 February 1986, Joan Hughes told author and former RAF officer Roland A. Hammersley that,

> on the day of the accident… she was riding/pushing her bicycle from her home at Clouds Hill, towards Bovington village. (Her sisters were bathing in one of the tanks of the three water towers on the west side of the road opposite Clouds Hill summer camp [i.e. Wool Camp].) She had to get off the bicycle several times as one tyre had punctured. She tried to maintain the air pressure by using the hand pump without success. As she walked she came in sight of the three water towers on her right (west) with the bell tents, etc, on her left (east) at Wool Camp. Just before the water towers were a number of soldiers in the road. There was a lorry and an Army ambulance which looked like the one that usually stood by the medical tent at Wool Camp. A motorcycle was lying in the road and two cycles, one of which was a delivery cycle from Bovington village.
>
> She stood by the crowd of soldiers as the ambulance door was closed. It was driven off followed by the lorry. A soldier by her said, 'The poor sod, if it hadn't been for those water butts he would have missed that tree.'

The inference here is that the presence of the water tower/butt nearest to the road prevented Lawrence from swerving onto the nearside verge to avoid the boys. The soldier added that he saw it happen. At no time from leaving her home at Clouds Hill did any vehicle, car or otherwise, pass her in either direction.[25]

Frank Fletcher, 1991

Interviewed by authors Marriott and Argent on 13 August 1991, Fletcher stated as follows.

> So as you go along a bit more there's two more hills, one down and one up, and then you get to your flat road again. Well we must have been on the second hill about 150 yards along the road at the time. When… we heard this motorbike come along. Like Bertie said we had better get inside [i.e. to the side of] the road. So we must have as he [Lawrence] was coming up the road. He must have seen us too late. That's the way I looked at it. And then, uh, he didn't have time to pull out.
>
> Well the next thing I knew, I heard Bertie's bike go down with a wallop as it [Lawrence's Brough] hit the back wheel.
>
> He [Lawrence] went over his handlebars before the bike went along there… Over like that, and then the bike skidded straight along

> the road. That's how I found him sitting up against the tree with blood coming down his face. [As regards the Brough] the wheels was out towards the road and the saddle was in towards the [nearside] kerb. He went in front a bit and I saw him go over, then the bike came to him and skidded like that there (demonstrates side skidding). The bike fell over afterwards.
>
> As he came out of the dip and onto a straight road he couldn't possibly have seen us because the hill's that steeper you know. He must have come up and saw us too late along there. And then Bertie's bike caught mine there.... We're on the side of the road. His [Bert's] front wheel just touched my back wheel, that was all.

Subsequently, said Fletcher:

> These guys came and they sent for an ambulance. Which presumably is the field ambulance which the camp [Wool Camp] used to have. The two casualties went [were stretchered] into the ambulance and then they went to Bovington Camp.[26]

Lyall Chapman, 1992

Patrick Knowles (known as Pat), born in 1906, was the son of Arthur and Henrietta who lived in the cottage across the road from Lawrence at Clouds Hill. After Arthur's death in 1933, Joyce Dorey, a farmer's daughter from nearby Wool, came to look after his widow and her son Patrick. Henrietta died in 1934, and a year later Pat and Joyce were married.

In their book *A Handful with Quietness*, published in 1992, Pat and Joyce Knowles stated as follows.

> The first person on the scene was a man well known to Joyce and me; a man who prefers to remain anonymous. He was employed as a lorry driver at the time and with his 'mate' was working about a hundred yards east of the road where the accident took place. They were loading gear and equipment which had been used for a weekend territorial camp.
>
> From where he was standing he saw the motorcycle come down the road into the camp, although at the time he was not aware that it was Shaw. Much later he heard the motorcycle again but didn't turn away from his task.
>
> This indicates that Lawrence had visited Wool Camp en route to Bovington.
>
> Then suddenly, when he heard the engine race, the wheels spinning uselessly, he turned and saw the motorcycle on its side and a figure lying nearby. With his companion he ran across quickly, and

> although the injured man's face was covered with blood, he realized from the Brough and the overalls that the man was wearing that it must be Lawrence. In surprise, he said 'Why it's Lawrence,' whereupon Shaw opened his eyes and smiled and raised his hand with one finger extended – a gesture which has caused much speculation. Shaw then went into a coma without saying a word, a coma from which he never regained consciousness.[27]

(Joyce Knowles later revealed that the anonymous person was her cousin, Lyall Chapman.)[28]

The state of the road

Tank Park Road, said Fletcher:

> was a rough sort of road where the tanks used to go along. They used to go on the moors…, then they used to cross this road on to the other moor. It was tar, a kind of tarry, but was rough with the tracks of the tanks.[29]

John B. Conolly, a soldier from Bovington who was ordered to attend the crash site in case extra help was required, said

> the piece of road near where the crash accident took place had been resurfaced by the usual method at the time, namely, sprayed with tar and stones simply thrown on the top.[30]

Chapter 39

A Reappraisal of the Crash

Is it possible to identify the exact location of Lawrence's motorcycle crash?

Evidence from maps and aerial photographs

According to the Ordnance Survey (OS) map of 1901 (revised in 1927[1]), what later became known as Tank Park Road ran north-north-westwards from Bovington Camp towards Clouds Hill in virtually a straight line, with only slight curvature apparent immediately south of Clouds Hill. The map also reveals that, in its course towards Clouds Hill, the road ascended a gentle gradient of about 2 degrees.

'Wool Camp' (or Clouds Hill Camp) is designated on the map as an area of approximately 150 acres, situated to the east and south east of Clouds Hill. Tented summer camps were held here, annually, for soldiers from Bovington who were often joined by personnel (such as Corporal Catchpole) from other units, or from the Territorial Army. They spent time under canvas in order to accustom themselves to life 'in the field'.

A sketch that Lawrence made of Clouds Hill in April 1934 shows Tank Park Road running southward from the cottage, before curving left and then, in a more pronounced manner, to the right (i.e. westwards), before straightening up and pointing towards Bovington.[2]

An aerial photograph taken by the RAF in 1947 shows Clouds Hill, together with both the War Department fence and the new tank track/fireguard as indicated by Lawrence in his sketch. There is no evidence of a long, straightish road, as shown on the 1901 OS map, but, instead, a more tortuous track to the immediate east of the newly constructed King George V Road. The place where this track joins the latter road is not discernible.[3]

On the modern-day Google aerial map of 2008, King George V Road (constructed during the Second World War) is easily identifiable, running in almost a straight line from Bovington to Clouds Hill.[4] Also, this map clearly shows a track running alongside King George V road on its west side. However, this track curves considerably more than the road depicted on the 1901 OS map, and is more similar in profile to the RAF map. Finally, this modern-day Google map is far more accurate and informative than maps of yesteryear. It may therefore be deduced that the 1901 OS map, as far as what later became known as Tank Park Road is concerned, is a gross simplification of the situation on the ground.[5]

Finally, Andrew R. B. Simpson has cleverly superimposed the position of King George V Road onto the 1901 OS map, thereby demonstrating that this (new) road was constructed almost entirely to the east of Tank Park Road; apart from where the two roads coincide in the immediate vicinity of Clouds Hill.[6]

Photographic evidence

In about 1930 a photograph was taken of the first section of Tank Park Road, leading from Bovington towards Clouds Hill.[7] The road is fairly straight, with a slight uphill gradient.

Four further photographs, taken shortly after the crash, are of particular interest.

i) From the crash site, looking southwards towards Bovington one mile or so distant (dated 14 May 1935, the day after the crash, by an unknown photographer).[8] The road, which curves gently to the right (i.e. westwards), ascends to a brow, as seen in the middle distance, then dips, before ascending to another brow. The right-hand (west) side is bordered by an ample covering of trees and bushes; some of the foliage of which overhangs it. On the left-hand (east) side of the road is low scrubland, the occasional tree, and a line of telegraph poles. Incidentally, the water towers/tanks are not visible on this photograph perhaps because a), they were hidden by foliage or b), because they were situated immediately to the right of the photographer, and therefore out of view. However, local historian Rodney Legg, stated that 'in 1935 there was a concrete water-tank on the west side of the road just south of the crash point….'[9]

ii) From the crash site, looking northwards towards Clouds Hill (dated 14 May 1935, by an unknown photographer, and featuring two motor vehicles).[10] The road begins to bend: first to the left and then more sharply to the right, before straightening up, once again. In the foreground on the left (west) side is a bank, with low scrubland and, in the middle distance, a tree, perched on a hillock and set back from the road. The fence marking the boundary of the Moreton Plantation is clearly visible. On the right (east) side, the telegraph poles continue northwards. It is possible that the position of the car shown facing north is where the Brough impacted with the bicycle, and the position of the more distant car with its adjacent tree (one of three) is where Lawrence's body came to rest.

iii) From the crash site, taken from the nearside verge of the road looking northwards towards Clouds Hill (mid-May 1935, by Joyce E. Knowles, featuring a single motor vehicle).[11] Here, the roadside telegraph poles are more clearly visible than in the previous photograph, and the curvature of the road is more clearly demonstrated.

iv) From the crash site, taken from the centre of the road looking northwards (mid-May 1935).[12]

Photographs taken from the crash site therefore indicate that Tank Park Road (on which the crash occurred) with its curves, had an entirely different configuration to King George V Road, which was constructed several years later. However, if Tank Park Road was simply straightened out to create King George V Road, then one would expect to see remnants of the former road criss-crossing the latter. This is not the case, because the two roads were different entities for virtually their entire lengths.

From the photographs it is clear that the carriageway was more than wide enough for two vehicles to pass abreast of one other. So, had Lawrence been travelling at a speed more appropriate for the road conditions, he would have had no difficulty in overtaking the two cyclists.

Evidence on the ground: the topography of Tank Park Road in 2013

At a point approximately 660 yards from Clouds Hill, and 1,200 yards from the centre of Bovington, a trackway is identifiable, running northwards alongside King George V Road and, to begin with, 30-50 yards or so from it on its west side. This track ascends a gentle slope of about five degrees, curving to the right at first and then more sharply to the left, as it skirts a hillock situated on its west side. At a distance of about 470 yards from Clouds Hill, a brow is reached. Forty-five yards or so beyond this brow is a dip, thirteen feet in depth. Twenty-four yards beyond the dip is a second, smaller brow, which is 4 feet higher than the lowest part of the dip. Then, still curving towards the left, the road begins a long, gentle descent of about three degrees, before subsequently curving right towards Clouds Hill, though this final section of the track is much overgrown and therefore difficult to identify.

Finally, an inch or so beneath the surface of the trackway is a blackish layer about an inch thick, below which is a layer of flintstones – presumably the foundation of the road.

The present-day view of this trackway, from just beyond the second brow, looking both northwards and southwards, bears an uncanny resemblance to the photographs taken from the crash site in May 1935. It is therefore virtually certain, beyond reasonable doubt, that this was the very place where the crash occurred – i.e. about twenty yards north of the second brow.[13]

Diagrams made of the crash site

In their biography of Lawrence, Marriott and Argent included 'Frank Fletcher's sketch map of the crash site on 13 May 1935'.[14] This is not an original sketch but appears to have been created by the authors from information given to them by Fletcher himself.

In the sketch, the accident spot is marked by an asterisk. Hargraves' body is lying on the nearside, near to the crown of the road with his bicycle beside him, also on the nearside. However, the asterisk is just *beyond* Hargraves and his bicycle, implying that both were knocked *backwards* - which is impossible. Fletcher is depicted lying on the nearside, beyond his bicycle which is also on the nearside, and level with the asterisk. As for Lawrence, he is shown on the offside (i.e. east side), lying half on the road and half on the verge, with his head almost touching a tree. On the nearside of the road is the Brough.

In 1986, as a result of his interview with Joan Hughes, Roland Hammersley made a sketch of how Joan remembered the site 50 years after the crash. The sketch depicts, on the east side of the road, Wool Camp with its tents, including the medical marquee, and the line of telegraph poles. On the west side are depicted the three water towers and a tree with damage to its bark. On the road itself, the positions of the ambulance and lorry are shown, and also a skid mark, then a gap, and beyond this, a score mark. Missing from the sketch is the position of Lawrence's body and the Brough, subsequent to the crash, and the position of the two boy cyclists and their bicycles.[15]

Both of the above sketches are misleading, in that they give the impression that the road was straight at this point, which is not the case, as has been demonstrated.

The weather

Did weather conditions play a part, as far as the crash was concerned? The evidence is, probably not.

> The morning was part sunshine part cloud, with half the sky covered with cloud at 10 a.m. (clock time) observation. The wind at 9:00 GMT was recorded as NNE Force 4, a moderate breeze. The maximum temperature was 53 degrees Fahrenheit (12 degrees Celsius), minimum temperature was 37 degrees F (3 degrees C). There was 7.9 hours of sunshine during the whole day, and no rain.[16]

The weather was therefore clement, and as he rode northwards towards Clouds Hill, Lawrence would have had both sun and breeze at his back.

Damage to the Brough

In view of the score marks on the road, it is not surprising that there was damage to the Brough. This included: offside footrest broken off; left handlebar bent; right gear-change lever pushed against petrol tank causing indentations; rear brake pedal grazed and bent; kick-start pedal bent upwards; silencer, rear toolboxes, saddle, and mudguards grazed; headlamp rim dislodged. Also, some of this damage may have been caused by the motorcycle's collision with Hargraves' bicycle. The Brough was discovered to be in second gear, and although it was capable of speeds of 85 mph in this gear,[17] it is possible that the machine was in third (top) gear at the time of the crash, and that the gear-change lever was jogged out of position on impact with the road.

Damage to Hargraves' bicycle

Three photographs taken after the crash[18] revealed severe damage to the rear wheel, the frame of which was dented into the shape of a U, the apex of which reached as far as the axle; bending of the rear forks, in particular, the offside one forwards and outwards; crumpling of the rear mudguard, and distortion of the spokes. The chain was still on its front and rear sprocket wheels, but slack, indicating that the rear section of the frame had been displaced forward by the impact, relative to the front.

In order to produce this pattern of damage, the Brough must have struck the bicycle from behind and from the nearside, but at a slight angle rather than straight on. This would have had the effect, not only of producing the observed dent in the wheel, but also of bending the forks, particularly the offside one. In other words, when viewed from above, the wheel would have been forced in an anticlockwise direction, putting extreme stress on the offside of the rear axle, a stress which was transmitted to the offside fork. This anticlockwise distortion of the axle (when viewed from above) on which the rear sprocket wheel was mounted also accounts for the slackness of the chain.

This said, the conclusion must be that immediately prior to impact, either a), Hargraves was steering towards the nearside – a natural reaction with a high-powered motorcycle approaching rapidly from behind – or b), that Lawrence was steering slightly towards the offside, in an attempt to avoid him. From the direction of the Brough skid mark in the Hammersley/Hughes sketch, which is slightly towards the offside direction, the latter appears to have been the case.

A statement by Pat Knowles

During those last years, he [Lawrence] was involved in several more-or-less serious accidents. It got so that each time he came I used to scan the bike for damage.... One afternoon we heard him arrive – the Brough's engine is unmistakable – but instead of going to the garage as he usually did he stopped outside our house and hooted, so I went out to see what was wrong.

He was clearly in pain and he was sitting uncomfortably. I also noticed a buckled footrest. I helped him to put the bike away and he was able to walk unsupported to the cottage, where with difficulty we got his top clothes off to inspect the damage. He was extensively bruised....[19]

A reconstruction of the crash

On the morning of Monday 13 May 1935, T. E. Lawrence is travelling on his motorcycle from Bovington northwards along Tank Park Road, on the return journey towards his cottage at Clouds Hill, a mile or so distant. To begin with, the road is long and fairly straight, as it ascends a gentle gradient, through open heathland. As Lawrence approaches the brow of the hill, the road begins to curve gently to the right. By the time he has reached this point, he has travelled approximately 1,400 yards, or just under one mile, at an average speed of 50-60 mph – based on what is known of his driving habits. Meanwhile, two boys, Frank Fletcher and Bert Hargraves, are cycling abreast and ahead of him in the same direction. On hearing the roar of the motorcycle, they move into single file, with Hargraves at the rear and Fletcher at the front. Even though the Brough was a powerful machine, the bend in the road, together with the presence of the hillock, may have meant that the boys did not hear the motorcycle until the final few seconds before impact.

Beyond the brow, the road commences a long, left turn, and descends into a dip before ascending to a second brow. To his right, is the military, tented summer camp. To negotiate this section at speed, Lawrence is obliged to lean inwards to counteract the centrifugal force which is acting on him and his machine. Being familiar with the road, a daredevil such as Lawrence would have found the prospect of zooming up the hill, down the dip, and up again exhilarating.

Having ascended the second brow, Lawrence and the Brough are almost airborne, when suddenly, immediately in front of him, is Hargraves. By now, according to Fletcher, he and Hargraves had ascended the second brow and were on the downslope. Lawrence slams on his brakes and the tyres leave their mark on the road, but a collision is inevitable, and the Brough's front wheel (which is 21 inches in diameter) impacts with the rear wheel of the errand boy's bicycle (26 inches in diameter). Given the relative speeds at which they were travelling, and their respective weights (excluding their riders), the momentum of the Brough was forty times that of the bicycle.[20] This, together with the disparity in size between the impacting wheels, and the fact that the two vehicles were travelling in the same direction so that the impact on the bicycle came from behind, causes the bicycle to be projected into the air in a forward direction, giving credence to Fletcher's assertion that Hargraves' bicycle fell on top of him.

Finally, because the Brough's front wheel struck Hargraves' rear wheel at a slight angle, and not in a straight line, the force of the impact would have caused Hargraves' bicycle to spin in an anticlockwise direction. Both boy cyclists are, needless to say, thrown off, but mercifully survived to tell the tale.

On impact, owing to the sudden deceleration of the Brough, Lawrence is immediately thrown off. His body flies upwards, and the centrifugal force which acts on it by virtue of the bend, causes it to be projected to the right (offside). As his only injuries were allegedly to his head, it is assumed that this impacted heavily, either with the road or, as seems more likely, with a roadside tree. (A crash helmet might have saved Lawrence's life, but it was not his custom to wear one. More will be said about this shortly.)

Meanwhile, the Brough's momentum carries it forwards until it finally topples over onto its side and subsequently comes to rest, leaving score marks on the road. As already mentioned, the front brakes of the Brough were substantially less efficient than the rear brakes. Had Lawrence been riding any other type of motorcycle, he might have been able to stop in time to avoid the fateful collision.

Time Frame

25 seconds from the moment of the crash

Lawrence is 350 yards south of the first brow.
The boys have reached the first brow and are beginning to descend into the dip.

The right-hand bend therefore obscures Lawrence's view of the boys (see Google map).

15 seconds from the moment of the crash

Lawrence is 250 yards south of the first brow.
The boys are in the bottom of the dip.

The left-hand bend, and the hillock and vegetation on the nearside of the road obscures Lawrence's view of the boys.

8 seconds from the moment of the crash

Lawrence is 120 yards south of the first brow.

The boys have reached the summit of the second brow and are about to begin their descent.

The boys are obscured from Lawrence's view, for the same reasons.

Was there a black car?

Whether or not a black car was travelling along the road from Clouds Hill towards Bovington at the time in question remains a mystery. Corporal Catchpole was adamant that he saw it, and Margaret Montague of Wimborne, in her letter to Bournemouth's *Daily Echo*, suggests a likely candidate – i.e. the black 'Hillman 10', which her husband had been driving that very morning on that very road, when he is alleged to have seen and exchanged greetings with Lawrence. However, neither boy cyclist saw any such car, and furthermore, according to the evidence of Inspector Drake of the Dorset Constabulary (given at the inquest)

> in consequence of receiving a statement about a motor-car being on the road at the time, inquiries had been made in the district of a number of people. No other person than Cpl Catchpole could say they saw a car, and the Lieutenant in charge of the Camp could not say he saw a car.[21]

Supposing Catchpole was right, and such a car did pass Lawrence immediately prior to the crash. Then Lawrence would have been obliged to move away from the crown of the road and towards his nearside, which would help to explain why he was unable to avoid a collision with Hargraves' bicycle. Why, therefore, did the owner of the black car not come forward subsequently? Probably because a), he had not been involved in any collision and b), he may not even have been aware, at the time, that a road traffic accident had occurred. But it is difficult to believe that in view of the publicity, the news did not reach him subsequently.

Is it possible that, for some unknown reason, the driver of the black car was visiting the camp, and having done so, emerged from it and turned left onto Tank Park Road just after the boy cyclists had passed it – hence their failure to observe it? But if so, how was it possible for the car to achieve a speed of 30 mph in the space of only twenty feet? The likelihood is, therefore, that there was no black car on the road at the time in question.

In the photograph 'From the crash site looking north', dated 14 May 1935 and featuring the two cars, three trees are visible at the point where the road begins to bend back towards Clouds Hill. Comparing this with the present-day topography of the site, it is possible to identify the likely location for the tree nearest to the road. And sure enough, just where one would expect it – i.e. about 44 yards northwards from the crest of the second brow – is the decomposing trunk of a large tree – presumably a pine about 80 cm or more in diameter. Perhaps this is indeed the tree in question.

Chapter 40

The Funeral: Aftermath

Lawrence's funeral was held on the afternoon of 21 May 1935 at the Church of St Nicholas, Moreton, and he was buried in Moreton cemetery. Mourners – of whom there were many – included Florence Hardy; Mr and Mrs Winston Churchill; Augustus John; Lady Astor; Mr and Mrs Siegfried Sassoon; Aircraftman Bradbury of the RAF; and Private Russell of the Royal Tank Corps. Also present were representatives of the King of Iraq and of the Emir Abdullah of Transylvania. The Shaws were absent on a cruise to South Africa; as was E. M. Forster, who later visited Clouds Hill with the Sassoons. Neither Trenchard nor Allenby, nor Robert Graves attended. Feisal had died in Switzerland two years earlier, and there was no representative of Lawrence's late father's family, the Chapmans. His brother Arnold was present, but not his mother Sarah, nor his brother Bob, who were on their way home from China and did not yet know of his death.

As for John Bruce, he stated that after Lawrence's motorcycle crash,

> I stayed in Bournemouth while waiting for his death to come. I stayed on at my hotel until the day of the funeral which was Tuesday, the twenty-first. I went to the cottage, waited outside till the cortege came, and followed him to his last resting place.[1]

The same day, a message from King George V to Arnold Lawrence was published in *The Times* newspaper.

> The King has heard with sincere regret of the death of your brother, and deeply sympathises with you and your family at this sad loss. Your brother's name will live in history, and the King gratefully recognizes his distinguished services to his country and feels that it is tragic that the end should have come in this manner to a life still so full of promise.

The inscription on Lawrence's tombstone, erected by his mother on her return to England, reads as follows:

TO THE DEAR MEMORY OF
T. E. LAWRENCE
FELLOW OF ALL SOVLS COLLEGE
OXFORD
BORN 16 AVGVST 1888
DIED 19 MAY 1935
THE HOVR IS COMING & NOW IS
WHEN THE DEAD SHALL HEAR
THE VOICE OF THE
SON OF GOD
AND THEY THAT HEAR
SHALL LIVE

In May 1985, a mysterious note appeared on the grave, which read: 'I have kept the secret still.' What could this secret have been?

For many years, on the anniversary of Lawrence's birthday (16 August), a bouquet of white roses was delivered to the Rector of Moreton Church, to be placed on Lawrence's grave. (The company Interflora, which delivered the flowers, confirmed that the order for them came from the USA.) The order also stipulated that on the same date, a single white rose was to be delivered to Lawrence's cottage, Clouds Hill.[2] Furthermore, each year, the bouquet contained one less rose. For example, in 1984 there were 36 roses and by 1993, the number had fallen to 27. In that year, 1993, an intriguing message accompanied the roses. It read, 'In memory of T.E.S. 2020 AD'. What was the significance of this date, which is the year after 2019, when the final rose was due to be delivered? Incidentally, another flower, a geranium, is also placed on Lawrence's grave annually, also from an anonymous donor.

In August 1990 there appeared in the *Sunday Express* newspaper an article by Gerard Kemp, describing an interview that he had conducted with a Doctor Susan Lawrence, a thirty-five-year-old cancer specialist from California, who confessed to having changed her name to 'Lawrence' and 'to being related in a way. I can't say any more or my confidentiality will be violated.' She also confessed to having seen David Lean's film *Lawrence of Arabia* at least 12 times. 'I fly over [to England] three times a year, each time for a week, for the anniversaries of Lawrence's death on May 19 and his birth on August 16,' she said. Her third visit always coincided with a date in November, which was the anniversary of the rape of Lawrence by Turkish soldiers in Deraa, a place which she herself had visited. Furthermore, she described Lawrence as having 'showed all the classic signs of being a rape victim.' However, Doctor Lawrence denied she was the sender of the annual box of white roses.

The late rector of Wareham, the Reverend Lionel Howe, in a letter donated to St Martin's-on-the-Walls Church in that town by his widow, referred to:

> old Mrs Lawrence [i.e. Lawrence's mother Sarah], whom we later [after the funeral] met and stood in awe of. I think E. K.

> [Eric Kennington the sculptor and friend of Lawrence who was responsible for the lettering on his tombstone and for the effigy of him in Wareham church] considers her rather 'a holy terror'.

The Reverend Howe said that if anyone put flowers on 'Ned's' grave at Moreton and she found them, she would fling them over the hedge:

> but I remember her once coming to the rectory at Wareham and admiring a plant in bloom and in full flower and I said would she like some and she said she would, and we learned later that she had put them on T. E's grave herself. E. K. told us that in her eyes Ned was almost God-like and she had wanted his memorial to take the form of a huge pyramid somewhere in the desert!

The roses: a possible explanation

How can the mystery of 'the roses' and 'the secret' (mentioned in the note placed on Lawrence's grave) be explained?

If the number 100 is subtracted from the year 2020 (the date when the last rose is due to be placed on the grave), this leads back 100 years to the year 1920. Is it possible that in 1920 – when Lawrence was aged 32 and at All Souls College, Oxford – he had a liaison with a female, which resulted in the birth of a child? This was despite his previous declaration that, 'knowledge of her [his mother Sarah] will prevent my ever making any woman a mother.'

If it was the case that Lawrence did father a child, then was this 'love child' sent, in order to avoid a scandal, for adoption (possibly to the USA, as was often the case in those days). And was it then decided that the secret of this love child (of whose existence Lawrence may not even have been aware) should be kept for 100 years after the child's birth – i.e. until the year 2020, the date mentioned in the 1993 message which accompanied the roses? And yet this flies in the face of Lawrence's protestations that he himself had never indulged in 'venery'. So, what is the explanation? Perhaps, in 2020, all will be revealed!

Meanwhile, on 18 August 1994, the following article by Thomas J. Brady, entitled 'Lawrence of Arabia and the Lure of the Roses', was published online.

> A mysterious bouquet of white roses, laid on British war hero Lawrence of Arabia's grave each year since he died in 1935, failed to appear Tuesday. The flowers had been ordered annually on his birthday, Aug. 16, by a U.S. admirer whose identity has never been revealed and who may have died or fallen ill. 'It appears the order has not been placed in America, which is very sad,' said Rosemary Wise, one of two local florists who used to place the bouquet on the grave at the English village of Moreton.[3]

In August 2013, Richard Harvey appeared on the BBC's programme, the Antiques Roadshow. His father John Hooper Harvey (born 1911) had once been articled to Sir Herbert Baker of 14 Barton Street, Westminster – the very place where Lawrence had written *Seven Pillars*.[4] On the table, Richard placed two items. The first was a swagger stick, the silver cap of which bore the insignia of the RAF. The second item was a whip, made of braided leather, well-worn, and about 3 feet in length. What relevance has this to Lawrence?

Lawrence's letters reveal that, following his return from India, he was resident at Barton Street for virtually the whole of February 1929, and this is when he and the 17-year-old John Hooper Harvey met. John, said his son Richard,

> did little jobs around the office, and probably took Lawrence his tea and the mail. They got chatting and discovered that they had common interests – in politics, travel, and architecture. Also, John was charged with the task of shooing away the press – who were anxious to interview Lawrence – from time to time.

When the time came for Lawrence to leave Barton Street, he presented John not only with the swagger stick and the whip, but also with a single stirrup iron complete with leather spur strap, and a spur with spiked rotating wheel, 'as a leaving present'.[5] These items were, presumably, part of the camel riding tack, as used by Lawrence in the Arabian desert. Also, a length of braided, maroon-coloured cord, about four feet in length to which two large tassels were attached, What was the function of the cord? It may have been an agal, worn doubled and used to keep the ghutra - traditional Arab headdress made of cotton - in place on the wearer's head. However, Leonard Woolley described how, at Carchemish, Lawrence 'always wore… pink, white shorts held up by a gaudy Arab belt with swinging tassels. It was a belt worn only by bachelors, and Lawrence had his tassels made bigger than anyone else's'.[6]

In *The Mint*, Lawrence had referred to his swagger stick thus: 'God's curse on that stick. A slip of lack cane with a silver knob'. This was an item which he and the other men were taught to carry as they underwent their basic training at RAF Uxbridge.

Was it a coincidence that two of the objects in Lawrence's possession were associated with discipline/punishment? (Traditionally, swagger sticks were used to direct military drill, or to administer punishment. Latterly, they were carried by those with the rank of regimental sergeant major, or above, as a symbol of authority.)

And so, yet more mystery attaches to the life and death of T. E. Lawrence.

Chapter 41

The Effigy

In the spring of 1920, Lawrence purchased two portraits of soldiers by Eric Henri Kennington RA (born in 1888) – sculptor and official war artist – at a London exhibition. Kennington subsequently visited Lawrence at Oxford and was told by him that he required illustrations for his book. Whereupon, to this end, Kennington visited the Middle East to make portraits at first hand, of some of Lawrence's former comrades-in-arms. He later became Art Editor of the splendid subscriber's edition of *Seven Pillars of Wisdom*, which was published in 1926.

Lawrence, who was to remain friends with Kennington, wrote to him in in August 1934 in his familiar, self-deprecatory way, saying:

> Both the *Seven Pillars* and *The Mint* stink of personality … One of the sorest things in life is to come to realize that one is just not good enough. Better perhaps than some, than many, almost – but I do not care for relatives, for matching myself against my kind. There is an ideal standard somewhere and only that matters: and I cannot find it. Hence this aimlessness.

Anticipating his forthcoming retirement, he said:

> Out I go. Clouds Hill awaits me, as home and I have nearly £2 a week of an income. So I mean to digest all the leisure I can enjoy: and if I find that doing nothing is not worse than this present futile being busy about what doesn't matter – why then, I shall go on doing nothing. But if doing nothing is not good – why then, I shall cast loose again and see where I bring up.[1]

On 6 May 1935, from Clouds Hill, he expressed to Kennington sentiments that, perhaps, many would share after having been retired for a period of two months.

> You wonder what I am doing? Well, so do I, in truth. Days seem to dawn, suns to shine, evenings to follow, and then I sleep. What I have done, what I am doing, what I am going to do, puzzle me and bewilder me. Have you ever been a leaf and fallen from your tree in autumn and been really puzzled about it? That's the feeling.[2]

Only 15 days later Kennington was to be one of the pall-bearers at Lawrence's funeral.

The story of the Lawrence effigy was told by its creator Eric Kennington, on 3 July 1945 at Wareham. The monument was commissioned by the Lawrence family through T. E. Lawrence's younger brother Arnold, and designed, originally, as a national memorial for London's St Paul's Cathedral. But as there was already a bust of Lawrence – also by Kennington, in the cathedral's crypt – it was considered to be superfluous.

Kennington explained how he had been commissioned to sculpt the effigy.

> The shock of T. E.'s death, yes, when we were getting over it I had a letter from Buxton [Robin Buxton, Lawrence's banker and former comrade-in-arms in Arabia] asking me to attend a committee meeting which would plan a national memorial. We met. I attended. As far as I can remember the other members were Buxton in the chair, Lady Astor who soon elbowed him out of it and was in it herself, Newcombe [Captain S. F. Newcombe of the Royal Engineers and formerly director of the Sinai survey], Storrs [Sir Ronald Storrs, formerly assistant to the British High Commissioner in Cairo], Lionel Curtis [administrator and political theorist who popularized the idea of a commonwealth of self-governing nations], Bernard Shaw, Sir Herbert Baker [architect, who provided Lawrence with the attic room in Barton Street, Westminster where he wrote much of *Seven Pillars*]. They said we should make a national appeal. Then Baker said he had asked T. E. once what his idea was for a monument to himself and his reply, 'the largest mountain in Arabia carved into a likeness of himself.' I lay low till Baker said, 'What about an effigy. We have a distinguished sculptor here.' That was the only meeting I attended but I was told my drawings had been accepted and I was to go ahead and await official confirmation. Next I wrote to A. W. Lawrence who can be spiteful and vindictive. He came and saw the effigy. 'What's this worth to you,' he said. My answer was, 'Two thousand pounds.' He pulled out a chequebook and wrote out a cheque for two thousand pounds. 'Now its mine and I can do what I like with it.'
>
> We went to Salisbury (cathedral) and looked at the site and met the Dean. He was against it. He said he wanted it in the south transept on a high table tomb. A. W. explained to him, elaborately and architecturally, that this was an effigy in the Early English style, and flattish for putting on a low base, not like the fifteenth-century figures, all knobbly and sticking up so you could see them from below. Of course he was right, but the Dean thought the height of the building demanded a tall base with a raised up figure … Then we went and saw the Bishop at the palace. A. W. wasn't giving in, nor

> was the Dean (terrible fellow). So having slain a bishop, murdered a dean, turned down a cathedral, A. W., quite ruthless, said, 'We'll go to Wareham.' We fairly danced and said, 'This is the place – St Martin's, Wareham [a reference to the tenth-century church of St Martin's-on-the-Walls]. Then back to Salisbury to tell the Bishop. He was a bit surprised to see us back so soon. He was delighted and said, 'I've always loved that church and from the first I thought it was the right place for the Lawrence effigy.'[3]

Richard Knowles (formerly of RAF Cattewater, Plymouth) gave an excellent description of the effigy, which is carved from a 3-ton block of Portland stone.

> Lawrence is represented in his Arab robes and headdress from the fabled period of his involvement with the Arab Revolt during the First World War. The right hand rests on the hilt of his dagger whilst the left lies loosely at his side. His feet rest upon a piece of Hittite sculpture representing his pre-war archaeological days at Carchemish, his head lies on a camel saddle and beside it are three unlabelled books which represent those that he always carried with him, including on the Arab Campaign – *Morte d'Arthur*, the *Oxford Book of English Verse*, and a *Greek Anthology*. The chest upon which the effigy lies carries only the simple text 'T. E. Lawrence 1888-1935'. The effigy is in an unashamed English fourteenth-century style with crossed legs, the Arab robes being treated rather as the medieval gown.[4]

Wing Commander Reginald G. Sims (with whom Lawrence had worked at Bridlington and who was an expert amateur photographer) photographed the sculpture at its various stages of development. Said Kennington of the results: 'The photos are welcome. I profit by these. They show me errors.' Undoubtedly it was this help from Sims which enabled Kennington to produce the exquisite likeness of Lawrence which he achieved.[5]

Chapter 42

Wendy Vallance: New Light on Lawrence's Final Days

Wendy Phyllis Vallance was born in Weymouth on 9 February 1944 to Henry Edward, an accountant, married to Florence Ivy (née Mogg). She was the middle sister of three. This was the 5th year of the Second World War. When the town was bombed by the enemy, the family relocated to the village of Godmanstone, 14 miles inland, where she grew up. During the war, Henry served as a major in the Royal Army Pay Corps. Wendy subsequently attended a preparatory school followed by a convent school in Dorchester. 'In fact, my whole life has been spent living in a variety of villages in Dorset, or within a 5-mile radius of the county town of Dorchester', she declared.[1]

From the age of 12, Wendy wanted to be a nurse, and at the age of 17 she embarked on a nursing career, first as a pre-student cadet nurse, at Dorchester County Hospital (DCH) in Princes St, under the matron, Miss Newport. The hospital was founded in 1840, originally as a charity to treat the 'working poor'. It was funded entirely by private subscriptions, notable benefactors being the Dorset poet and novelist Thomas Hardy, and the renowned surgeon Sir Frederick Treves. The hospital was designed by architect Benjamin Ferry.

Wendy was a dedicated student, winning Weymouth and Dorchester Hospitals' Orthopaedic, Gynaecology, and Ophthalmic prizes in 1964 and the Senior Nursing Prize in 1965.

In 1966 Wendy married Colin Victor Vallance and the couple set up home at Crossways, near Moreton where Lawrence was buried. She bore him two sons and a daughter.

One night in 1975 or 1976, Wendy spent a single night working as a staff nurse on night duty at the Private Patients' Annex, Dorchester County Hospital, to which patients with various medical and surgical conditions were admitted. She was alone, and during a quiet period she opened the medicine cupboard, where Casualty Record Ledgers for the DCH were being temporarily stored. 'There were many volumes', she said, 'red or green in colour, about 3 inches thick and 18 inches tall, and each inscribed with dates of the relevant period'. Having an inquiring mind, Wendy was interested to discover details, amongst other matters, about soldiers who had been admitted to the DCH during the course of the First World War.

Suddenly to Wendy's great surprise, halfway down the left-hand side page in the admissions ledger for the year 1935, she came across the entry 'T. E. Shaw'. The date was 13 May. Wendy was aware that 'T. E. Shaw' was the name that Lawrence adopted when he joined the army at Bovington. She was also aware that 13 May 1935 was the exact same date of his motorcycle accident. The entry also stated that the patient had sustained a head injury. Beside the entry were the names of several eminent medical specialists from London, who had arrived on the scene in order to try and save his life. Although Wendy could not remember the names specifically, they would almost certainly have included Hugh W. B. Cairns, neurosurgeon; Sir Farquhar Buzzard, Physician-in Ordinary (a permanent appointment) to King George V and Honorary Colonel in the service of the RAMC; Lord Dawson of Penn, Physician-in Ordinary to King George V and lung specialist and pathologist; Dr Alfred Hope Gosse, heart and lung specialist. The entries, said Wendy, were made in various colours of (presumably fountain pen) ink.

Sadly, the best efforts of the medical experts were to no avail, and according to the records which Wendy was privy to, Lawrence died in Dorchester County Hospital on Sunday 19 May 1935.

Wendy concluded that, having been first taken to Bovington Military Hospital (BMH), Lawrence was almost immediately transferred to the DCH, and when he died 6 days later, his body was returned to the BMH.

If, as Wendy stated, Lawrence was transferred from the BHM to the DCH, this would have made perfect sense. After all the county hospital would have had better facilities and highly qualified staff for coping with such a serious case. Furthermore, not knowing that Lawrence was in the DCH meant that the journalists and the 'paparazzi' (freelance photographers) would have been put completely off the scent!

'I know what I saw' said Wendy, referring the entry 'T. E. Shaw' in the DCH leger, and there is absolutely no doubt that she was telling the truth. Unfortunately, it has not been possible to trace the ledger, possibly because this was a time of great upheaval when DCH's casualty department was being transferred to Weymouth. Nevertheless, Wendy's detailed recollections of events make her account entirely credible.

Furthermore, the two local doctors who attended Lawrence were in no way qualified to deal with such serious injuries as a fractured skull and brain damage. Geoffrey Anderton had the qualifications MRCS (Member of the Royal College of Surgeons), LRCP (Licentiate of the Royal College of Physicians), 1924, and in 1925 he obtained the degrees BM (Bachelor of Medicine) and BS (Bachelor of Surgery) from the University of London. Likewise, Charles Philip Allen gained a Bachelor of Medicine and a Bachelor of Surgery from the University of Liverpool in 1925.[2] In the case of both doctors, these are basic qualifications for entry to the medical profession, but they are not the specialist qualifications as required for a qualified surgeon of physician. This, of course, adds weight to the fact that Bovington Military Hospital did not have doctors with the clinical expertise necessary to treat a casualty such as T. E. Lawrence, and it would not have possessed the necessary medical equipment either.

As already mentioned, journalists who were besieging the gates of Bovington Military Camp would have been unaware Laurence had been transferred to the DCH – after all, ambulances were presumably coming and going all the time. Therefore, access to the military base having been denied to them, and hungry for a dramatic story to transmit back to London, they invented fanciful tales, such as that Lawrence had been murdered, and it was all a plot of the British intelligence services, etcetera: whereas in fact his death was a simple accident.

How could anyone possibly have contrived a murder, which depended on two boys cycling on a blind bend in the road just at the very moment when Lawrence was approaching from behind, causing him to swerve and his body to crash into a pine tree, which just happened to be in his path?

From 1986 Wendy worked as a community Macmillan nurse in Weymouth, caring for patients suffering from cancer in their homes, which she described as a privilege.

Chapter 43

T. E. Shaw – 'Lawrence of Arabia' – Happy Years Spent as Mechanic and Boatman: Lawrence's Contribution to Air-Sea Rescue

Lawrence's time spent at RAF Mount Batten, the seaplane base in Plymouth Harbour, from 1929 to 1933, was to have important repercussions when it came to the important matter of air-sea rescue.

Visitors to the upstairs room of Lawrence's cottage, 'Clouds Hill', may admire two three-branched chromium-plated candelabra which have pride of place on the mantelpiece. These pieces, useful because of the absence of electricity in the house, were a retirement present which he received from two of his colleagues after leaving the RAF in February 1935. They are a reminder of the happy friendships forged during his time with the Motor Boat Development Unit during the last five years of his time in the service.

From 1927 until 1929, Lawrence, as 'T. E. Shaw', had been in India; first, in the depot in Karachi and latterly, at a fort on the North West Frontier. However, when his whereabouts was discovered by journalists, rumours began to circulate that Shaw was involved in espionage in Afghanistan. The RAF responded to these inaccurate reports by bringing him back to Britain on the first available ship!

Shaw was greeted in February 1929, as he came ashore at Plymouth, by Wing-Commander Sydney W. Smith, whom he had met in Cairo some years before. Smith was the commanding officer of a seaplane squadron based in Plymouth Harbour. Whereupon Shaw was assigned to him to be his clerk and secretary.

At this time, the RAF was taking part in the biennial races for the Schneider Trophy, a biennial race for seaplanes and flying boats, and Smith was the officer responsible for the RAF team which represented the UK.

Seaplane: an aircraft with floats or skis instead of wheels, designed to land on and take off from water.[1]

Flying boat: a large seaplane that lands with its fuselage in the water.[2]

During the 1929 races for the Schneider Trophy, Major Colin Cooper, a wealthy supporter of the competition, made his motor yacht available to Smith and Shaw. This was a 'Biscayne Baby' speedboat, manufactured in the USA, which was now provided for them for use as a tender. After the race was over, Cooper gifted this boat to Smith and Shaw, who took it back to RAF Mount Batten. It was a vessel in need of repairs, both to the hull and to the engine and during the winter of 1929-30, Shaw carried out this work and this began his transformation from clerical duties to those of a marine mechanic and boat builder.

Throughout 1930, Shaw carried out routine duties at RAF Mount Batten and that summer he used the Biscayne Baby speedboat to explore the backwaters of Plymouth Harbour and to develop his skills as a boatman. He was often accompanied on these excursions by his commanding officer's wife, Clare Sydney Smith, or by Lady Astor, the Member of Parliament for Plymouth. Both ladies expressed their admiration for Shaw: Clare Sydney Smith wrote her recollections in a book entitled *The Golden Reign* which was published in 1940, and Lady Astor welcomed him into her influential social circle at her stately home, 'Cliveden' in Berkshire.

On 4 February 1931 a Blackburn Iris Mark III (3-engined biplane) flying boat of No. 209 Squadron, RAF crashed into the sea at Batten Bay, Plymouth, Devon. Its pilot was Flight Lieutenant Maurice H. Ely, but prior to landing, Wing Commander Charles Tucker had taken over the controls. The waters were calm, but despite this, the aircraft nosedived into the water at a speed of approximately 70 mph.

First on the scene were Wilfred Little, a harbour pilot and Harry Hole, who were sailing nearby, assisted in the rescue attempt, as did Wing Commander Sydney Smith, the Mount Batten station commander, and Aircraftsman Shaw (T. E. Lawrence), who reached the scene an RAF launch. The survivors were:

Flight Lieutenant Maurice H. Ely (injured)
Flight Lieutenant Charles Ryley (injured)
Corporal William M. Barry (unhurt)

However, nine of the crew perished. They were:

Wing Commander Charles G. Tucker (aged 44)
Flying Officer Frederick K. Wood (aged 23)
Sergeant Edmund Walter H. Wilson (aged 24)
Leading aircraftman William H. Stark (aged 22)
Leading aircraftman Cecil G. Davies (aged 22)
Leading aircraftman Louis C. Oates (aged 25)
Leading aircraftman Harold C. Ongley (aged 25)
Leading aircraftman William S. Rutledge (aged 24)
Leading aircraftman William G. Stevens (aged ?)

At the public inquest, at which Shaw appeared as a witness, the cause of the crash was stated to have been pilot error.[3]

Shaw's rescue attempt was severely hampered by the slowness of the rescue craft available – i.e. seaplane tenders used to carry men, supplies, and equipment to and from seaplanes and flying boats. This incident made plain the need for faster rescue craft to be on hand for such mishaps and Shaw, upon who the crash had had a profound psychological effect, began to press for this work to be given urgent attention. Instead of slow craft which displaced the water through which they travelled, the aim was to produce craft which planed – i.e. skimmed over the surface, and were therefore faster.

To Lady Astor on 2 March 1931 Shaw wrote in respect of the proposed development of fast rescue boats for the RAF:

The best results all coming, though slowly. They have set the reforms afoot, and I think they may be trusted to push them through. I am watching very closely and will move another little lever or two when or if it is necessary.

Tomorrow, I get a change from Mount Batten, for I go to Hythe near Southampton, for ten days instruction in a new fast motor boat being built for the RAF. Not very fast, I'm afraid, but faster than the old crocks.[4]

To Basil H. Liddell Hart on 13 April 1931, Lawrence wrote:

My two-year war with the Air Ministry over the type of motor boats suited to attend seaplanes is bearing results and experimental boats are being offered by contractors.[5]

On 19th April 1931, Lawrence wrote to Dick Knowles to say:

Just now I am wholly M.B.C. [Motor Boat Crew], for the RAF is at last trying to get some marine craft of modern design, a need I have been urging on them … for 18 months.[6]

Meanwhile, another story was unfolding. Hubert Scott-Paine was an engineer who founded the Supermarine Aircraft Company in 1916. He sold it in 1923 and became a director of Imperial Airways. Scott-Paine's particular interest was in the design of power boats, which he raced. In 1927, he purchased a shipyard at Hythe and created the British Power Boat Company.

Scott-Paine began to develop an improved seaplane tender for the RAF and in 1930, he invited Flight-Lieutenant William E. G. Beauforte-Greenwood, senior officer at the Marine Section of the Air Ministry, of the unit, for a preview of the new vessel. Beauforte-Greenwood was favourably impressed and accepted the prototype, the 200-Class High-Speed Launch (200-Class HSL). Specifications for the 200-Class HSL Mark I were as follows:

Built in 1931; length 37ft 6 inches; displacement 4.5 tons; powered by 2 x 100 horsepower Meadows engines; range 140 miles at cruising speed of 24 knots; top speed 29 knots.

Furthermore, RAF Mount Batten was chosen as the site for testing and development.

In the summer of 1931, Smith was promoted to the rank of group-captain and appointed to be the station commander at RAF Manston in Kent. Suggestions were made that Shaw should accompany him, but no transfer could be arranged. Nonetheless, Shaw's abilities with speedboats were recognized by Air Ministry and he found himself under the direction of Beauforte-Greenwood.

Throughout the remaining months of 1931 and into the following year, trials of the new 200-Class HSL took place, both in Plymouth Harbour and at Hythe, near the premises of the British Power Boat Company.

Early in 1932, and seeking publicity for the high-speed launch project, Shaw contacted his friend Geoffrey Dawson, editor of *The Times* newspaper, whose aeronautical correspondent was E. Colston Shepherd. In April, Shepherd and Shaw under the command of a Flying-Officer Rogers, made a voyage in a 200-Class HSL from Calshot Royal Naval Air Station near Southampton, along the English Channel and through the North Sea to Donbristie Royal Naval Air Station on the Firth of Forth in Scotland. Rough seas persisted throughout the trip but an average speed of 18 knots was maintained, night and day, over a distance of 742 miles: the time taken was 35 hours and 10 minutes. No faults were reported on arrival. Shepherd wrote his report of the adventure, and a good measure of public attention was gained.

In March 1932 Beauforte-Greenwood was asked by the Air Ministry to investigate the possibility of fitting out a 200-Class HSL for use as a bombing target. Clearly a fast-moving object would present a more challenging target for RAF bombing crew. On the negative side, however, such a conversion was costly, and highly dangerous for the RAF 200's crew! Nevertheless, in May 1932, two prototypes were ordered, numbered 'RAF 190' and 'RAF 191', speedily constructed, and delivered to RAF Bridlington which was the location of an established bombing range.

To Robert Graves on 24 January 1933 Lawrence wrote:

I'm now a [mechanical] fitter, very keen and tolerably skilled on engines, but in no way abstract. I live all of every day with real people and concern myself only in the concrete. The ancient self-seeking and self-devouring T.E.L of Oxford (and T.E.S. of *The Seven Pillars* and *Mint*) is dead. Not regretted either. My last ten years have been the best of my life. I think I shall look back on my [aged] 35-45 period as golden.[7]

In the early months of 1933, Shaw was offered an early termination of his contract of service with the RAF. But aware as he was that more development work remained to be done on the high-speed launches, he decided to stay on and complete his twelve-year engagement.

In May 1933, Shaw was posted to Suffolk, to RAF Felixstowe's Marine Aircraft Experimental Establishment (MAEE). Here, he helped develop motor torpedo boats.

On 11 May 1934, in a rare interview given to J. M. Pughe of the *News Chronicle*, Shaw revealed his current thinking:

'I like my work on aeroplanes, power boats, machines. It is an ordinary man's job. It gives me pleasure. There is no mystery about me. I am just an ordinary man trying to earn his living in the way that he likes. The mystery is fictitious. I want to be left alone, not hounded from pillar to post, not forced to leave my lodgings because I am supposed to be a notorious character. I want to be left alone.'[8]

In autumn 1934, Shaw relocated to Bridlington, Yorkshire, where he was made responsible for liaison between Beauforte-Greenwood, Scott-Paine, and the Marine Aircraft Experimental Establishment (MAEE) at Felixstowe. In February 1935, Shaw's period of service with the RAF formally ended.

Shaw summed up his contribution to the development of high-speed launches for the RAF in a letter to Air Commodore George L. S. Dawson-Damer, Lord Carlow on 4 January 1935. The new vessels, he said:

> 'had three times the speed of their predecessors, less weight, less cost, more room, more safety, more seaworthiness. As their speed increases, they rise out of the water and run over its face. They cannot roll more pitch having no pendulum nor period, but a subtly modelled planing bottom and sharp edges.

Now I do not claim to have made these boats. They have grown out of joint experience, skill, and imagination of many men. But I can (secretly) feel that they owe to me their opportunity and their acceptance. The pundits met them with a fierce hostility: all the RAF sailors, and all the Navy, said that they would break, sink, wear, be unmanageable. Today we are advising the War Office in refitting the coast defences entirely with boats of our own model, and the Admiralty has specified them for the modernised battleships: while the Germans, Chinese, Spanish, and Portuguese Governments have adopted them.[9]

It is sad to note that, after a busy working life, Shaw had only a few weeks to enjoy the quietness of his Dorset cottage. During those days, his thoughts must have gone back to recall, with satisfaction, the successful results of his last five years in the RAF. He would have been delighted when Beauforte-Greenwood and Flight-Lieutenant Harry Norrington (Beauforte-Greenwood's subordinate in the Marine Craft Section at the Air Ministry) invited him to take lunch with them at RAF Hythe in Hampshire. At that meeting, they presented him with the two candelabra which can still be seen at 'Clouds Hill'. They are inscribed:

A SOUVENIR OF A VERY HAPPY PARTNERSHIP

1930-35

FROM B. G. AND NORRY

Surely, these were the terms of affection with which Lawrence addressed his colleagues Beauforte-Greenwood and Norrington.

Clearly, in his final five years of employment Lawrence had found happiness, contentment, and a sense of purpose once again. Beauforte-Greenwood and Norrington, for their part, would have been delighted with the letter of thanks, dated 5 May 1935, which reached them a few days later. In that letter, Shaw makes it clear that he is already finding his way by candlelight; of the candelabras he wrote: 'They look lovely. By day they sit on a brown oak mantelshelf above a Stainless Steel fender. By night they move to my writing table (as at present) or to my reading chair. They clean easily, stand solidly, and feel good'.[10]

Within two weeks of his writing these lines, Shaw, that remarkable man of so many talents, was no more.

From the 200-class High-Speed Launch, was developed the standard vessel used by the RAF Air-Sea Rescue Service from 1937, namely the 100-Class High-Speed Launch (100-Class HSL). Specifications for 100-Class HSL Type I were as follows:

Built 1936; length 64 feet; beam 14 feet 6 inches; displacement 19 tons; hull mahogany; powered by 3x 500 horsepower Napier Sea Lion engines; range 500 miles; top speed 35 knots. (The Type II, built between 1940 and 1942, had a top speed of 39 knots.)

Shaw was closely involved in this work which involved modifications to the vessel's hull. Various combinations of engine installation were also tested. An additional bonus for Shaw was that he loved speed, whether overland on his Brough Superior, or over water!

During the years of the Second World War alone, in excess of 13,000 lives were saved by the crews of the high-speed rescue launches, the motto of the RAF's Air-Sea Rescue Service being 'The Sea Shall Not Have Them'. The launches were involved at Dunkirk (May-June 1940); Dieppe (August 1942); and during Operation Overlord, the Allied invasion of northern France, (commencing on D-Day, 6 June 1944).

RAF Air-Sea Rescue launches also supported operations in the Middle East, Malta and Italy and also in the Far East, India, Burma, Malaya and Ceylon. They were also used for clandestine operations in Greece, Turkey and occupied Europe. After the war, the RAF's Air-Sea Rescue Service 'was involved in secret submarine location work, surveys and anti-terrorist patrols'. However, by 1986 'the more versatile helicopter had taken over the rescue work'.[11]

It was therefore largely thanks to the work and foresight of T. E. Lawrence ('Shaw') and his colleagues that countless lives have been saved by the RAF's Air-Sea Rescue Service, in particular during the Second World War.

Chapter 44

T. E. Lawrence: Sir Hugh Cairns and Road Safety

T. E. Lawrence's untimely death, following a motorcycle accident on 13 May 1935, was to benefit mankind in a way that perhaps no one could have foreseen, with the exception of one man, namely the visionary Australian neurosurgeon Hugh Cairns. Cairns attempted, unsuccessfully to save Lawrence's life. He also performed the postmortem, in the course of which he made a thorough examination of the victim's skull and brain.

Hugh William Bell Cairns was born on 26 June 1896 at Port Pirie, South Australia, to father William, a carpenter, and mother, Amy Florence (née Bell). He was educated at Adelaide High School.

In 1917, the 3rd year of the First World War, Cairns graduated in medicine at the University of Adelaide. He was commissioned into the Australian Army Medical Corps and saw active service in the Middle East and France.

Having been awarded the annual South Australian Rhodes Scholarship for 1919, Cairns entered Balliol College, Oxford. Here, he became President of the Balliol College Boat Club and rowed for Oxford as a bow in the Boat Race of 1920.

In December 1921 Cairns became a Fellow of the Royal College of Surgeons (FRCS). Having held resident posts at Oxford's Radcliffe Infirmary and at the London Hospital, Cairns travelled to Boston, Massachusetts on a Rockefeller Travelling Fellowship. Here he was mentored by US neurosurgeon, pathologist, and pioneer of brain surgery Harvey Cushing (1869-1939), whereupon he decided on a career in neurosurgery.

On his return to the UK, Cairns was appointed surgeon to the Hospital for Paralysis and Epilepsy, Maida Vale (1931-34) and to the National Hospital for Nervous Diseases, Queen Square (1934-37).[1]

In 1937, Cairns set about creating a school of neurosurgery at Oxford's Radcliffe Infirmary and in that year he was appointed Oxford's first Nuffield Professor of Surgery. This was thanks to the munificence of motorcar manufacturer Lord Nuffield.

In the late 1930s, as war loomed ever nearer, Cairns and Consultant Neurologist to the Royal Air Force, Charles Symonds, trained the staff of the Mobile Neurosurgical Units, the first of which, 'No 1 Mobile Neurosurgical Unit' accompanied the British Expeditionary Force to France.

At the start of the Second World War in 1939, Cairns was appointed adviser on head injuries to the Ministry of Health and Consulting Neurosurgeon to the British Army. Whereupon he researched head injuries sustained by military motorcycle dispatch riders. The outcome was that on 4 October 1941 his paper, entitled 'Head Injuries in Motor-Cyclists: The Importance of the Crash Helmet', was published in the *British Medical Journal* (BMJ). In his paper, Cairns reported that during the first twenty-one months of the Second World War, 'the number of motor-cyclists and pillion passengers killed on the road [i.e. on British roads] was 2,279'. 'In a number of cases', said Cairns, 'the fatal outcome might have been avoided if adequate protection for the head had been worn'.

Although very few motorcyclists wore crash helmets in those times, Cairns did encounter 'seven cases or motorcyclists injured while wearing a crash helmet' and 'in all of them the effects of the head injury had been unusually mild'. Although this sample could not be 'regarded as representative' he said, nevertheless, the findings were 'encouraging'. Whereas the crash helmets used by these 7 motorcyclists 'did not invariably prevent fracture of the skull', Cairns continued, it was 'probable that it did prevent the fracture from spreading as far as it otherwise would have done'. Most importantly, 'the brain damage in all cases was remarkably slight, as judged by the absence of neurological signs and by the promptness and completeness of the recovery of intellectual functions'.[2]

In November 1941 and doubtless as a result of Cairns's meticulous research, all Army motorcyclists were required to wear crash helmets whilst on duty.

During the Second World War St Hugh's College, Oxford became the British Army's Military Hospital for Head Injuries. 'To meet the requirements' of the war, Cairns 'gave a large part his time to devising and putting into effect plans for the optimal treatment of head injuries under battle conditions'.[3]

On 15 May 1943, Cairns co-authored with physicist A. H. S. Holbourn a second paper on the subject entitled 'Head Injuries in Motor-Cyclists: With Special Reference to Crash Helmets'. 'We now have records of 106 accidents in which we have been able to examine the crash helmet and, usually, the patient', said the authors. Furthermore, this 'enables us to compare the relative values of different types of helmet'. Two main types of helmet were currently in use. 'In one the outer shell' was 'composed mainly of hard vulcanized rubber; in the other, of compressed wood pulp'. The authors concluded that the 'pulp helmet' was 'superior to the vulcanized rubber helmet'. Here, it should be mentioned that although motorcycle helmets had been invented in 1914, by Eric Gardner, a medical officer at the Brooklands Race Track near Weybridge in Surrey, the helmets were generally used only for racing.

The authors studied 46 fatalities 'in one Army Command'. Of these, 'approximately 20%' died 'on the road'. Of those admitted to hospital, those not wearing a crash helmet had double the incidence of fractured skull and a 50% greater incidence of amnesia (memory loss) when compared with those with helmets.[4]

In 1946, Cairns was awarded a well-deserved knighthood. On 7 September of that year, he published a third paper on the subject, entitled simply 'Crash Helmets'.

'After the crash helmet was made compulsory in the Army', he said, 'there was a considerable sustained fall in the total death rate of motorcyclists in Britain'. In conclusion, 'there can be little doubt that adoption of a crash helmet as standard wear by all civilian motorcyclists would result in a considerable saving of life, working time, and the time of hospitals'.

Cairns now explained how the crash helmet protected the skull and brain of the wearer in cases of impact: 'the crash helmet modifies both the local and the remote effects. Locally the shell of the helmet spreads the blow over a wide area and protects the scalp and skull from the pointed pieces of road metal or whatever object is struck. In some cases it prevents fracture of the skull; in others, where a fracture is produced, it prevents the fracture from becoming depressed. The shell lessens bending of the skull, and therefore the local bruising of the brain'.[5]

Cairns died of cancer in 1952. Sadly, it was not until 1973, more than three decades after his initial 1941 report, the wearing motorcycle helmets became compulsory in the UK.

Of the connection between Lawrence's fatal accident, Cairns, and the campaign to make the wearing of helmets by motorcyclists compulsory, there is no doubt. Cairn's former Oxford colleague Gustav J. Fraenkel, who subsequently became Dean of the School of Medicine at Flinders University, South Australia in 1991, stated that he had 'always believed that Cairns's lifelong passionate interest in the prevention of injuries to motorcyclists - not only head injuries – stemmed from the death of T. E. Lawrence'. This was despite the fact that on 20 March 1946, at a meeting of the Royal Society of Medicine, Cairns had declared that his 'interest in crash helmets arises solely from the fact that during the war, I spent a considerable part of my time treating injured motorcyclists'.

Oxford pathologist Alastair Robb-Smith, in a letter to *The Times* newspaper of 21 May 1987, stated that Cairns, in reference to the death of Lawrence, 'never forgot that … he was powerless in this case' - i.e. powerless to save Lawrence's life. 'The outbreak of war resulted in a very high death rate amongst Army dispatch riders', Robb-Smith continued, 'so Cairns instituted an inquiry in which he and I determined the precise site and nature of the brain injuries. This enabled Cairns to introduce a scientifically designed helmet …. It is not suggested that none of these things would have happened had Cairns not been invited to go to Bovington camp in May 1935, but it focussed his mind on the problem and for 'Hugo', problems were there to be solved'.[6]

Epilogue

In 1936, Lawrence's brother Arnold donated Clouds Hill to the National Trust. Joyce Knowles became its caretaker and curator, a role which she fulfilled for more than 50 years. Lawrence's mother, Sarah, outlived her husband Thomas by forty years, and died in 1959 at the age of 98. Lawrence's eldest brother Bob, died in 1971. His youngest brother Arnold, who was the only one of the five to marry, became Professor of Classical Archaeology at Cambridge, and lived, for some years, in Ghana, where he established a museum. He died on Easter Sunday 1991, aged 90 years.

Of the fact that the character of T. E. Lawrence was a complex one, there is no doubt: masochism and Sexual Aversion Disorder being part of his make-up. However, it was the mental trauma that he suffered, following his rape by the Turks, which brought him low and almost destroyed him.

In Lawrence's day rape was a taboo subject. However, one would like to think that had he lived in the modern world, this once strong, purposeful, honourable, and heroic man would have received the advice and support which he so desperately needed, when in his latter years he became dejected, confused, and rudderless. And yet, despite all, his spirit somehow endured and in his secluded Dorsetshire cottage, with his beloved music, and in the company of his colleagues from the army camp at nearby Bovington, together with literary and artistic friends, he finally found peace.

How will Lawrence be judged by future generations? Field Marshal Viscount Allenby, Commander-in-Chief, Egypt and Palestine, 1917-19, and High Commissioner for Egypt, 1919-25, said of him:

> His cooperation was marked by the utmost loyalty, and I never had anything but praise for his work, which, indeed, was invaluable throughout the campaign.[1]

Said Field Marshal Earl Wavell, who served in Egypt (1917-1920)

> On the theoretical side, he had read more and thought more on military history and the military art than probably any great

> commander: physically he had courage and endurance beyond the ordinary: morally, he had the gift of inspiration and leadership, he had vision, determination in plenty, and an absence of the personal ambition that has marred the character of many great soldiers; he knew the common man; and, best of all, he had no hampering shackles of long professional training and prejudice.[2]

Sir Winston Churchill said of Lawrence:

> Alike in his great period of adventure and command or in those later years of self-suppression and self-imposed eclipse, he always reigned over those with whom he came in contact. They felt themselves in the presence of an extra-ordinary being. They felt that his latent reserves of force and will-power were beyond measurement. If he roused himself to action, who should say what crisis he could not surmount or quell? If things were going very badly, how glad one would be to see him come round the corner. Part of the secret of his stimulating ascendancy lay, of course, in his disdain for most of the prizes, the pleasures and comforts of life.

And he concluded:

> King George the Fifth wrote to Lawrence's brother, 'His name will live in history.' That is true. It will live in English letters, it will live in the traditions of the Royal Air Force, it will live in the annals of war and the legends of Arabia.[3]

And so, the abiding image remains of sunshine, streaming in through the stained-glass window of St Martin's-on-the-Walls Church, Wareham, onto the effigy of a man who, once so tortured and tormented, is at last, serene and at peace.

Lawrence's legacy

As an undergraduate at Oxford, Lawrence had a keen interest in military strategy, and he studied the military theories of German, French, Prussian, Carthaginian, Byzantine, and US military theorists. However, the one to whom he was most attracted was German military commander Maurice de Saxe (1696-1750) who 'provided Lawrence' with 'the theoretical foundation for his own theory of guerrilla war'.

In *Seven Pillars of Wisdom*, Lawrence described the algebraic, biological, and psychological elements of warfare. *Seven Pillars of Wisdom*, pp.192-5. The algebraic element was concerned with the topography of the landscape where the battle was being fought; the biological element was concerned with capitalising upon the 'genius of our tribesmen' in conducting guerilla warfare; the psychological element was concerned with the struggle for the hearts and minds of those whom a leader led into battle.

Said US history professor George W. Gawrychl:

'Much to his credit, Lawrence demonstrated the importance of military theory in warfare. Officers today should study his career and writings for the ways in which they challenge the profession of arms. First, officers should set aside time for serious reflection on their profession, and military theory is an important tool in this endeavour. Reading the military classics is essential for intellectual development in peacetime. Second, coalitions, whether in war or peace support operations, will remain a feature of the United States' military deployments in the future. Lawrence offered some necessary principles and guidelines that are indispensable for officers who are assigned to work with an allied army. Third, officers should study Lawrence's theory of guerrilla warfare and the way he arrived at it. Studying Lawrence will help prepare American officers for the unexpected challenges of the profession of arms in the future.' This, of course, applies to army officers worldwide if they wish to be successful.[4]

The enthusiasm and expertise which Lawrence applies in respect of the development of fast RAF rescue boats resulted in countless lives being saved, both before, during, and after the Second World War.

Finally, a sad consequence of Lawrence's fatal crash highlighted the need for crash helmets to be worn by motorcyclists, and again, this has resulted in the saving of countless lives.

Appendix 1

Rape and the United Nations

In June 2008, 92 years after T. E. Lawrence's rape at the hands of Turkish forces at Deraa, the 15 members of the United Nations Security Council voted unanimously to classify rape as a weapon of war. Rape, it said, was no longer merely a by-product of war, it was,

> A tactic of war [designed] to humiliate, dominate, instil fear in, disperse and/or forcibly relocate civilian members of a community or ethnic group.

UN Secretary General Ban Ki-moon declared that the problem had, 'reached unspeakable and pandemic proportions in some societies attempting to recover from conflict,' the former Yugoslavia, Sudan's region of Dafur, the Democratic Republic of Congo, Rwanda, and Liberia being places where deliberate sexual violence had occurred on a massive scale.

Appendix 2

Brough Superior SS-100 GW2275, 1932, List of Owners

T. E Shaw (T. E. Lawrence) of Clouds Hill, Moreton, Dorset, who registered the machine on 27 February 1932

Following Lawrence's crash, his brother A. W. Lawrence, returned the machine to the Brough factory in Nottingham. Once the repairs had been carried out it was then sold to motorcycle dealers King & Harper Limited, Bridge Street, Cambridge.

3 September 1935, sold to ophthalmic surgeon Robert Munro, 7 Malbrook Road, Putney, London SW15. After a year of ownership, Munro returned the machine to King & Harper

3 October 1936, registered to South African army officer Johannes Leon Pretorius of The Deanery, Rochester, Kent

14 August 1937, registered to army officer Ronald Merriman Barry, also of the The Deanery, Rochester, Kent

1 January 1947, registered to artist Alexander Ramsey Rae of Enabert New Road, Hythe, Southampton

17 April 1948, sold to engineer John Richard Reed of 31 South East Crescent, Sholing, Southampton

2 January 196l, sold to engineer Leslie Perrin of 55 Lone Valley, Portsmouth, Hampshire

18 February 1977, sold to present owner, Jonathan M. Weekly (who kindly supplied the above information)

Appendix 3

Bovington Camp

'On 16 February 1899, the War Office agreed to pay Mrs Louisa Mary Fetherstonhaugh Frampton of Moreton the sum of £4,300 for just over 1,000 acres of heathland' situated in various parishes in Dorsetshire, including Bovington, 'to be used as a Rifle Range or for any other Military use or purpose'. According to the Ordnance Survey map of 1901, Bovington then consisted only of heathland, woods, and two small homesteads, with Bovington Farm to the south.

The size of the camp was enlarged, both prior to and during the First World War, which commenced in August 1914. The following year, wooden huts were built to house the troops, and also a hospital block. On nearby Gallows Hill an elaborate system of trenches was dug, to enable soldiers to practise trench warfare.

A Royal Warrant, dated 18 October 1923, stated as follows:

> Whereas we have noted with great satisfaction the splendid work that has been performed by our Tank Corps during the Great War, our will and pleasure is that the Corps shall enjoy the distinction of 'Royal' and shall henceforth be known as our 'Royal Tank Corps'.

On Tuesday 4 April 1939, Mr Leslie Hore-Belisha, the Secretary of State for War, announced in the House of Commons that the newly mechanised regiments of cavalry were to combine with the RTC [Royal Tank Corps] battalions to create a single corps, to be known as the Royal Armoured Corps [RAC].

The RAC duly saw service during the Second World War (1 September 1939 - 2 September 1945), both on the mainland of Europe and in North Africa.

In 1947 at Bovington, the Tank Museum of the Royal Armoured Corps and Royal Tank Regiment was first opened to the public.[1]

1. From *Bovington Tanks*, by George and Anne Forty.

Appendix 4

Clouds Hill: Occupancy over the Years

1808: According to an estate diary, this was the year in which Clouds Hill was built. From about this year until the early 1820s, the cottage was occupied by William Hallett, his wife, and two of his children.

1820s: Jonathan Chilcott, a brother-in-law of Williams Hallett's son, occupied the cottage with his family for the next 30 years. He and all the farmworkers who succeeded him were woodmen.

1850s and 1860s: Several families occupied Clouds Hill during this period, the family of Edward Pride and his wife Elizabeth being the last. The Pride family occupied the cottage for almost 40 years until 1906. Their eldest son, William lived in the cottage until 1912.

1914-1918: during the First World War the cottage was evacuated.

1923: By the summer of 1923, Sergeant Arthur Knowles had made temporary repairs to the cottage, including the roof, with the idea of making it his family home. However, T.E. Lawrence persuaded Knowles to sublet the cottage to him from September 1923, for the sum of 10 shillings per month. Source: 'History of Clouds Hill', The National Trust, online.

Notes

Chapter 1: His Mother, Sarah

1. Mack, John E., interview with Arnold Lawrence, 21 July 1968, in Mack, John E., *A Prince of Our Disorder: The Life of T. E. Lawrence*, p. 33.
2. Brown, Malcolm (editor), *The Letters of T. E. Lawrence*, to Charlotte Shaw, 14 April 1927.
3. Ibid, to his Mother, 13 August 1905.
4. Ibid, April 1907.
5. Ibid, 26 August 1907.
6. Ibid, 28 August 1908.
7. Lawrence, A.W. (editor), *T. E. Lawrence by His Friends, p. 23.*
8. Ibid, p. 47.
9. Soanes, Catherine and Angus Stevenson (editors), *Oxford Dictionary of English.*
10. Liddell Hart, Basil, *T.E. Lawrence to his Biographer*, p. 50.
11. Brown, Malcolm, op. cit., to his Mother, circa 1915 (undated).

Chapter 2: His Father, Thomas

1. Wilson, Jeremy, *Lawrence of Arabia*, p. 409.
2. Brown, Malcolm (editor), *The Letters of T. E. Lawrence*, to his Mother, 14 August 1906.
3. Ibid, 2 August 1908.
4. Lawrence, M.R. (editor), *The Home Letters of T. E. Lawrence and his Brothers*, p. 103.
5. Wilson, Jeremy, op. cit., p. 409.

Chapter 3: Dr Hogarth and Syria

1. Mack, John E., *A Prince of Our Disorder: The Life of T. E. Lawrence*, p. 69.
2. Brown, Malcolm (editor), *The Letters of T. E. Lawrence*, to his Mother, 11 April 1911.
3. Lawrence, A.W. (editor), *T. E. Lawrence by His Friends*, p. 78.

Chapter 4: Dahoum

1. Brown, Malcolm (editor), *The Letters of T. E. Lawrence*, to his Mother, 24 June 1911.
2. Lawrence, T. E., *Seven Pillars of Wisdom*, p. 40.
3. Ibid, p. 40.
4. Ibid, p. 41.
5. Brown, Malcolm, op. cit., *The Letters of T. E. Lawrence*, to C.F. Bell, 12 August 1913.

Chapter 5: Lord Kitchener

1. Lord Kitchener died in June 1916, when the cruiser HMS *Hampshire*, which was carrying him on an urgent visit to Russia, was mined and sank off the Orkney Islands.
2. Brown, Malcolm (editor), *The Letters of T. E. Lawrence*, to his Mother, 4 January 1914.

Chapter 6: Emir Abdulla

1. Brown, Malcolm and Julia Cave, *A Touch of Genius: The Life of T. E. Lawrence*, Kitchener: telegram to Storrs, p. 55.

Chapter 7: Lawrence's Role

1. Lawrence, A.W. (editor), *T. E. Lawrence by His Friends*, p. 207.

Chapter 8: Gertrude Bell

1. Brown, Malcolm (editor), *The Letters of T. E. Lawrence*, to his Mother, 23 May 1911.
2. Bell, Gertrude, Gertrude Bell Archive, Newcastle University Library, 21 May 1911.
3. Bell, Lady, *The Letters of Gertrude Bell*, Volume 2, 9 April 1916.

Chapter 9: Sherif Hussein

1. Brown, Malcolm (editor), *The Letters of T. E. Lawrence*, Cable to Foreign Office, 4 August 1921, p. 189, in Wilson, Jeremy, *Lawrence of Arabia*, p. 567.
2. Brown, Malcolm and Julia Cave, *A Touch of Genius: The Life of T. E. Lawrence*, p. 55.
3. Lawrence, T. E., *Seven Pillars of Wisdom*, p. 49.

Chapter 10: Emir Feisal

1. Lawrence, T. E., *Seven Pillars of Wisdom*, p. 91.
2. Ibid, p. 91.
3. Ibid, p. 64.
4. Brown, Malcolm and Julia Cave, *A Touch of Genius: The Life of T. E. Lawrence*, p. 60.
5. Lawrence, Arnold W., *Secret Dispatches*, pp. 37-8, from *Arab Bulletin*, 26 November 1916, I, p. 482.
6. Lawrence, T.E., op. cit., p. 93.
7. Ibid, p. 104.
8. Ibid, p. 105.
9. Ibid, p. 106.
10. Ibid, p. 111.
11. Ibid, p. 114.
12. Ibid, p. 119.
13. Ibid, p. 126.
14. Joyce, Pierce, transcript of BBC broadcast of 30 April 1939, in 'Akaba Papers', King's College, London.

Chapter 11: The Arab Campaign

1. Lawrence, T. E., *Seven Pillars of Wisdom*, p. 127.
2. Ibid, p. 137.
3. *Report of a Journey of Lawrence through Arabia on Military Intelligence*, 17-25 January 1917. Harvard University, Houghton Library.
4. Brown, Malcolm and Julia Cave, *A Touch of Genius: The Life of T. E. Lawrence*, pp. 86-8.
5. Ibid, p. 90.

Chapter 12: General Allenby

1. Lawrence, T. E., *Seven Pillars of Wisdom*, p. 313.
2. Ibid, pp. 321-2.
3. Brown, Malcolm (editor), *The Letters of T. E. Lawrence*, to Charlotte Shaw, 4 March 1927.
4. Lawrence, T. E. to Alan Dawnay, 14 April 1927, Bodleian Reserve Manuscripts d43.
5. Allenby, General, Radio Interview, 19 May 1935, in *The Listener*, 22 May 1935.
6. Lawrence, T. E., op. cit., p. 326.
7. Ibid, pp. 367.
8. Ibid, p. 369.
9. Ibid, p. 379.
10. Ibid, p. 380.

11. Ibid, p. 381.
12. Ibid, p. 383.
13. Ibid, p. 383.
14. Ibid, p. 387.
15. Hogarth Papers, St Antony's College, Oxford, 7 and 11 November 1917.

Chapter 13: Disillusionment

1. Lawrence, T. E., *Seven Pillars of Wisdom*, pp. 275-6.
2. Lawrence, T. E., Notebook jottings, undated but circa 5 May 1917, British Library Add. MS 45915 fo. 55v.

Chapter 14: Degradation

1. Lawrence, T. E., *Seven Pillars of Wisdom*, pp. 441-7.

Chapter 15: Was Lawrence Recognised by the Turks? Was he Betrayed?

1. Brown, Malcolm (editor), to Major W. F. Stirling, Deputy Chief Political Officer, Cairo, 28 June 1919.
2. Lloyd, The Lord, *Letters and Diaries*, 9/10, Churchill College Cambridge.
3. Lawrence, T. E., *Seven Pillars of Wisdom*, p.389.
4. Ibid, p. 390.
5. Ibid, p. 402.
6. Ibid, p. 415.
7. Ibid, p. 448. Lawrence subsequently described Kadir as 'a fanatical Moslem who had been much annoyed by the sherif [of Mecca, Feisal's father]'s friendship with the British'. He told Stirling that al-Qadir had worked on behalf of the Ottoman government to set up an anti-British propaganda campaign in Egypt, and to launch a campaign against the Sherif of Mecca. He was also instrumental in advising Jemal Pasha, Commander of the Ottoman 4th Army and Military Governor of Syria, and in raising volunteers for Pasha to fight against the British at Amman and at Deraa. El Kadir and his brother Mohammed Said (who had worked for Leo Frobenius, head of the German Military Mission to the Middle East) had, subsequently, attempted to seize control of the government of Damascus with their Algerian volunteer forces, and had also attempted to enlist the support of the Druse religious sect against the British. Abd el Kadir died in a shooting in 1918.
8. Lawrence, T. E., op. cit., p. 441.
9. Ibid, p. 442.
10. Colarusso, John, Professor in the Anthropology Department of McMaster University, online.
11. Lawrence, T. E., op. cit., p. 444.

12. Mack, John E., *A Prince of Our Disorder: The Life of T. E. Lawrence*, Fareedah el Akle to Professor John E. Mack, 20 June 1969, p. 78.
13. Lawrence, T. E., op. cit., p. 443.
14. Ibid, p. 446.
15. Lawrence, T. E., op. cit., p. 447.

Chapter 16: Rape as a Weapon of War

1. Brown, Malcolm (editor), *The Letters of T. E. Lawrence*, to Deputy Chief Political Officer, Cairo, 28 June 1919.
2. *Human Rights Watch. No Escape: Male Rape in US Prisons*, p. 96.
3. Ibid, p. 70.
4. Godl, John, 'The Disputed Sexuality of T. E. Lawrence', 22 August 2009, firstworldwar.com.
5. Groth, Nicholas A., *Men Who Rape: The Psychology of the Offender*.

Chapter 17: Onward to Victory

1. Lawrence, T. E., *Seven Pillars of Wisdom*, p. 453.
2. Ibid, p. 526.
3. Ibid, p. 527.
4. Ibid, p. 455.
5. Ibid, p. 465.
6. Ibid, p. 467.
7. Ibid, p. 502.
8. Mack, John E., *A Prince of Our Disorder: The Life of T. E. Lawrence*, p. 159.
9. Lawrence, T. E., op. cit., p.503.
10. Ibid, p. 502.
11. Ibid, p. 586.
12. Lawrence, T. E., *Seven Pillars of Wisdom*, 1926 edition, Jonathan Cape, Introductory Chapter, p. 24.
13. Lawrence, T. E., op. cit., p. 624.
14. Ibid, p. 504.
15. Ibid, p. 537.
16. Ibid, p. 176.
17. Ibid, p. 171.
18. Ibid, pp. 175-6.
19. Ibid, p. 565.
20. Ibid, p. 580.
21. Ibid, p. 646.
22. Bell, Gertrude, *The Desert and the Sown*, p. 134.
23. Mack, John E., op. cit., Hogarth to his wife, 16 December 1917, Hogarth Papers, St Antony's College, Oxford, p. 157.

Chapter 18: Discord

1. Lawrence, T. E., *Seven Pillars of Wisdom*, pp. 659-660.
2. Wilson, Jeremy, *Lawrence of Arabia*, pp. 567-8, and p. 1109.
3. Joyce, Pierce, in BBC radio broadcast, 14 July 1941.

Chapter 19: Churchill and the Paris Peace Conference

1. Churchill, Winston, *Lawrence of Arabia as I Knew Him.*
2. Brown, Malcolm and Julia Cave, *A Touch of Genius: The Life of T. E. Lawrence*, *Sunday Times*, 22 August 1920, p. 156.
3. Mack, John E., *A Prince of Our Disorder: The Life of T. E. Lawrence*, Feisal to Justice Felix Frankfurter, March 1919, p. 269.
4. Lawrence, A. W. (editor), *Letters to T. E. Lawrence*, from Gertrude Bell, 10 July 1920.
5. Hogarth, D. G., *Mecca's Revolt Against the Turk*, p. 411.

Chapter 20: *Seven Pillars of Wisdom*

1. Liddel Hart, Basil, *T. E. Lawrence to his Biographer*, p.129.
2. Lawrence, T. E., *Seven Pillars of Wisdom*, p.351.
3. Churchill, Winston, *Lawrence of Arabia as I Knew Him.*
4. Lawrence, T. E., op. cit., p. 13.

Chapter 21: Churchill Attempts to Make Amends

1. Churchill, Winston, *Lawrence of Arabia as I Knew Him.*
2. Ibid.
3. Gertrude Bell died in Baghdad, where she had held the post of Director of Antiquities, on 12 July 1926.
4. Lawrence, T. E., *Seven Pillars of Wisdom*, p. 562.

Chapter 22: Dream and Reality

1. Brown, Malcolm (editor), *The Letters of T. E. Lawrence*, to G. J. Kidson, 14 November 1919.
2. Ibid, to Eric Kennington, 25 August 1921.
3. Churchill, Winston, *Lawrence of Arabia as I Knew Him.*
4. Brown, Malcolm, op. cit., to R. D. Blumenfield, 11 November 1922.
5. Ibid, to Charlotte Shaw, 18 October 1927.
6. Knightley, Phillip, and Colin Simpson, *The Secret Lives of Lawrence of Arabia*, pp. 188-9.
7. According to Lawrence's Pocket Diary, he was at Umtaiye on 14, 18, and 24 September 1918.
8. Knightley, Phillip, and Colin Simpson, op. cit., pp. 190-1.

9. Brown, Malcolm, op. cit., to R. A. M. Guy, 25 December 1923.
10. Brown, Malcolm and Julia Cave, *A Touch of Genius: The Life of T. E. Lawrence*, to Sir Herbert Baker, 17 July 1928, p. 167.
11. Lawrence, T. E., Notebook jottings, undated but circa 5 May 1917, British Library Add. MS 45915 fo. 55v.

Chapter 23: Sir Hugh Trenchard and the RAF

1. Brown, Malcolm (editor), *The Letters of T. E. Lawrence*, to Sir Hugh Trenchard, January 1922.
2. Garnett, David (editor), *The Letters of T. E. Lawrence*, to Dr Hogarth, 13 June 1923.
3. Royal Air Force: Aircraftman Shaw, Thomas Edward, Royal Tank Corps, Character Certificate 338171. Wareham Town Museum.

Chapter 24: Bovington Camp and Clouds Hill

1. Brown, Malcolm and Julia Cave, *A Touch of Genius: The Life of T. E. Lawrence*, p. 176, Note 1.
2. University of Texas Counselling and Mental Health Center and Wisconsin Coalition Against Sexual Assault, USA. Dr Michael Hunter, Ph.D. Article, 'The Disputed Sexuality of T. E. Lawrence', in First World War.com. 1 December 2002.
3. Brown, Malcolm (editor), *The Letters of T. E. Lawrence*, to Sir Hugh Trenchard, 1 March 1924.
4. Lanning, G. E., 'From Rifle Range to Garrison: An Essay on Bovington Camp (1899 – 1925)', in *Bovington Garrison & The Armour Centre: A History*, online.
5. Knowles, Patrick and Joyce, *A Handful with Quietness,* p. 20.
6. Lawrence, A.W. (editor), *T. E. Lawrence by His Friends*, p. 226.
7. Ibid, p. 235.
8. Garnett, David (editor), *The Letters of T. E. Lawrence*, to Mrs Eric Kennington, 18 October 1932.
9. Lawrence A. W, op. cit., p. 226.
10. Ibid, p. 286.
11. Brown, Malcolm, op. cit., to Charlotte Shaw, 26 March 1924.

Chapter 25: John Bruce's Story

1. This word is omitted from the typed transcript of the original text.
2. Ibid.
3. Bruce, John, 'Papers Relating to the Medical History of T. E. Lawrence' (Misc 196 (2904)), courtesy of the Imperial War Museum.
4. Mack, John E., *A Prince of Our Disorder: The Life of T. E. Lawrence*, p. 431.
5. Ibid, p. 433.

6. Ibid, p. 434. Had Lawrence not died suddenly and unexpectedly, he would in all probability have destroyed the letters and diary jottings described above.
7. Lawrence, Arnold, 'My Knowledge of Bruce', 1970, quoted in Mack, John E., op. cit., p. 428
8. *Mercury*, *The*, 19 June 1939.
9. Bodleian Library, University of Oxford, Fethertonhaugh Frampton Family, Transcripts of letters to T. E. Lawrence, MS. Eng. d. 3341, fols. 484-7, 588-9.
10. Information kindly supplied by The Seven Pillars of Wisdom Trust.
11. Lawrence, A. W. (editor), *T. E. Lawrence by his Friends*, Editor's postscript, Jonathan Cape, London, 1937, in Knightley, Phillip and Colin Simpson, *The Secret Lives of Lawrence of Arabia*, p. 15.

Chapter 26: A Return to the RAF

1. Brown, Malcolm (editor), *The Letters of T. E. Lawrence*, to Sir Hugh Trenchard, 6 February 1925.
2. Boyle, Andrew, *Trenchard: Man of Vision*, p. 516.
3. Brown, Malcolm, op. cit., to Sir Hugh Trenchard, 20 November 1926.
4. Ibid, to Sir Hugh Trenchard, 17 March 1928.
5. Ibid, to Ralph H. Isham, 10 August 1927.
6. Ibid, to Charlotte Shaw, 10 November 1927.
7. Ibid, to C. F. Bell, 14 December 1927.
8. Lawrence, T. E. to Edward Garnett, 25 December 1927, Bodleian Reserve Manuscripts d43.
9. Garnett, David (editor), *The Letters of T. E. Lawrence*, op. cit., to Edward Garnett, 1 December 1927.
10. Ibid, to William Rothenstein, 14 April 1928.
11. Brown, Malcolm, op. cit., to Sir Hugh Trenchard, 21 December 1928.
12. Lawrence, T. E. to Sir Hugh Trenchard, 27 December 1928, Bodleian Reserve Manuscripts d46.
13. Lawrence, A. W. (editor), *T. E. Lawrence by His Friends,* p. /247.
14. Legg, Rodney, *Lawrence in Dorset*, pp. 70,75.

Chapter 27: *The Mint*

1. Lawrence, T. E., *The Mint*, pp. 19-20.
2. Ibid, pp. 24,26.
3. Ibid, p. 28.
4. Ibid, p. 41.
5. Ibid, p. 50.
6. Ibid, p. 53.
7. Ibid, p. 72.
8. Ibid, p. 84.
9. Ibid, pp. 65,66

10. Ibid, p. 67.
11. Ibid, p. 76
12. Ibid, p. 108
13. Ibid, p. 109.
14. Ibid, pp. 109-10
15. Ibid, pp. 134,147.
16. Ibid, p. 75.
17. Ibid, p. 199.
18. Ibid, pp. 205-6.
19. Lawrence, T. E. to K. W. Marshall, Bodleian Reserve Manuscripts d58.
20. Brown, Malcolm and Julia Cave, *A Touch of Genius: The Life of T. E. Lawrence*, p. 201.
21. Lawrence, A. W. (editor), *Letters to T. E. Lawrence*, from King Feisal I of Iraq, 18 December 1932.
22. Ibid.

Chapter 28: E. M. Forster

1. Brown, Malcolm (editor), *The Letters of T. E. Lawrence*, to E. M. Forster, 20 February 1924.
2. Ibid, to E. M. Forster, 6 April 1924.
3. The National Trust, 1998, *Clouds Hill.*
4. Lawrence, A. W. (editor), *T. E. Lawrence by His Friends*, p. 97.
5. Ibid, p. 248.
6. Brown, Malcolm, op. cit., to E. M. Forster, 17 June 1925.
7. Ibid, 21 December 1927.
8. Ibid, 28 August 1928.
9. Lawrence, Arnold W. (editor), *Letters to T. E. Lawrence*, from E. M. Forster, 5 July 1928.
10. Brown, Malcolm, op. cit., 1 April 1929.
11. Ibid, 22 October 1932.

Chapter 29: George Bernard Shaw

1. Brown, Malcolm (editor), *The Letters of T. E. Lawrence*, to Bernard Shaw, 17 August 1922.
2. Lawrence, A. W. (editor), *Letters to T. E. Lawrence*, from Bernard Shaw, 1 December 1922.
3. Garnett, David (editor), *The Letters of T. E. Lawrence*, to George Bernard Shaw, 20 December 1923.
4. Lawrence, A. W., op. cit., from Bernard Shaw, 4 January 1923.
5. Bernard Shaw, private memorandum to Mr Baldwin, 31 May 1923.
6. Mack, John E., *A Prince of Our Disorder: The Life of T. E. Lawrence*, Bernard Shaw to T. E. Lawrence, 7 October 1924, p. 352.

7. Brown, Malcolm, op. cit., to his Mother, 10 July 1928.
8. Lawrence, A. W., op. cit., from Bernard Shaw, 12 April 1928.
9. Brown, Malcolm, op, cit., to Bernard Shaw, 19 July 1928.
10. Ibid, to Sir Hugh Trenchard, 5 February 1929.

Chapter 30: Charlotte Shaw

1. Dunbar, Janet, *Mrs G.B.S.: A Biographical Portrait*, p. 7.
2. Knightley, Phillip and Colin Simpson, *Sunday Times Weekly Review*, 23 and 30 June, and 7 and 14 September 1968,
3. Brown, Malcolm (editor), *The Letters of T. E. Lawrence*, to Bernard Shaw, 27 December 1922.
4. Dunbar, Janet, op. cit., pp. 266-7, Charlotte Shaw to T. E. Lawrence, 31 December 1922.
5. Brown, Malcolm, op. cit., to Charlotte Shaw, 26 March 1924.
6. Ibid, 10 June 1924.
7. Ibid, 31 August 1924.
8. Ibid, 28 September 1925.
9. Ibid, 17 June 1926.
10. Ibid, 24 February 1927.
11. Ibid, 14 April 1927.
12. Dunbar, Janet, op. cit., p.281, T. E. Lawrence to Charlotte Shaw, 17 May 1927.
13. Brown, Malcolm, op. cit., to Charlotte Shaw, 18 August 1927.
14. Ibid, 18 October 1927.
15. Ibid, 20 March 1928.
16. Ibid, 17 May 1928.
17. Ibid, 20 November 1928.
18. Ibid, 27 April 1929.
19. Ibid, 27 March 1930.
20. Ibid, 5 December 1930.
21. Ibid, 23 August 1933.
22. Ibid, 18 May 1934.
23. Ibid, 31 December 1934.
24. Lawrence, A. W. (editor), *T. E. Lawrence by His Friends,* p. 221.
25. Ibid, p. 248.
25. Lawrence, A. W., op. cit., p. 64.

Chapter 31: Thomas Hardy

1. Brown, Malcolm (editor), *The Letters of T. E. Lawrence*, to Robert Graves, 20 March 1923.
2. Ibid, to Mrs Thomas Hardy, 25 March 1923.
3. Garnett, David (editor), *The Letters of T. E. Lawrence*, to Eric Kennington, 30 March 1923.

4. Brown, Malcolm, op. cit., To Mrs Thomas Hardy, 25 March 1923.
5. Garnett, David, op. cit., to D.G. Hogarth, 23 August 1923.
6. Ibid, to Robert Graves, 8 September 1923.
7. Titterington, Ellen E., *The Domestic Life of Thomas Hardy*.
8. Original letters at University of Texas, Austin, to Mrs Thomas Hardy, 11 January 1927.
9. Garnett, David, op. cit., to William Rothenstein, 14 April 1928.
10. Ibid, to Mrs Thomas Hardy, 16 April 1928.

Chapter 32: Florence Hardy

1. Garnett, David (editor), *The Letters of T. E. Lawrence*, to Robert Graves, 8 September 1923.
2. Atkins, Norman. *Thomas Hardy and the Hardy Players*.
3. Ibid.
4. Mack, John E., *A Prince of Our Disorder: The Life of T. E. Lawrence*, p. 451.
5. Hart-Davis, Rupert (editor), *Siegfried Sassoon Diaries*, 6 and 7 August 1924.
6. Brown, Malcolm (editor), *The Letters of T. E. Lawrence*, to Mrs Thomas Hardy, 26 August 1925.
7. Ibid, to Mrs Thomas Hardy, 9 November 1925.
8. Ibid, 15 January 1928.
9. Ibid, p. 361, Note 1.
10. Ibid, to Mrs Thomas Hardy, 3 December 1932.
11. Legg, Rodney, *Lawrence in Dorset*, Florence Hardy to Robert Graves, 13 June 1927, p. 57.

Chapter 33: Robert Graves

1. Brown, Malcolm (editor), *The Letters of T. E. Lawrence*, to Robert Graves, 18 January 1923.
2. Ibid, to Charlotte Shaw, 28 September 1925.
3. Ibid, to Robert Graves, 20 March 1923.
4. Ibid, to Robert Graves, 6 November 1928.
5. Ibid, p. 387, Note 1.
6. Ibid, to Robert Graves, 6 November 1928.
7. Ibid, to Robert Graves, 13 September 1929.
8. Ibid, to Robert Graves, 21 April 1931.
9. Lawrence, A. W. (editor), *T. E. Lawrence by His Friends* p. 312.
10. Brown, Malcolm, op. cit., to Robert Graves, 4 February 1935.

Chapter 34: Lady Astor

1. Brown, Malcolm (editor), *The Letters of T. E. Lawrence*, p. 395.
2. Ibid, to Sir Hugh Trenchard, 16 April 1929.

3. Brown, Malcolm and Julia Cave, *A Touch of Genius: The Life of T. E. Lawrence*, p. 195.
4. Brown, Malcolm, op. cit., to Lady Astor, 13 March 1929.
5. Ibid, to Lady Astor, 31 December 1930.
6. Ibid, to Lady Astor, 11 December 1933.
7. Ibid, to Lady Astor, 12 July 1929.
8. Ibid, to Lady Astor, 11 May 1934.
9. Brown, Malcolm and Julia Cave, op. cit., p. 197 Note 1.
10. Ibid, p. 197.
11. Brown, Malcolm and Julia Cave, op. cit., to Lady Astor, p. 195.
12. Brown, Malcolm, op. cit., to Lady Astor, 5 May 1935.
13. Ibid, to Lady Astor, 8 May 1935, and p. 537, Note 1.

Chapter 35: Deraa and the Alleged Rape: Was Lawrence Telling the Truth?

1. This volume is in the possession of the Arents Collection, New York Public Library.
2. Mack, John E., *A Prince of our Disorder: the Life of T. E. Lawrence*, p.229.
3. 'Lawrence of Arabia: The Battle for the Arab World', 2003, Lion Television.
4. Day, Elizabeth, 'Lawrence of Arabia "Made Up" Sex Attack by Turk Troops', 14 May 2006, online.
5. Lawrence, T. E., *Field Diary*, Courtesy British Library.
6. Lawrence, T. E., *Seven Pillars of Wisdom*, pp. 425,432.
7. Lawrence, T. E., *Field Diary*, op. cit.
8. Lawrence, T. E., *Seven Pillars of Wisdom*, op. cit., p. 385.
9. Ibid, p.441.
10. Ibid, p.441.
11. Brown, Malcolm (editor), *The Letters of T. E. Lawrence*, to his Mother, 14 November 1917.
12. Ibid, to Colonel Pierce Joyce, 13 November 1917.
13. Ibid, to his Parents, 14 December 1917.
14. Ibid, to Major W. F. Stirling, Deputy Chief Political Officer, Cairo, 28 June 1919.
15. Ibid, to Charlotte Shaw, 26 December 1925.
16. Tank Corps Documents, 12 March 1923, Army Forms B.203 and B.178. In Royal Air Force file AIR 1/2696. 338171. Shaw, Thomas Edward. 'Secret File'. Army Form B.178. Medical History Sheet. National Archives, Kew.
17. August 21 1925, Royal Air Force file AIR 1/2696. 338171. Shaw, Thomas Edward. 'Secret File'. RAF Form 35. Entry (medical) Examination record card. Medical History Sheet. National Archives, Kew.
18. Brown, Malcolm, op. cit., to Edward Garnett, 22 August 1922.
19. Korda, Michael, *Hero: The Life and Legend of Lawrence of Arabia*, p. 302.

Chapter 36: Rape Trauma Syndrome

1. Koss, Mary P. and Mary R. Harvey, *'The Rape Victim, Clinical and Community Intervention*', pp. 48-54.
2. Groth, A. Nicholas and Ann W. Burgess, Male Rape: Offenders and Victims, *American Journal of Psychiatry*, 137:7, pp. 806-810, 1980.
3. Brown, Malcolm (editor), *The Letters of T. E. Lawrence*, to Deputy Chief Political Officer, Cairo, 28 June 1919.
4. Oxford Dictionaries online.
5. Lawrence, T. E., *Seven Pillars of Wisdom*, p. 631.
6. Brown, Malcolm, op. cit., to Charlotte Shaw, 26 March 1924.
7. Lawrence, T. E., op. cit., p.502.
8. Brown, Malcolm, op. cit., to Alan Dawnay, 27 July 1924.
9. Walker, Jayne, John Archer and Michelle Davies, 'Effects of Male Rape on Psychological Functioning', *British Journal of Clinical Psychology* (2005), 44, pp. 445–51.
10. Brown, Malcolm, op. cit., to Lionel Curtis, 27 March 1923.
11. Ibid, to Charlotte Shaw, 19 July 1924.
12. Ibid, to Charlotte Shaw, 26 March 1924.
13. Ibid, to Charlotte Shaw from RAF Karachi, 28 January 1927.
14. Ibid, to Lady Astor, 8 May 1935.
15. Ibid, to Charlotte Shaw, 26 March 1924.
16. McMullen, Richie J., *Male Rape*, p.74
17. Leitenberg, H., and Henning, K. (1995). 'Sexual Fantasy', *Psychological Bulletin*, 117(3), pp. 469-96.
18. Brown, Malcolm and Julia Cave, *A Touch of Genius: The Life of T. E. Lawrence, p. 177.*
19. Walker, Jayne, John Archer and Michelle Davies, 'Effects of Rape on Men: A Descriptive Analysis', *Archives of Sexual Behaviour*, Volume 34, Number 1, February 2005, pp. 69-80.
20. Lawrence, T. E., *The Mint*, pp. 205-6.
21. Brown, Malcolm, op. cit., to Lady Astor, 12 July 1929.
22. McMullen, Richie J., *Male Rape*, p.65.
23. *Diagnostic and Statistical Manual of Mental Disorders,* American Psychiatric Association, pp. 463-6.
24. Mack, John E., *A Prince of Our Disorder: The Life of T. E. Lawrence*, p. 232.

Chapter 37: Lawrence's Sexual Orientation

1. Hart-Davis, Rupert (editor), *Siegfried Sassoon Diaries*, March 1924.
2. Brown, Malcolm (editor), *The Letters of T. E. Lawrence*, to E.M. Forster, 21 December 1927.
3. Ibid, to E. M. Forster, 21 December 1927.

4. Ibid, to Robert Graves, 6 November 1928.
5. Ibid, to F. L. Lucas, 26 March 1929.
6. Ibid, to Ernest Thurtle, 1 April 1929.
7. Lawrence, T. E. to Ernest Altounyan, 28 December 1933, Bodleian Reserve Manuscripts, d49.
8. Lawrence, T. E., *The Mint*, p. 129.
9. Mack, John E., *A Prince of Our Disorder: The Life of T. E. Lawrence*, p. 67.
10. *Diagnostic and Statistical Manual of Mental Disorders,* American Psychiatric Association, pp. 541-2.
11. Lawrence, A. W. (editor), *T. E. Lawrence by His Friends*, p. 278.
12. Ibid, p. 364.
13. The word 'masochism' was invented by Austrian psychiatrist Richard F. von Krafft-Ebing (1840-1902), after writer, journalist, and fellow countryman Leopold von Sacher-Masoch, who wrote about masochism and was a masochist himself.
14. Oxford Dictionaries online.
15. Lawrence, T. E., *Seven Pillars of Wisdom*, p. 446.
16. Oxford Dictionaries online.
17. Mack, John E., op. cit., p. 433.
18. *Diagnostic and Statistical Manual of Mental Disorders,* op. cit., p. 573.
19. Brown, Malcolm, op. cit., to Charlotte Shaw, 14 April 1927.
20. Rousseau, Jean-Jacques, *The Confessions of Jean-Jacques Rousseau*, Book I.
21. Krafft-Ebing, Richard von, *Psychopathia Sensualis: eine Klinisch-Forensische Studie*, p. 104.
22. Hirschfeld, Magnus, *Sexual Anomalies: The Origins, Nature, and Treatment of Sexual Disorders*, p. 301.
23. Brame, Gloria D., William D. Brame, and Jon Jacobs, *Different Loving: The World of Sexual Dominance and Submission*, p. 232.
24. Townsend, Larry, *The Leatherman's Handbook*, in McAnulty, Richard D., and M. Michelle Burnette, *Sex and Sexuality*, Preager, Westport, CT, 2006, p. 22.
25. Korda, Michael, *Hero: The Life and Legend of Lawrence of Arabia*, p. 583.
26. Lawrence, T. E., *The Mint*, p. 42.
27. *Diagnostic and Statistical Manual of Mental Disorders,* op. cit., p. 573.
28. The concept of 'sexual script' was created by sociologists John H. Gagnon and William Simon in their book *Sexual Conduct: The Social Sources of Human Sexuality*, published in 1973.

Chapter 38: The Crash

1. Brown, Malcolm and Julia Cave, *A Touch of Genius: The Life of T. E. Lawrence*, p. 205.
2. Brown, Malcolm (editor), *The Letters of T. E. Lawrence*, to B. H. Liddell Hart, 31 December 1934.

3. From Brough Works Record Sheet, information kindly supplied by Jonathan M. Weekly
4. Lawrence, A. W. (editor), *T. E. Lawrence by His Friends,* pp. 227-8.
5. Garnett, David (ed.), *The Letters of T. E. Lawrence*, to George Brough, 5 March 1932.
6. Brown, Malcolm, op. cit., to George Brough, 3 May 1934.
7. This was originally reported in *The Life and Times of Joyce Knowles* by E. V. G. 'Bob' Hunt., in Andrew B. Simpson, *Another Life: Lawrence After Arabia*, p.241.
8. Simpson, Andrew B., *Another Life: Lawrence After Arabia*, p.241.
9. *Inquest Number 160, County of Dorset*, 21 May 1935.
10. Ibid.
11. Corporal No. 7581979 Ernest Catchpole. Catchpole rose to the rank of staff sergeant. He committed suicide at Cairo in July 1940 and was buried in Cairo's War Memorial Cemetery.
12. *Inquest Number 160*, op. cit.
13. Ibid.
14. *Daily Echo*, 15 May 1935.
15. *Inquest Number 160*, op. cit.
16. Alfred Russell, interviewed by Malcolm Brown and Julia Cave, 30 May 1986. In Marriott, P. J., and Yvonne Argent, *The Last Days of T. E. Lawrence: A Leaf in the Wind*, p. 149.
17. Albert Hargraves, interviewed by Stewart Rigby, 1982, in Marriott, P. J., and Yvonne Argent, p. 140.
18. Marriott, P. J., and Yvonne Argent, op. cit., p. 141.
19. *Daily Echo*, Bournemouth, early May 1985.
20. Fletcher, Frank, statement to Bournemouth's *Daily Echo*, 18 May 1985.
21. Frank Gordon, interviewed by Andrew R.B. Simpson at Bovington, 25 May 1985, in Marriott, Paul J., and Yvonne Argent, *The Last Days of T. E. Lawrence: A Leaf in the Wind*, pp. 147-8.
22. Montague, Margaret, 'There was a Car', Bournemouth's *Daily Echo*, 5 September 1985.
23. Legg, Rodney, *Lawrence in Dorset*, p. 113
24. Simpson, Andrew, 'The Crash that Killed T. E. Lawrence', interview with Margaret Montague, November 1985, privately printed, in Marriott, Paul J., and Yvonne Argent, op. cit., p. 146.
25. Joan Hughes, interviewed by Roland A. Hammersley, 10 February 1986, courtesy Wareham Town Museum.
26. Marriott, P. J., and Yvonne Argent, op. cit., interview with Frank Fletcher, 13 August 1991, pp. 130-7.
27. Knowles, Patrick and Joyce, *A Handful with Quietness,* p. 46.
28. Marriott, P. J., and Yvonne Argent, op. cit., p. 144.
29. Ibid, pp. 133-4.
30. Ibid, p. 142.

Chapter 39: A Reappraisal of the Crash

1. Ordnance Survey Map originally produced in 1901 but modified in 1927.
2. Lawrence's sketch of Clouds Hill, 17 April 1934, Marriott, P. J., and Yvonne Argent, *The Last Days of T. E. Lawrence: A Leaf in the Wind*, Map 10.
3. RAF aerial photograph, 1947.
4. Google map, 2008.
5. Ibid.
6. Simpson, Andrew B., *Another Life: Lawrence After Arabia*, p. 233.
7. Marriott, P. J., and Yvonne Argent, op. cit., Plate 35.
8. Ibid, Plate 38A.
9. Legg, Rodney, Lawrence in Dorset, p. 89.
10. Marriott, P. J., and Yvonne Argent, op. cit., Plate 37A.
11. Ibid, Plate 36B.
12. Ibid, Plate 36A.
13. Based on the personal observations of the author.
14. Marriott, P. J., and Yvonne Argent, op. cit., Map 8.
15. Roland A. Hammersley, sketch of crash site, based on his interview with Joan Hughes on 10 February 1986, courtesy Wareham Town Museum.
16. Information kindly supplied by Met Office National Meteorological Archive. Times given are clock times – i.e. one hour ahead of GMT.
17. Information kindly supplied by Jonathan M. Weekly.
18. Marriott, P. J., and Yvonne Argent, op. cit., Plates 39A, B and C.
19. Knowles, Patrick and Joyce, *A Handful with Quietness*, p.37.
20. Not including the fuel, the Brough weighed 440 lb. It may come as a surprise to learn that the weight of an errand boy's bicycle of the time was in the region of 60lb, with an additional 12 lb for the basket and, in Hargraves' case, an extra 15 lb for the 'parcel orders' – parcels of meat for delivery – (Marriott p. 131) making a total of 87 lb. (Based on the weight of a similar 1930s tradesman's delivery bicycle, courtesy of Borough of Poole Museum Services.) This was probably not far short of the weight of Hargraves himself!
21. *Daily Telegraph*, report on the Inquest, 22 May 1935.

Chapter 40: The Funeral: Aftermath

1. Legg, Rodney, *Lawrence in Dorset*, p. 129.
2. Brady, Thomas J., 'Lawrence of Arabia and the Lure of the Roses', 18 August 1994, Philly.com
3. Antiques Roadshow, 18 August 2013, BBC Television.
4. J. Richard Harvey, conversation with the author, 20 August 2013. John Hooper Harvey became an architect, medieval historian, expert on medieval gardens, and author. His *magnum opus*, *English Mediaeval Architects: a Biographical Dictionary down to 1550*, was published in 1954. He died in 1997.

Chapter 41: The Effigy

1. Brown, Malcolm (editor), *The Letters of T. E. Lawrence*, to Eric Kennington, 6 August 1934.
2. Ibid, to Eric Kennington, 6 May 1935.
3. Eric Kennington, 3 July 1945, Wareham. Courtesy of the Rector and Churchwardens of St Martin's-on-the-Walls, Wareham.
4. *Tale of an 'Arabian Knight': the T. E. Lawrence Effigy*, by Richard Knowles. *The T. E. Lawrence Society Journal*, 2:1.
5. *Story of the Lawrence Effigy*, told by Eric Kennington at Wareham on 3 July 1945. Courtesy of the Rector and Churchwardens of St Martin's-on-the-Walls, Wareham.

Chapter 42: Wendy Vallance: New Light on Lawrence's Final Days

1. Wendy Vallance, personal discussion with the author, 5 September 2023.
2. *The Medical Register*, 1935

Chapter 43: T. E. Shaw – 'Lawrence of Arabia' – Happy Years Spent as Mechanic and Boatman: Lawrence's Contribution to Air-Sea Rescue

1. Soanes, Catherine and Angus Stevenson (editors), *Oxford Dictionary of English.*
2. Ibid.
3. Aviation Safety Network: ASN Wikibase Occurrence # 145650.
4. Garnett, David, *The Letters of T. E. Lawrence*, to Lady Astor, 2 March 1931.
5. Garnett, David, *The Letters of T. E. Lawrence*, to B. H. Liddel Hart, 13 April 1931.
6. Garnett, David, *The Letters of T. E. Lawrence*, to Dick Knowles, 19 April 1931.
7. Garnett, David, *The Letters of T. E. Lawrence*, to Robert Graves, 24 January 1933.
8. 'Lawrence of Arabia Talks (Exclusive)', *News Chronicle*, 11 May 1934.
9. Garnett, David, *The Letters of T. E. Lawrence*, to Lord Carlow, 4 January 1935.
10. Lawrence, A. W. (editor), *T. E. Lawrence by His Friends*. Shaw to B. G. & N., 5 May 1935.
11. Courtesy of Air-Sea Rescue & Marine Craft Section Club.

Chapter 44: T. E. Lawrence: Sir Hugh Cairns and Road Safety

1. *Plarr's Lives of the Fellows*: a biographical register of the Fellows of the Royal College of Surgeons of England.

2. Cairns, Hugh, 'Head Injuries in Motor-Cyclists: The Importance of the Crash Helmet', *British Medical Journal*, 4 October 1941, pp.465-471.
3. Hughes, J. T., 'Lawrence of Arabia and Hugh Cairns: Crash Helmets for Motorcyclists', *Sage Journals*, Volume 9, Issue 4.
4. Cairns, Hugh, and H. Holbourn, 'Head Injuries in Motor-Cyclists: With Special Reference to Crash Helmets', *British Medical Journal*, 15 May 1943, pp.591-8.
5. Cairns, Sir Hugh, 'Crash Helmets', *British Medical Journal*, 7 September 1946, pp.322-3.
6. Fraenkel, G. J., *Hugh Cairns, First Nuffield Professor of Surgery,* pp.97-8.

Epilogue

1. Lawrence, A. W. (editor), *T. E. Lawrence by His Friends*, p. 120.
2. Ibid, pp. 124-5.
3. Churchill, Winston, *Lawrence of Arabia as I Knew Him*.
4. Gawrychl, George W. 'T. E. Lawrence and the Art of War in the Twenty-First Century', *The History Reader* online, from Charles M. Stang, *The Waking Dream of T. E. Lawrence: Essays on His Life, Literature, and Legacy*.

Bibliography

American Psychiatric Association, *Diagnostic and Statistical Manual of Mental Disorders* (DSM-IV-TR) (American Psychiatric Association, Washington, DC, 2000)

Atkins, Norman J., *Thomas Hardy and the Hardy Players* (Toucan Press, Guernsey, Channel Islands, UK, 1980)

Bell, Lady, (editor), *The Letters of Gertrude Bell* (Penguin, London, 1939)

Boyle, Andrew, *Trenchard: Man of Vision* (Collins, London, 1962)

Brame, Gloria D., William D. Brame, and Jon Jacobs, *Different Loving: The World of Sexual Dominance and Submission* (Villard, New York, 1993)

Brown, Malcolm, *The Letters of T. E. Lawrence* (J.M. Dent, London, 1988)

Brown, Malcolm and Julia Cave, *A Touch of Genius: The Life of T.E. Lawrence* (J.M. Dent, London, 1988)

Carter, Jan, *The Maltreated Child* (Priory Press, London, 1974)

Churchill, Winston, *Lawrence of Arabia as I Knew Him* (*Sunday Dispatch*, 19 May 1940)

Daily Echo, Bournemouth

Dixon, J & B. Jones (editors), *Macmillan Dictionary of National Biography, The* (Macmillan Reference Books, London, 1981)

Dunbar, Janet, *Mrs G.B.S.: A Biographical Portrait* (George G. Harrap, London, 1963)

Forty, George and Anne, *Bovington Tanks* (Wincanton Press, Wincanton, Somerset, 1988)

Fraenkel, G. J., *Hugh Cairns, First Nuffield Professor of Surgery, University of Oxford* (Oxford University Press, 1991).

Gagnon, John H. and William Simon, *Sexual Conduct: The Social Sources of Human Sexuality* (Aldine Books, Chicago, 1973)

Garnett, David (editor), *The Letters of T. E. Lawrence* (Jonathan Cape, London, 1938)

Graves, Robert, *Lawrence and the Arabs* (Jonathan Cape, London, 1927)

Hart-Davis, Rupert (editor), *Siegfried Sassoon Diaries* (Faber & Faber, London, 1981, 1985)

Hirschfeld, Magnus, *Sexual Anomalies: The Origins, Nature, and Treatment of Sexual Disorders* (Emerson, New York, 1956)

Hogarth, D.G., *Mecca's Revolt Against the Turk* (*Century Magazine*, 100, London, 1920)

Human Rights Watch, 'No Escape: Male Rape in US Prisons' (Human Rights Watch, New York, April 2001)

James, Lawrence, *The Golden Warrior* (Weidenfeld & Nicholson, London, 1990)

Knight, Ronald D., *T. E. Lawrence and the Max Gate Circle* (R.D. Knight, Bat & Ball Press, Weymouth, Dorset, 1995)

Knightley, Philip & Colin Simpson (*Sunday Times Weekly Review*, 23 and 30 June, and 7 and 14 September 1968)

Knowles, Patrick and Joyce, *A Handful with Quietness* (E.V.G. Hunt, Weymouth, March 1992)

Korda, Michael, *Hero: The Life and Legend of Lawrence of Arabia* (JR Books, London, 2010)

Koss, Mary P. and Mary R. Harvey, *The Rape Victim, Clinical and Community Interventions*, New York: Sage Library of Social Research 185 (Sage, London, 1991)

Krafft-Ebing, Richard von, *Psychopathia Sensualis: eine Klinisch-Forensische Studie* (Arcade Publishing, New York, 1998)

Lawrence, A.W. (editor), *Letters to T. E. Lawrence* (Jonathan Cape, London, 1962)

Lawrence, A.W. (editor), *Secret Dispatches from Arabia* (Golden Cockerell, London, 1939)

Lawrence, A.W., *T. E. Lawrence by His Friends* (McGraw-Hill, New York, 1963)

Lawrence, M. R. (editor), *The Home Letters of T. E. Lawrence and his Brothers* (Macmillan, Oxford, 1954)

Lawrence, T. E., 'An Essay on Flecker' (Corvinus Press, London, 1937)

Lawrence, T. E., *Seven Pillars of Wisdom* (Jonathan Cape, London, 1935)

Lawrence, T. E., *Minorities*, edited by J. M. Wilson, (Jonathan Cape, London, 1971)

Lawrence, T. E., *The Mint* (Jonathan Cape, London, 1955)

Legg, Rodney, *Lawrence in Dorset* (Dorset Publishing Company, Wincanton, Somerset, 1997)

Liddel Hart, Basil, *T. E. Lawrence to his Biographer* (Liddel Hart, London, 1938)

Mack, John E., *A Prince of Our Disorder: The Life of T. E. Lawrence* (Weidenfeld & Nicholson, London, 1976)

Marriott, Paul J., and Yvonne Argent, *The Last Days of T. E. Lawrence: A Leaf in the Wind*, (Alpha Press, Portland, Oregon, 1996)

McMullen, Richie J., *Male Rape* (GMP Publishers, London, 1990)

The Medical Register, published for the General Medical Council (Constable & Co., London,
1935)

Peterkin, A., W. Johnston, and R. Drew, *Medical Officers Serving in the Army 1660-1960* (The
Wellcome Historical Medical Library, 1968).

Rousseau, Jean-Jacques, *The Confessions of Jean-Jacques Rousseau* (Privately printed for members of the Aldus Society, London, 1903)
Scarce, Michael, *Male on Male Rape* (Plenum Press, New York, 1997)
Stewart, Desmond, *T. E. Lawrence* (Paladin, London, 1979)
Sunday Express
Inquest Number 160, County of Dorset, 21 May 1935
Sassoon, Siegfried, *Diaries* (Faber & Faber, London, 1924)
Scarce, Michael, *Male on Male Rape* (Perseus Books Group, New York, 1997)
Schwartz, Dr Allan N., LCSW, Ph.D., 'A Discussion of Sexual Fetishism and Masochism', updated 20 May 2008 (Online)
Simpson, Andrew B., *Another Life: Lawrence After Arabia* (Spellmount, Stroud, 2011)
Soanes, Catherine and Angus Stevenson, *Oxford Dictionary of English* (Oxford University Press, 2006)
Stang, Charles M. *The Waking Dream of T. E. Lawrence: Essays on His Life, Literature, and Legacy* (Palgrave Macmillan, London, 2002)
Titterington, Ellen E., 'The Domestic Life of Thomas Hardy'. *Thomas Hardy Year Book,* Monograph 4, courtesy of G. Stevens Cox MA (Oxon) PhD, editor (Toucan Press, Guernsey, Channel Islands, UK, 1963)
Townsend, Larry, *The Leatherman's Handbook* (Modernismo Publications, New York, 1983)
Wilson, Jeremy, *Lawrence of Arabia* (Heinemann, London, 1989)
Wilson, Jeremy and Nicole (editors), *T. E. Lawrence: Correspondence with Bernard and Charlotte Shaw 1922-1926* (Castle Hill, Woodgreen Common, Hants, 2000)

By the Same Author

By Swords Divided: Corfe Castle in the Civil War. Halsgrove, 2003.
Thomas Hardy: Christmas Carollings. Halsgrove, 2005.
Enid Blyton and her Enchantment with Dorset. Halsgrove, 2005.
Tyneham: A Tribute. Halsgrove, 2007.
Agatha Christie: The Finished Portrait. Tempus, 2007.
The Story of George Loveless and the Tolpuddle Martyrs. Halsgrove, 2008.
Father of the Blind: A Portrait of Sir Arthur Pearson. The History Press, 2009.
Agatha Christie: The Pitkin Guide. Pitkin Publishing, 2009.
Arthur Conan Doyle: The Man behind Sherlock Holmes. The History Press, 2009.
HMS Hood: Pride of the Royal Navy. The History Press, 2009.
Purbeck Personalities. Halsgrove, 2009.
Bournemouth's Founders and Famous Visitors. The History Press, 2010.
Thomas Hardy: Behind the Mask. The History Press, 2011.
A Brummie Boy goes to War. Halsgrove, 2011.
Winston Churchill: Portrait of an Unquiet Mind. Pen & Sword Books, 2012.
Charles Darwin: Destroyer of Myths. Pen & Sword Books, 2013.
Beatrix Potter: Her Inner World. Pen & Sword Books, 2013.
T.E. Lawrence: Tormented Hero. Fonthill, 2014.
Agatha Christie: The Disappearing Novelist. Fonthill, 2014.
Lawrence of Arabia's Clouds Hill. Halsgrove, 2014.
Jane Austen: Love is Like a Rose. Fonthill, 2015.
Kindly Light: The Story of Blind Veterans UK. Fonthill, 2015.
Thomas Hardy at Max Gate: The Latter Years. Halsgrove, 2016.
Corfe Remembered. Halsgrove, 2017.
Thomas Hardy: Bockhampton and Beyond. Halsgrove, 2017.
Mugabe: Monarch of Blood and Tears. Austin Macauley, 2017
Making Sense of Marilyn. Fonthill, 2018.
Hitler's Insanity: A Conspiracy of Silence. Fonthill, 2018.
The Unwitting Fundamentalist. Austin Macauley, 2018.
Robert Mugabe's Lost Jewel of Africa. Fonthill, 2018.
Hitler: Dictator or Puppet? Pen & Sword, 2011, 2020.
Halsewell: A Shipwreck that Gripped the Nation. Fonthill, 2020.
The Amazing Story of Lise Meitner. Pen & Sword, 2021.
Paul Robeson: A Song For Freedom. New Haven Publishing, 2022
Francoise Hardy: A Musical Tale of Love and Loss. New Haven Publishing, 2022.
The Real Sir Arthur Conan Doyle. Pen & Sword, 2023.
A Dorset Childhood: Growing up in the Land of the Tolpuddle Martyrs at the Time of the Cold War. Pen & Sword, 2023.
A Purbeck Romance: Set in Thomas Hardy's Glorious Wessex. Pen & Sword, 2023.

Index